HEALTH, MEDICINE, AND SOCIETY IN VICTORIAN ENGLAND

Recent Titles in
Victorian Life and Times

HEALTH, MEDICINE, AND SOCIETY IN VICTORIAN ENGLAND

Mary Wilson Carpenter

VICTORIAN LIFE AND TIMES
Sally Mitchell, Series Editor

PRAEGER
An Imprint of ABC-CLIO, LLC

A B C ☰ C L I O

Santa Barbara, California • Denver, Colorado • Oxford, England

Library of Congress Cataloging-in-Publication Data
Carpenter, Mary Wilson, 1937-
   Health, medicine, and society in Victorian England / Mary Wilson Carpenter.
      p. cm. — (Victorian life and times)
   Includes bibliographical references and index.
   ISBN 978-0-275-98952-1 (hard copy : alk. paper) — ISBN 978-0-313-
06542-2 (ebook) 1. Social medicine—England—History—19th century. 2. Medicine—
England—History—19th century. 3. Public health—England—History—
19th century. I. Title.
   RA418.3.G7C37 2010
   362.1—dc22   2009031084

ISBN: 978-0-275-98952-1
EISBN: 978-0-313-06542-2

14 13 12 11 10   1 2 3 4 5

This book is also available on the World Wide Web as an eBook.
Visit www.abc-clio.com for details.

Praeger
An imprint of ABC-CLIO, LLC

ABC-CLIO, LLC
130 Cremona Drive, P.O. Box 1911
Santa Barbara, California 93116-1911

This book is printed on acid-free paper ∞

Manufactured in the United States of America

CONTENTS

ILLUSTRATIONS

SERIES FOREWORD

Although the nineteenth century has almost faded from living memory—most people who heard firsthand stories from grandparents who grew up before 1900 have adult grandchildren by now—impressions of the Victorian world continue to influence both popular culture and public debates. These impressions may well be vivid yet contradictory. Many people, for example, believe that Victorian society was safe, family-centered, and stable because women could not work outside the home. Yet, every census taken during the period records hundreds of thousands of female laborers in fields, factories, shops, and schools as well as more than a million domestic servants (often girls of fourteen or fifteen) whose long and unregulated workdays created the comfortable, leisured world we see in Merchant Ivory films. Yet it is also true that there were women who had no household duties and desperately wished for some purpose in life but found that social expectations and family pressure absolutely prohibited their presence in the workplace.

The goal of books in the Victorian Life and Times series is to explain and enrich the simple pictures that show only a partial truth. Although the Victorian period in Great Britain is often portrayed as peaceful, comfortable, and traditional, it was actually a time of truly breathtaking change. In 1837, when eighteen-year-old Victoria became queen, relatively few of England's people had ever traveled more than ten miles from the place where they were born. Little more than half the population could read and write, children as young as five worked in factories and mines, and political power was entirely in the hands of a small minority of men who held property. By the time Queen Victoria died in 1901, railways provided fast and cheap transportation for both goods and people, telegraph messages sped to the far corners of the British Empire in minutes, education was compulsory, a man's religion (or lack of it) no longer barred him from sitting in Parliament, and women were not only wives and domestic servants but also physicians, dentists, elected school-board members, telephone operators, and university lecturers. Virtually every aspect of life had been transformed either by technology or by the massive political and legal reforms that reshaped Parliament, elections, universities, the army, education, sanitation, public health, marriage, working conditions, trade unions, and civil and criminal law.

The continuing popularity of Victoriana among decorators and collectors, the strong market for historical novels and for mysteries set in the age of Jack the Ripper and Sherlock Holmes, the new interest in books by George Eliot and Charles Dickens and Wilkie Collins whenever one is presented on television, and the desire of amateur genealogists to discover the lives, as well as the names, of nineteenth-century British ancestors all reveal the need for accurate information about the period's social history and material culture. In the years since the first edition of my book *Daily Life in Victorian England* was published in 1996, I have been contacted by many people who want more detailed information about some area covered in that overview. Each book in the Victorian Life and Times series will focus on a single topic, describe changes during the period, and consider the differences between country and city, between industrial life and rural life, and above all, the differences made by class, social position, religion, tradition, gender, and economics. Each book is an original work, illustrated with drawings and pictures taken from Victorian sources, enriched by quotations from Victorian publications, based on current research, and written by a qualified scholar. All of the authors have doctoral degrees and many years' experience in teaching; they have been chosen not only for their academic qualifications but also for their ability to write clearly and to explain complex ideas to people without extensive background in the subject. Thus the books are authoritative and dependable but written in straightforward language; explanations are supplied whenever specialized terminology is used, and a bibliography lists resources for further information.

The Internet has made it possible for people who cannot visit archives and reference libraries to conduct serious family and historical research. Careful hobbyists and scholars have scanned large numbers of primary sources: nineteenth-century cookbooks, advice manuals, maps, city directories, magazines, sermons, church records, illustrated newspapers, guidebooks, political cartoons, photographs, paintings, published investigations of slum conditions and poor people's budgets, political essays, inventories of scientists' correspondence, and many other materials formerly accessible only to academic historians. Yet the World Wide Web also contains misleading documents and false information, even on educational sites created by students and enthusiasts who don't have the experience to put material in useful contexts. So far as possible, therefore, the bibliographies for books in the Victorian Life and Times series will also offer guidance on using publicly available electronic resources.

Among the massive changes affecting much of the world since Queen Victoria's reign ended in 1901, one of the most significant is the alteration in medical practice, medical treatment, and health itself as measured by life expectancy and by the likelihood of surviving (or even catching) a serious disease. Yet although the antibiotics, the increasingly complex surgical interventions, and the vaccines to banish once-deadly childhood diseases were not developed until the twentieth century, much of the practical and scientific understanding that led to these discoveries took place during the Victorian years.

But was this indeed a story of science triumphant? Mary Wilson Carpenter's *Health, Medicine, and Society in Victorian England* is, first and foremost, a social history of medicine: an account of health and disease as experienced by ordinary patients and understood by society as a whole. The facts about medical training and practice, the analysis of terrifying epidemics and the ever-present specter of tuberculosis (the greatest single cause of death throughout the century), and the information about disabilities such as blindness are enriched by vivid examples drawn from patients' memories and physicians' diaries as well as from fiction, household advice books, and medical texts. Thus in addition to describing nineteenth-century discoveries that turned into twentieth-century realities, the book suggests attitudes and contexts that continue to be important as we think about medical research and resources in contemporary society.

Sally Mitchell, Series Editor

ACKNOWLEDGMENTS

I would first like to thank Jacalyn Duffin, MD, FRCP (C), PhD, and my colleague at Queen's University, Canada, who generously read my first proposal for this book and offered insightful comments that were fundamental to its final shape. Her experience in teaching the history of medicine to medical students, who generally know as little about the history of their field as most students do about the respective history of their own disciplines, was invaluable. And her own books, especially *History of Medicine: A Scandalously Short Introduction*, and *To See with a Better Eye: A Life of R. T. H. Laënnec*, have been not merely instructive but a pleasure to read.

I also wish to thank my general readers, nonspecialists in the field of history of medicine, especially Jane Wegscheider Hyman, Andrea Broomfield, Nancy Sconyers, John Tener, and my sister, Julia Davenport Stevens. Although they cannot be considered nonspecialist readers, Abigail Siegal, MD, and Elizabeth LeQuesne, MD, also read parts of the manuscript, and I thank them for their time and encouragement.

Graduate students at Queen's helped me explore the new field of disability studies, and their lively and engaged classroom discussion of issues in this field has certainly enabled my own work. Beyond this, I wish to mention especially former graduate students and present colleagues Jennifer Esmail and Vanessa Warne, whose conference presentations and published work have made important contributions to disability studies, as well as to my own thinking.

Colleagues in the Northeast Victorian Studies Association (NVSA), North American Victorian Studies Association (NAVSA), and the Victorian Studies Association of Ontario (VSAO) have heard papers drawn from various parts of this book, and their interest and questions have been most useful. I have been privileged to participate in the Victorian Literature and Culture Seminar at the Humanities Center at Harvard University, and this ongoing community of Victorianists active in teaching and research has been both encouraging and enlightening. I wish to thank particularly Anna Henchman, James Buzard, John Plotz, and John Picker, all of whom have served as seminar chairs at various times.

Staff members at the Widener Library at Harvard University have answered many questions, solved a number of apparently insoluble research problems, and been unfailingly helpful. I also wish to thank staff members at the Countway Medical Library at Harvard University and the Medical Historical Library at Yale University.

I thank staff members at the Wellcome Trust in London, especially Rachael Johnson, for invaluable assistance in obtaining appropriate illustrations for the book. Without Ms. Johnson's expert, efficient, and always kind help, I would have been far less able to make good use of the Trust's rich library of virtual images.

No amount of thanks can be sufficient to my husband, who has dedicated considerable time to gophering books in a field alien to his own research and generally to putting up with irrational hours and the inevitable tensions of meeting deadlines.

I also wish to thank Suzanne Stazak-Silva and Michael Millman, publishing editors for this series, both of whom have been most helpful. Last, and perhaps most important, I wish to thank Sally Mitchell, who first offered me this opportunity to write on a subject I had always wanted to study, and who has been a discriminating reader of each chapter, offering the benefit of her extraordinary knowledge of Victorian history and literature. Like other writers in this series, I have found her guidance invaluable.

Lastly, I would have liked to thank Barbara Johnson, whose brilliant scholarship and quiet, witty yet potent feminism have inspired me from the beginnings of my academic career. Her amazing courage and determination to continue her own writing in the face of a disabling illness during the last few years have proven an inspiration beyond my capacity to describe. Her death on August 27, 2009, has precluded my chance to thank her in person, but her work in literary and feminist theory will continue to delight and invigorate not only me but her many other grateful students and friends.

CHRONOLOGY

1764	Braidwood Academy, first school (private) for deaf-mutes in Britain, founded.
1791	Liverpool School for Indigent Blind founded.
1792	London Asylum for the Deaf and Dumb founded.
1796	Edward Jenner introduces cowpox vaccination to prevent smallpox.
1801	Egyptian Ophthalmia, contagious eye infection that could cause blindness, contracted by British soldiers fighting in Napoleonic wars in Egypt.
1815	Apothecaries Act sets national (England and Wales) standards for licensing of apothecaries.
1819	Stethoscope invented.
1823	The *Lancet*, first medical journal in England, founded by Thomas Wakley.
1831–32	First cholera epidemic in Britain.
1832	Anatomy Act empowers medical schools to appropriate unclaimed bodies.
1836	University of London founded, offers medical degrees that combine academic instruction with clinical practice in medicine.
1840	Vaccination Act makes vaccination free as administered by Poor Law medical officers.
1846	Anesthesia introduced to Britain.

1847	James Simpson Young first uses chloroform for woman in labor.
1847	Ignaz Phillip Semmelweis proves that puerperal fever could be largely prevented by washing hands in chlorine solution before contact with woman in labor.
1848	Public Health Act in England sets up General Board of Health, permits local authorities to take over water companies, but only if the companies agreed.
1848–49	Second cholera epidemic in Britain.
1850	Ophthalmoscope invented.
1853	Compulsory Vaccination Act requires vaccination of all infants before four months.
1853–54	Third cholera epidemic in Britain, including "Broad Street pump" epidemic.
1854–56	Crimean War: Florence Nightingale organizes hospitals and nursing services.
1855	John Snow publishes second edition of *On the Mode of Communication of Cholera*, based on studies of London water system, proposing that cholera is transmitted through polluted water.
1858	Medical Act of 1858 calls for registration of all qualified practitioners annually, but does not specify whether physicians, surgeons, or apothecaries and does not impose national requirements.
1859	Elizabeth Blackwell becomes first woman to register under Medical Act of 1858, but does not set up practice in England.
1862	Florence Nightingale establishes Nightingale School for Nurses at St. Thomas' Hospital.
1864, 1866, 1869	Contagious Diseases Acts, which permit police to have surveillance over, arrest, and require medical treatment of prostitutes suspected of having venereal disease.
1865	Elizabeth Garrett awarded License of the Society of Apothecaries, becomes second woman to register under Medical Act of 1858.
1866–67	Fourth and last cholera epidemic in Britain.
1867	Joseph Lister publishes discovery of antiseptic technique.
1870–71	Most severe epidemic of smallpox to occur in Britain during the nineteenth century.
1871	Elizabeth Garrett opens New Hospital for Women, first hospital in Britain to have only women appointed to its medical staff.
1874	London School of Medicine for Women established by Sophia Jex-Blake and others to provide medical education for women.

1882   Identification of tubercle bacillus by Robert Koch.

1883   Identification of cholera bacterium by Robert Koch.

1886   Repeal of Contagious Diseases Acts.

1886   Medical Act Amendment Act makes triple qualifications in medicine, surgery, and midwifery mandatory for registration as medical practitioner.

1886   British Royal Commission on the Blind and the Deaf and Dumb calls Edward Miner Gallaudet and Alexander Graham Bell to testify on the use of sign languages in deaf education.

1888   British Nurses Association founded with specific goal of achieving legal status for professional nurses.

1890   First Congress of the British Deaf and Dumb Association (later changed to British Deaf Association) affirms sign language as "most natural and indispensable."

1893   Elementary Education Act (Blind and Deaf Children) requires provision of free schools for blind and deaf children.

1894   Diphtheria antitoxin introduced as first agent capable of actually curing an existing disease.

1896   Sphygmomanometer invented.

1898,   New Vaccination Acts permit parents to refuse vaccination for their children on grounds of conscientious objection.
1907

1902   Midwives' Act sets qualification standards for midwives for first time in British history.

1905   Bacterium that causes syphilis, *Treponema pallidum,* identified.

1906   Wassermann blood test for syphilis invented.

1910   Salvarsan, first drug to effectively treat syphilis, formulated.

1911   National Insurance Act provides for health insurance for working men to which government contributed.

1919   Nurses Registration Act sets up General Nursing Council to establish qualifications for registration.

1948   National Health Service founded.

INTRODUCTION

"History may seem to be about the past, but it is really about the present."
Jacalyn Duffin, an MD and a historian of medicine, begins a chapter in her
book, *History of Medicine: A Scandalously Short Introduction*, with this
short and perhaps scandalous truth about history.[1] The questions we ask,
the subjects we choose to research, and the way we put together our findings
about the past, all proceed from our position in the present. Until the last
quarter of the twentieth century, the history of medicine was largely written by medical men concerned with the intellectual history of medicine and
with the lives and work of medicine's great men. It was a story of progress,
of the defeat of disease, of the invention of marvelous new surgical techniques, of continual improvement in the health and longevity of national populations. Smallpox had been eradicated from the globe in 1977, public
health measures were effective in banishing epidemics of cholera and similar
diseases primarily spread through unsanitary practices, vaccinations had
been developed to prevent most of the old childhood killers such as diphtheria and measles, and antibiotics were able to cure most diseases, even that
guilt-ridden terror, syphilis. The future of medicine seemed rosy, and the
past tended to be viewed as a steady progress toward that future via a successful and self-congratulatory present.

Then in 1981 a new, and terrifying, disease appeared. Called AIDS for
"acquired immune deficiency syndrome," it was invariably fatal and its victims died after suffering a number of horrific symptoms. It was at first
blamed on homosexual men, but was later found to be capable of infecting
both sexes and people of any sexual orientation. Since it weakens the
immune system, people with AIDS were found to be much more vulnerable

to other diseases, especially tuberculosis. Tuberculosis, in turn, like many other diseases, seemed to be becoming resistant to the antibiotics that had been thought to be a sure cure. The traditional, "triumphalist" narrative of medical history suffered a fatal attack from this new disease.

But that fatal attack was in fact only the final blow to medical history as a triumphal progress, for historians had been raising new questions since the 1960s. In 1965, as Dorothy Porter comments in her 1995 essay, "The Mission of Social History of Medicine: An Historical View," members of the newly formed British Society for the History of Medicine were concerned with "social medicine" or "the relationship of medicine to society." By the early 1970s, meetings of the Society were devoted to such new topics as "midwifery in the context of feminist politics, the social history of tuberculosis and the history of general practice."

In 1976, Charles Webster's presidential address in effect rewrote the manifesto of the Society. He suggested that medicine should be examined from the "perspective of the beliefs, values, social organization, and professional activities of every *stratum* within the ranks of medical practitioners; and by regarding patients as more than passive objects of disease. It should be an essential part of our brief to resurrect the patient." Indeed, he concluded, "there are few questions in modern social history which are devoid of a medical dimension, although it is only very recently that English historians, following in the wake of their French counterparts, have become aware of the full relevance of medicine to the understanding of social structure, social transformation, and collective mentality."[2]

Among the French counterparts Webster surely had in mind was Michel Foucault, whose *The Birth of the Clinic: An Archaeology of Medical Perception*, originally published in 1963 and translated into English in 1973, continues to be regularly cited in works on the history of medicine today. In this work, Foucault identifies a significant turning point in medical history around the beginning of the nineteenth century when "the clinic," or the institution of the teaching hospital where large numbers of medical students and their professors gathered not just to treat the sick but to study their diseases, first took modern form. In the great hospitals of postrevolutionary Paris, practitioners of medicine began to focus on the patient's body as a material object to be examined while living and dissected when dead. This new focus, termed the "clinical gaze," signaled a radical departure from the traditional theorizing of the patient's disease based on the principles of ancient Greek medicine and on the patient's own interpretation of his or her symptoms. Foucault makes the startling proposal that the clinical gaze produced not only a new system of medical knowledge but also a new system of power relations. The producers of this new medical knowledge—medical students, and even more so the titled professors of medicine—rose to a new power and authority in this system, but patients were reduced to examples of disease.

As Ludmilla Jordanova has commented in another 1995 essay, "The Social Construction of Medical Knowledge," Foucault's work has become foundational in what Jordanova calls "social constructionism," or the critical examination of how medical ideas or knowledge are shaped by social forces. But Jordanova also argues that this approach to the social history of medicine was "well-established among English-speaking historians long before Foucault had a major impact." And she points out that "it has not proved possible to formulate a neat definition of social history of medicine."[3] Among the diverse intellectual and political currents that Jordanova discusses as contributing to the new social history of medicine are the analysis of power relations in society, the study of professionalism, and feminist criticism, not to mention a general revolt against triumphalist history. Jordanova thus emphasizes the work done in social history of medicine by those "who had neither been medically trained nor had their ideas shaped by history and philosophy of science."[4]

I write this book on the history of health, medicine, and society in Victorian England from the perspective of one trained in the field of literary studies, particularly Victorian literature, cultural studies, and feminist criticism. The book is intended for general readers who have no specialist knowledge of any of these fields and who are also newcomers in the complex universe of health and disease, practitioners and patients, and medicine and society in nineteenth-century England. That universe is represented as a history of "medicine from below," or medicine as seen by ordinary nineteenth-century people, whether patients or practitioners. Like most histories of medicine written since the 1980s, this book is a *social* history of Victorian medicine: it sets medicine in its social and political contexts, rather than schematizing it as a history of ideas in which medical advances follow logically from intellectual developments. But this study also situates nineteenth-century medicine in its literary contexts—fiction, poetry, biography, letters, and diaries—in order to demonstrate how Victorians themselves thought and wrote about health and medicine outside their medical and scientific contexts. Because so many nineteenth-century medical texts are now freely available on the Internet, this book may be considered as interleaved with the actual medical writings of the nineteenth century. Readers are encouraged to read John Snow's revolutionary work on the transmission of cholera, for example, for themselves. His work was formerly available only in an early twentieth-century reprint edition generally found only in rare book libraries, but can now be read in its entirety on the Internet.

This book may also be considered a *cultural* history of Victorian medicine. There are many definitions of culture, but I will here use the term to refer to groups whose social relations and individual identities are formed by their common interest in and interaction with a particular issue, though differing in professional or nonprofessional status, political position, health, or illness. Such medically associated cultures as Victorian invalidism, the "fallen woman" and her female "rescuers," antivaccinationists, and advocates of the "pure oral method" of teaching the deaf and dumb will be discussed.

The nineteenth century saw a transformation in medicine in Britain, as it did in France and other European countries and also in the United States. But the history of medicine differed from nation to nation, and even from region to region within nations. At the beginning of the century, medicine was practiced in England by an assortment of physicians, surgeons, and apothecaries whose educations ranged from many years of university study in the classic Greek theory of the body as a system of humors (fluids) to a few years of apprenticeship with a local surgeon or apothecary, which might or might not have been accompanied by a few months of hospital attendance or a short course of medical lectures, or perhaps both. There were also many people, women as well as men, who practiced as midwives, venereologists (specialists in venereal diseases), smallpox inoculators, itinerant oculists, traveling quacks or healers, and those who simply advertised themselves as surgeons or practitioners of "physic." Most hospitals functioned primarily as charities: they took in the sick poor, or simply the poor. Most of those who were sick remained in their homes and paid the practitioner of their choice to give them the care they preferred, whether a tonic to stimulate their constitution or bleeding, or purgatives to calm it down or lower it. There weren't many other forms of medical treatment, and because of the pain and the danger of infection, most surgery was confined to relatively minor operations such as pulling teeth or setting simple fractures. Surgical penetration of the abdomen, the chest, or the skull was rarely attempted because such operations led to almost certain death from infection or hemorrhage or both.

By the end of the nineteenth century, the modern medical profession had emerged, organized essentially as we know it today. All medical practitioners had to have legally defined qualifications, including hospital training, in order to be registered by the General Medical Council (GMC). Because women had always been excluded from hospital training and formal medical education of any kind, the medical profession at this time was still almost entirely male. But women had begun to breach the barriers in the latter half of the nineteenth century, and by the turn of the century, a few had managed to earn a medical degree or a license from one of the nineteen licensing corporations, such as the Society of Apothecaries or the King and Queen's College of Physicians in Ireland, and had set up medical practice in Britain. Women midwives, who had only been tolerated during the nineteenth century and were largely without formal training, now had their training and qualification regulated with the passage of the Registration of Midwives Act of 1902. Although the Nurses Registration Act wasn't passed until 1919, the training of nurses had begun to be standardized with the foundation of the Nightingale School for Nurses at St. Thomas' Hospital in London in 1860, and by the turn of the century nurses were recognizably similar to nurses today: educated in medical knowledge and trained in specific nursing practice. Medicine had become the *science* of medicine, informed by laboratory as well as clinical research. Hospitals had become thoroughly medicalized: they functioned as centers of medical training and clinical research as well as institutions for the care and treatment of the sick, who now included members of the middle and upper classes. Most surgery was now performed in hospitals, under antiseptic or aseptic conditions, and with the benefits of anesthesia.

At the beginning of the nineteenth century, medical diagnosis of a patient's condition depended largely on what the patient told the practitioner or what the practitioner could see with his own eyes. During the nineteenth century, the stethoscope, the speculum, the microscope, the ophthalmoscope, the thermometer, the sphygmomanometer, the x-ray machine, and other instruments were invented or came into common medical use, allowing the practitioner to detect a patient's illness before the patient herself was aware of it. Today we take it for granted that a doctor can learn crucial information about our health that we would never have been aware of ourselves from a blood test or examination with one of the instruments above, but this development was one of the most revolutionary aspects of medical history in the nineteenth century. Practitioners became like prophets, able to see things about the body that were not visible to the naked eye, and thereby to forecast the patient's future, though they were not necessarily able to make any therapeutic intervention in that future. Patients were no longer the first authority about their bodily condition; with his, or sometimes now her, array of specialized knowledge about the body, the doctor had become the first and most valid authority. In the hospitals of the late nineteenth century, patients found themselves seen as cases: they were exhibits to be studied and demonstrated to classes of medical students, sometimes to be written up in case reports and published in medical journals for the benefit of other doctors. Publication, of course, also enhanced the doctor's own prestige and standing with peers.

This study often refers to medicine in Britain, but the reader should be warned that most research on nineteenth-century so-called British medical history is based on data from England and, to a lesser extent, Scotland. Although Wales was included with England in medical legislation, very little has been written specifically on the history of medicine in Wales. Similarly, the history of medicine in nineteenth-century Ireland, which appears to have followed quite a different course from that of England and Scotland, is only just beginning to be studied by historians. Except where specified otherwise, then, the reader should be aware that the history of medicine here discussed is largely that of England. Even though Scotland's medical history is intertwined with that of England, it nevertheless differs in important respects from English medical history.

The reader should also note that, though commonly referring to Victorian medicine, the chronological focus of this book actually takes in the "long nineteenth century," a period beginning with roughly the time of the French Revolution and usually extending beyond Queen Victoria's death in 1901 to the beginning or end of World War I (or the Great War), 1914–1918. In the case of certain disease histories, I have thought it useful to extend my historical focus even further back, to the time when a particular disease is thought to have originated, and also to look forward to the status of those diseases today.

Although the focus of this book is on the social history of medicine in England, that history is necessarily situated in the context of other European countries, especially France and the German-speaking countries (the boundaries and governments of the latter changed dramatically over the nineteenth century), as well as the United States. During the nineteenth century, medicine became cosmopolitan: students often studied in more than one country; military practitioners and missionaries practiced in the colonies; professors of medicine were invited to lecture in the medical schools of other countries; and medical journals, pamphlets, and books circulated internationally, both in the language in which they had been written and in translation. No nation developed its medicine in isolation. The radical transformation of medicine which took place over the course of the nineteenth century could not have happened without this international circulation of medical knowledge. Yet the profession of medicine developed differently in different nations.

In this internationally situated, regionally differentiated, and yet unique realm of Victorian medicine, it has not been possible to cover every subject of importance in that realm. The reader will not find a discussion of psychiatric or neurological disorders, which the Victorians would have lumped together under such terms as epilepsy, idiocy, lunacy, insanity, and hysteria, or simply mental infirmity. Nor have I discussed the culture of antivivisectionists, though it intersected with other Victorian medically associated cultures. The topics selected for study are those I feel are not only most representative of Victorian medicine and society, but also those that fit into a reasonably short and comprehensible narrative history of an enormously complex subject.

Chapter 1, "Practitioners and Patients in Victorian England," describes first the changing education and qualifications of practitioners (who, with the single exception of Elizabeth Garrett, were exclusively men until the 1870s) throughout the century. This chapter focuses particularly on the medical education of John Snow, who came from a very low rank of society (his father started out as a common laborer) but who attained the highest degree of medical education possible, the MD or doctor of medicine. The story of John Snow forms a continuing thread in the book, which returns to his work on cholera in chapter 2, and his work as an anesthesiologist in the final chapter. In the second part of chapter 1, the differing experience of patients of upper- and lower-class status is discussed, focusing particularly on the unique invalid culture that emerged in Victorian England. Finally, chapter 1 also describes the burgeoning of hospitals in the Victorian era and the experience of one intrepid patient, Margaret Mathewson, who wrote a "Sketch" of her months in the Royal Infirmary of Edinburgh, where she underwent surgery at the hands of the famed professor of clinical surgery, Joseph Lister.

Chapters 2–5 take four infectious diseases as their subjects: cholera, tuberculosis, syphilis, and smallpox. Infectious disease was the overwhelming medical concern in the Victorian era. Britain was the first nation to be industrialized; its mushrooming cities spawned infectious disease through filthy streets, crowded living quarters, and polluted water. At the same time, Britain and France were the two great empires, and the global travel of vast numbers of people spread infectious disease at a rate hitherto unprecedented. The particular diseases discussed in this book all had some particular relevance for the nineteenth century. Cholera had never been seen outside of India until the nineteenth century: the great pandemics of cholera (there were four of them in Britain), sweeping around the globe, were specifically the product of mass population movements, especially those resulting from military and commercial interests. Tuberculosis was the single biggest killer of the nineteenth century, accounting for far more deaths than all the cholera epidemics combined. The number of deaths caused by syphilis, by contrast, and the even larger toll of disabilities caused by the disease—blindness, deafness, paralysis, and insanity—is not known. But it was in the nineteenth century that the most significant medical features of the disease were first understood, i.e., that it appeared and disappeared in three different stages, all of which were the same disease, but that it was not the same disease as the other commonly known venereal disease, gonorrhea. It was also in the nineteenth century that Britain and other European countries instituted campaigns to arrest and forcibly examine prostitutes, who were blamed as the sole reservoir of the disease. The bacteria that cause these three diseases—cholera, tuberculosis, and syphilis—were all first identified in the late nineteenth century or very early twentieth, and an effective drug for the treatment of syphilis, Salvarsan, was first produced in 1910.

The cause of smallpox, a disease that had decimated nations and toppled governments through the deaths of entire royal families for many centuries, was not discovered in the nineteenth century, but a way to prevent the disease was discovered in the last decade of the eighteenth century. In 1796, an

English country practitioner named Edward Jenner tried out a practice of infecting healthy people with matter from cows who had cowpox. Because of his privileged social position in the elite medical world of the time (he was a protégé of the well-known London surgeon John Hunter), he was able to promulgate the practice, which he called vaccination; it spread worldwide. Over the course of the nineteenth century in England, vaccination was gradually though erratically extended to a large part of the population. A strong culture of antivaccinationists emerged, however, and by the end of the century vaccination was no longer compulsory. Nevertheless, smallpox epidemics after the turn of the twentieth century in Britain were never as widespread or as terrifying as those in the nineteenth, and by the last quarter of the twentieth century, the disease had been entirely eradicated from the globe.

Chapters 6 and 7 discuss the social and medical treatment of the deaf and the blind. Although these conditions are now referred to as disability, in the Victorian era they were spoken of as infirmity or affliction, and those so afflicted were considered to be among the most unfortunate members of society. Literary representations of the deaf and the blind, both fictional and nonfictional, are extremely useful in helping us to understand not only how Victorians perceived the blind and the deaf as they did but why.

Chapter 8 describes Victorian women as patients and as practitioners. During the course of the nineteenth century, practitioners developed the new "science of woman," or gynecology, and women were constituted as a special kind of patient. There was no similar development of andrology, or a science of man. The notion that women were specialized for reproduction became increasingly prominent in medicine and led to a range and degree of surgical interventions without proven benefit that were both extreme and dangerous. Childbirth also became largely the province of medical men with inadequate training in obstetrics, and maternal and infant mortality rates remained shockingly high until the 1930s. Meanwhile, Victorian gender ideology promoted the development of the "Nightingale nurse," who was expected to be properly subordinate to medical men, while the entry of women into the medical profession was vehemently resisted. By the time of Queen Victoria's death in 1901, however, a few women had managed to qualify as physicians and to set up practice in England. They joined what had now become a modern profession with uniform standards of education and ethics. Though much remained to be learned, scientific knowledge was beginning to transform medical practice.

1

Practitioners and Patients
in Victorian England

Lydgate did not mean to be one of those failures, and there was the
better hope of him because his scientific interest soon took the form
of a professional enthusiasm: he had a youthful belief in his bread-
winning work, not to be stifled by that initiation in makeshift called
his 'prentice days; and he carried to his studies in London, Edinburgh,
and Paris, the conviction that the medical profession as it might be
was the finest in the world; presenting the most perfect interchange
between science and art; offering the most direct alliance between intellectual conquest and the social good.[1]

On his arrival in the provincial town of Middlemarch, George Eliot's idealis-
tic young doctor represents the best in the medical scene in England around
the time of the first Reform Bill (1832). Identified as a surgeon, he has
rounded off his early makeshift apprentice days with a cosmopolitan education in the most important centers of medical study in the world: London,
Edinburgh, and Paris. He has chosen to buy a practice in Middlemarch
because he wants to promote reform in the medical profession and to "keep
away from the range of London intrigues, jealousies, and social truckling."[2]
He particularly wants to "resist the irrational severance between medical
and surgical knowledge in the interest of his own scientific pursuits," and
he is very much in favor of building a new fever hospital in the town, with
the idea that it might even become "the nucleus of a medical school."[3]

But Lydgate finds himself as much in the midst of "intrigues, jealousies,
and social truckling" in rural Middlemarch as in urban medical politics.

Neither his colleagues nor his patients share his vision of a medicine that will combine science and art, medical and surgical knowledge, let alone benefit that undefined entity, the social good. Lydgate's upper-class patients, like Lady Chettam, expect their physician to be a kind of servant who will cater to their beliefs about their constitution and dole out medicines to their liking. His lower-class patients, like Mrs. Dollop, are sometimes convinced that he means "to let the people die in the Hospital, if not to poison them, for the sake of cutting them up without saying by your leave or with your leave."[4] Ultimately, Lydgate's high ideals are defeated by his need to make more money in order to support his wife in the style she desires. He becomes a doctor to wealthy patients at a fashionable watering-place or spa, and thus in his own eyes a failure. At the end of the novel, we hear that he dies of diphtheria, an infectious disease that has today virtually disappeared due to routine vaccination of infants, but that was new to England in the 1840s. The career of this fictional Victorian doctor thus casts a highly skeptical light on the medical profession he imagines to be "the finest in the world."

Both literary critics and historians have commented on the accuracy of George Eliot's picture of provincial English medicine in the early decades of the nineteenth century. Readers of this magnificent novel may take its representation of medical practice in the 1830s as very close to the actual, often cheerless, condition of both patients and practitioners in early Victorian England. But we should also be aware that Eliot began work on *Middlemarch* in 1869 (it was published in 1871–72), and that she was looking back over a forty-year perspective in medical history in which she had herself participated as a patient, as well as having studied the topic with her usual thoroughness of research. What we see in her novel is medicine as it was in England before microscopic science had begun to make much in the way of actual changes in the practice of medicine or in the education of medical students, and before it had had any effect on the health of Victorians. Eliot and her partner, George Henry Lewes, were thoroughly familiar with the use of the recently improved microscope and its seemingly miraculous revelations, as is especially evident in one of Lewes's books, *Studies in Animal Life* (1862). Lewes enthusiastically urges his readers to buy a microscope because "few purchases will yield you so much pleasure." Eliot and Lewes were also familiar with Charles Darwin's *On the Origin of Species* (1859), a work that was both the product of Victorian science and a founding text in modern biology. But Eliot and Lewes were also only too aware of the ongoing inability of the medical profession to cure most diseases. In the months just preceding the writing of *Middlemarch*, the two had nursed Lewes's twenty-five-year-old son, Thornie, through an agonizing period of slow death from a cause—probably tuberculosis of the spine—which one of the most prestigious physicians of the day, Sir James Paget, had been unable to diagnose or to treat. Only a few years before, in December 1861, Prince Albert, beloved husband of Queen Victoria, had died of typhoid fever, a disease that, though known to be infectious, still escaped efforts to control its spread, even among the most privileged classes. (In the novel, Lydgate's unusually advanced medical knowledge is demonstrated by his correct diagnosis of Fred Vincy's illness as typhoid and his immediate imposition of precautionary measures to prevent its spread.) In London, where Eliot and Lewes lived, a cholera epidemic had recently devastated the East End, though the epidemic fortunately did not extend to their neighborhood. Eliot was not to know that this epidemic of cholera, the fourth to hit England, would also be the last because public health authorities had finally learned how to search out and eliminate the source of contamination, even though they had no knowledge of the bacterium, *Vibrio cholerae*, that caused the devastating disease.

Indeed, the entire decade of the 1860s and the first years of the 1870s were perhaps the most unhealthful in the history of Victorian England. Analysis of the statistics on deaths gathered by the General Register Office (GRO) since 1837 documented the fact that the death rate for England and Wales, which had been at the high point of 22.4 per thousand for 1841–50, actually rose to 22.5 per thousand between 1861 and 1870. In addition to typhoid fever which, like cholera, was spread by contaminated water and food, typhus fever (spread by the body louse) raged not only in London but in the Lancashire textile districts, where the workers had been thrown out of work by the cotton famine, for most of the 1860s.[5] Measles increased in fatality, as did smallpox, and a serious epidemic outbreak of that new disease, diphtheria (first described by Pierre Bretonneau in 1826), struck London between 1858 and 1865. Parliament became so concerned about the increase of venereal disease in the military forces that the Contagious Diseases Acts of 1864, 1866, and 1869 were passed to permit surveillance, arrest, and forcible examination and treatment of prostitutes, who were thought to be the source of such disease. Smallpox had been increasing in virulence throughout the 1860s, but in 1870 the severest epidemic of this terrible disease to occur in the entire nineteenth century swept the country, despite the fact that vaccination had been made compulsory in 1853. British hospitals also witnessed what seemed to be an epidemic of wound disease, though infection of wounds had always been common.

It's entirely understandable, then, that Eliot's perspective on the medical profession and on a patient's chances of receiving effective treatment should be a skeptical one. Yet after 1870, the death rate began a continuous, though unsteady, decline, and by 1900 it stood at 18.2 per thousand. By 1939, it had reached 12 per thousand. Had *Middlemarch* been written about three decades later, at the end of Queen Victoria's reign (1901), the writer's perspective might have been much more optimistic. By then the Medical Act Amendment Act (1886) had been passed, an act that for the first time made both medical and surgical qualifications, as well as qualification in midwifery, compulsory for all medical practitioners. German scientist Robert Koch had not only identified the bacterial causes of tuberculosis and cholera but also formulated postulates for proving a particular bacterium to be the cause of a particular disease. Effective treatments for most infectious diseases were still not known, but medical practitioners were forced to believe in contagion, and steps were now routinely taken to prevent the spread of disease. It was also now recognized that the provision of clean drinking water and uncontaminated food were not only necessary to prevent disease but should be the legal right of the population. Smallpox vaccination, even though no longer compulsory in Britain, had nevertheless undercut this terrifying disease from major, widespread epidemics to sporadic and much more localized outbreaks. Middle- and even upper-class patients were beginning to enter hospitals, as antiseptic and aseptic technique, along with the use of anesthesia, rendered operations safer and no longer accompanied by pain so hideous as sometimes to cause death by shock alone. The experience of both practitioners and patients had been transformed during the nineteenth century by the change from a largely prescientific medicine to a medicine informed, if not always reformed, by advances in scientific knowledge.

Yet that change in England had been only slowly and unevenly gained, and by the end of the century new problems both in patient care and in the medical profession replaced some of those that had been resolved. The surgeon, now termed the doctor, had been romanticized in literature and art as the kind of physician Eliot's Lydgate had hoped he would become: revered by patients and colleagues alike for seemingly miraculous cures brought about through the combination of scientific knowledge and selfless devotion to the patient's care. Those who became patients in the modernized, bureaucratic hospitals of the twentieth century were wont to look back on the Victorian era as a golden age when doctors made home visits and spent hours nursing, as well as doctoring, their patients. But it was in the nineteenth century that medicine changed from treatment based largely on the patient's own account of her or his constitution to one based more on the physician's specialized knowledge of the patient's body, and then to the scientist's knowledge of the microscopic constitution of the patient's body and its environment. The Victorian era in England saw the formation of the medical profession as we know it now, but it was also the era in which, as doctors gained in knowledge and authority, patients were made increasingly passive objects, viewed as instances of a disease, a "case," or collection of symptoms that correlated with some phenomenon observed in a laboratory test tube far removed from the patient's bedside. Hospitals, increasingly important for both care of the patient and education of the practitioner, were also increasingly scientific, efficient, and bureaucratic.

THE STRUGGLE FOR REFORM: THE PRACTITIONER'S PERSPECTIVE

Wednesday 19 July, 1848

Mr. Allen. Visit. Somewhat less feeble. Good appetite. Rheumatism subsided.

Administered Chloroform to Martha Swindle aged 15 at University College Hospital whilst Mr. Morton divided the tendons of the ham string muscles. The narcotism [anesthesia] was carried little if at all beyond the 2nd. Degree, yet she showed no sign of any impression being caused by the operation.

Mr. Dubois. Visit. Much the same.

Mr. Frankum's Child. Cough better, but more feverish and some diarrhea, his food passing undigested. Magnesia C 3ss P Ipecac gr iv Aqua _ iv Tr Rhei Co 3ii [th].[6]

An 1848 entry from the casebooks of Dr. John Snow includes only one item of his medical practice that differs significantly from the kind of medicine he had been practicing for years in London, where he had lived and worked since his student days: the administration of chloroform anesthesia. Otherwise, his entry shows repeated visits to the homes of ailing Londoners, whose improved or worsened condition he noted, and for whom he prescribed standard medicines. Those prescribed for Frankum's child, ill with cough, fever, and diarrhea, included milk of magnesia, a laxative; ipecac, an emetic (substance used to induce vomiting); and tincture of rhubarb, another mild laxative. These were common medications, considered gentle and beneficial means of purging a sick person's system and thus removing whatever poison was causing the problem, and they were about all Snow could, or would, prescribe. Had he been an advocate of heroic medicine, as some British practitioners still were at this time, he would also have let blood, either by the lance or the use of leeches, and the purgatives prescribed would have been far more severe. But Snow, like an increasing number of physicians during the Victorian era, believed in the practice of *vis medicatrix naturae*, or providing care intended simply to aid nature in recovery and not to make any violent (and perhaps harmful) intervention in that process.

Snow, who was to become well known both for his work with the new anesthetic agents, ether and chloroform, and for his brilliant researches in the mode of transmission of cholera, was as highly qualified as a doctor could be in Victorian England. He was, in fact, far less typical than Eliot's fictional surgeon, Lydgate, who is reported to have studied in London, Edinburgh, and Paris but not to have taken a degree at any of these universities. Although Snow also started out as an apprentice, he ultimately qualified as an MD, or doctor of medicine, at the University of London, which had been offering MD degrees only since 1838. Snow's career exemplifies both the diversity and the full range of medical education available in England during the first half of the nineteenth century.

Snow's initial medical education was shaped by the requirements of the Apothecaries Act, passed by Parliament in 1815. The Apothecaries Act set standards for all of England and Wales for the qualification and licensing of apothecaries. As such, it was not only the first national regulation of medical education and practice but also marked the first time Parliament had intervened in medical affairs, previously governed only by local corporations.

John Snow

(Autotype from a Presentation Portrait, 1856, and Autograph facsimile.—B. W. R.)

John Snow, 1856. © Wellcome Library, London.

The Apothecaries Act was a step taken in the direction of the revolutionary reforms in France, where the division between medicine and surgery had been abolished, and all practitioners were required to have the same hospital-based education. When a group of London practitioners first met in 1812 to protest a new tax on glass that fell especially heavily on apothecaries (they sold medicines in glass bottles), they found themselves turning instead to the more serious problems caused by the ongoing traditional English divisions between three kinds of medical men: apothecaries, surgeons, and physicians. Originally chartered in 1617 by James I, the Worshipful Society of Apothecaries had begun as tradesmen who sold herbs and spices as well as "drugs," or medicinal compounds. Surgeons were originally classed with barbers, or barber-chirurgeons, having only been separated into the Company of Surgeons in London in 1745. They were regarded as skilled craftsmen, workers with their hands, and often had only rudimentary education, if any. In 1800 the Royal College of Surgeons in London was chartered, but it could set qualifications only for surgeons practicing in London. Physicians were the oldest medical professional group, having been incorporated in 1518 by Henry VIII, who chartered them for the treatment of internal complaints, or the practice of physic. They were typically educated at Oxford or Cambridge where, as the universities had no hospitals, they gained no experience with actual patients until they began practicing. They spent their university years becoming learned scholars of ancient Greek or Galenic medicine, in which the body was seen as a balanced system of "humors," or fluids.

But by 1812, most practitioners were in fact general practitioners. Surgeons, whether they held the MRCS (Member of the Royal College of Surgeons) or not, commonly practiced physic, as well as midwifery, and often compounded and sold their own drugs. Apothecaries, who might or might not hold the LSA (License of the Society of Apothecaries), not only compounded and sold their own drugs but also diagnosed and prescribed for their patients, performed surgery, and often practiced midwifery. Both groups found themselves sharing patient populations with men (and women) who were totally unqualified: hucksters, itinerants, and quacks. Not only were their profits undercut, but the lack of any national standard for medical qualification meant their status was low, as anyone could call themselves an apothecary or, for that matter, a surgeon.

Those who met to discuss the glass tax thus found themselves debating the far more complex matter of medical reform. This group first called itself the London Association of Apothecaries, but changed its name to the London Association of Apothecaries and Surgeon-Apothecaries. The name change said a lot about the status of practitioners and the problems they hoped the act would address. In 1813, it was proposed that the name of their profession should be changed to "general practitioners," and by 1826 it actually was changed to the Associated General Medical and Surgical

Practitioners, thus naming apothecaries and surgeons for what most of them actually were, practitioners of both physic and surgery.[7] In this time of agitation for political reform in England, the practitioners hoped to accomplish medical reform by abolishing the traditional, hierarchical structure of medical practice, and also by raising the standard of the general practitioner, i.e., the surgeon-apothecary.

But the Apothecaries Act as finally passed in 1815 was a reactionary law. It explicitly reinforced the traditional tripartite division by restricting apothecaries to the compounding and sale of drugs as prescribed by a physician. The act also mandated an apprenticeship training for apothecaries, thus keeping the apothecary in the skilled tradesman category, although it also stated that the candidate must have "sufficient medical education," or a certain number of medical lecture courses, spend six months in attendance at a hospital, pass an oral examination, and be at least twenty-one years old. On the other hand, because the act required that all practitioners in England or Wales who wished to compound and sell drugs must have the LSA, it encouraged the acquisition of a dual qualification by surgeons.

The Apothecaries Act proved to be virtually impossible to enforce. There were nowhere near enough licensed physicians to go around (less than 5 percent of medical practitioners were physicians at the beginning of the nineteenth century). Apothecaries went right on advising patients and prescribing drugs, which they also sold to the patients. Surgeons (like Lydgate) took care of patients with internal as well as external complaints, advertised themselves as "man-midwives," and also (unlike Lydgate) continued to sell drugs because that was their major source of income. And because the Apothecaries Act allowed for dual qualification as both apothecary and surgeon, the act actually worked against the very separation of medical specialties it had been intended to reinforce. By the 1830s or 1840s, most medical men not only thought of themselves as "general practitioners" but used this term in professional communications. The public nevertheless continued to speak of the apothecary, the surgeon, and the doctor. The first two were addressed as Mister; only those with a university degree were addressed as Doctor.

The Apothecaries Act also excluded those who had trained in Scotland, despite the facts that the University of Edinburgh continued to be a major resource for medical education and hospital experience and that other medical schools proliferated in Scotland as demand grew for hospital-based medical education. Since 1726, when the city of Edinburgh had appointed Alexander Monro I as professor of anatomy (he was to be succeeded by his son, Alexander Monro II or secundus, and his grandson, Alexander Monro III, or tertius), students had flocked to this medical school to attend lectures by internationally acclaimed professors, to gain experience with patients in the hospital, and to observe and perhaps actually perform dissections on dead bodies. Bodies were hard to come by, however, and even after the passage of the Anatomy Act of 1832, which allowed bodies of paupers who had died in a hospital to be claimed by the hospital, the supply was always limited. Poor people like Mrs. Dollop in *Middlemarch* feared that doctors' strongest motive in admitting them to the hospital was to acquire their bodies after death, not to make those bodies well again.

The general medical practitioners of the time also resented the Apothecaries Act for its failure to replicate in England the signal reforms of Paris medicine. Foremost among these was the abolition of the distinction between medicine and surgery, the senselessness of which was becoming increasingly apparent. In addition, the centralization of care for the poor in large hospitals in Paris resulted in an abundant supply of bodies for dissection. After the Battle of Waterloo in 1815, British (and American) students flocked to Paris for study. Here Xavier Bichat made advances in pathological anatomy by his dissection of hundreds of patients' bodies and correlation of what he saw there with observation of the patients before death. Here Pierre Louis invented "numerical medicine," a careful counting of mortality rates among patients who underwent different treatments. He proved, for example, that bloodletting made no difference in the outcome of pneumonia, no matter at what stage of the disease it was performed. René Laënnec invented the stethoscope and taught students how to analyze the sounds from the body's interior, thus for the first time making it possible for a doctor autonomously to detect changes in a patient's condition of which the patient himself might be unaware. These innovations, combined with the large numbers of patients hospitalized in Paris, brought about a major conceptual change in the theory and practice of medicine that Michel Foucault has characterized as "the gaze." In *The Birth of the Clinic* (1963), Foucault proposes that medical men began to focus on the patient's body and its disease at this time, as opposed to the preclinical practice of listening to the patient's account of her condition as the major source of knowledge for diagnosis and treatment.

In addition to attempting to reinforce the traditional divisions between apothecaries, surgeons, and physicians instead of doing away with them, the Apothecaries Act was also disappointing because it failed to remedy what was seen as a general decline in standard of living for apothecaries and surgeons. In the eighteenth century, most practitioners expected to be able to make a good living, but in the nineteenth century, they faced heightened competition from larger numbers of practitioners. Medical practitioners were also very little regulated at this time, with the result that almost anyone could practice as an apothecary or surgeon, a midwife, or a venereologist (one who specialized in the treatment of venereal diseases), including many women. Most learned their art entirely by apprenticeship, often to members of their own families, although from the mid-eighteenth century on, a period of attendance at a hospital and perhaps at a course of lectures on medical topics became increasingly common.

By the nineteenth century, especially from 1820 to 1850, medicine had become a very crowded field. In Scotland, not only Edinburgh but Glasgow medical schools were attracting many students. In London, both private medical schools and hospitals where professors lectured increased, as students flocked to the city to fulfill the hospital attendance requirement of the new LSA. By 1834 there were also no fewer than thirteen provincial medical schools in England. A provincial town with a population of 20,000 might have as many as 20 general practitioners, as well as a couple of physicians and two or three surgeons. Perhaps another motive for the Apothecaries Act of 1815, though unspecified, was to exclude women from the field, and thus limit competition. By setting standards for education and for licensing, women were effectively barred from most forms of medical practice, although they were tolerated as midwives. Only in the latter part of the nineteenth century did women begin to reenter medicine (see chapter 8).

Snow's medical education demonstrates both the diversity of experience possible for those seeking qualification for the post-1815 LSA and the full range of education available for those who wished to go beyond the LSA in early nineteenth-century England. In 1827 his parents apprenticed the fourteen-year-old boy to William Hardcastle, a surgeon-apothecary in Newcastle-upon-Tyne. Snow's parents were unusual in arranging a medical apprenticeship for their son in that they were of the laboring class. Snow's father was at first a common laborer, though he eventually moved up to the status of "carman," or carter who transported goods in a horse-drawn cart, and then farmer. As a landowning farmer, he became eligible to vote after the Reform Act of 1832 was passed. Most boys intended for the medical profession at this time were of the middle classes, sons of tradesmen, clergy, lawyers, and especially medical men. Snow's parents not only bettered themselves but managed to provide a primary education for all of their eight surviving (one child died in infancy) children.[8]

The teenage Snow was an "indoor" apprentice, meaning that he lived in the house with his master's family. He performed a wide variety of tasks, from sweeping the shop floor to preparing drug prescriptions and delivering them to patients' homes, and perhaps also taking down patient information from his master's dictation. After the first few years, apprentices served as unsupervised assistants, making house calls and even being assigned responsibility for care of entire outlying villages or collieries (mines), especially during epidemics when their masters were busy with cases in the home town. Snow, for example, was sent to the mines near Killingworth during the first cholera epidemic to reach Britain (1831–32). Apprentices performed the full range of medical and surgical procedures, such as pulling teeth, setting fractures, lancing abscesses, using that new instrument the stethoscope, and even conducting autopsies.

Sometimes masters paid for apprentices to take medical courses or lecture series. In Snow's case, Hardcastle did not send him away for such courses because several physicians and surgeons in Newcastle founded a medical school there in 1832 that was eventually accredited by the Society of Apothecaries. Snow was among eight students who enrolled and were given courses in *materia medica* (drugs and other material treatments), chemistry, theory and practice of medicine, surgery, and anatomy and physiology. For an additional fee, Snow was able to attend clinical presentations at the Newcastle Infirmary, which in 1832–33 contained 150 beds for patients with acute medical complaints or those needing surgical treatment.

In April 1833, Snow took on a second apprenticeship, this time to a rural apothecary, apparently hoping that he would be able to earn enough money in this position to eventually be able to afford the two years of London medical schooling he would need to gain dual qualification as a surgeon-apothecary. Snow's new master in the village of Burnop Field (about 100 houses), John Watson, was a pre-1815 medical man without formal training who had established his practice before the Apothecaries Act became law. Snow again lived with the family and worked in his master's "shop" (surgery).

An incident from his apprenticeship with this pre-1815 apothecary illustrates the ignorance even of the most basic hygiene such a poor man's apothecary might display. Snow found Watson's surgery in a very disorderly state and decided to clean it out for him, emptying every drawer, among other things. When the doctor returned, he was "quite taken by storm with the change," until he tried to find a blister (a poultice or piece of gauze to which a substance capable of raising a blister on the skin had been applied) in a drawer. "To his horror, the drawer was cleansed. Goodness! Cried he, why where are all the blisters? The blisters, I replied, the blisters in that drawer? I burnt them all; they were old ones. Nay, my good fellow, was the answer, that is the most extravagant act I ever heard of; such proceedings would ruin a parish doctor. Why I make all my parochial people return their blisters when they have done with them. One good blister is enough for at least half a dozen patients."[9]

This anecdote, which Snow recounted to his physician friend of later years, Sir Benjamin Ward Richardson, shows that Watson was a parish medical officer, one paid by a parish to care for people in the parish who were too poor to pay for their treatment themselves. Such medical officers sent itemized bills for attendance and for "therapeutics," not only drugs but such items as blisters, to their regular patients who were able to pay the bills. But the parish or parochial poor, being paid for by the parish, were less profitable, so the apothecary tried to save money by reusing as many items as he could.

Snow left Watson in April 1834 and took on yet a third position, this time being hired as an assistant to Joseph Warburton, a licensed apothecary practicing in Pateley Bridge. Snow again moved in with the doctor's family. But this time he became part of a medical team consisting not only of the doctor and himself but of the doctor's son, Joseph Jr., who was apprenticed to his father—a typical example of a medical family in which the son was expected to follow his father's profession. Here Snow in effect worked as a provincial general practitioner, diagnosing and prescribing for internal complaints, compounding his own prescriptions, treating external lesions, setting fractures, and performing minor surgery.

Snow left this position after two years and, after visiting with his family in York, *walked* to London, a distance of almost four hundred miles, to study medicine there. He rented a single room for himself near Soho Square and began his studies at the Hunterian School of Medicine, named after the famed anatomist William Hunter, located nearby on Great Windmill Street. By 1836, the year of Snow's arrival, there were twenty-one medical schools in London, and they competed for students by advertising their star faculty, a process attacked as "puffs and pretensions" in the *Lancet*, the radical medical journal founded in 1823 by Thomas Wakley.[10] Nevertheless, London was at this time on its way to becoming the center for medical education in England and an alternative to the previously unique University of Edinburgh. In England it was the location of the most important hospitals and also of the most prestigious medical corporations, the Royal College of Surgeons and the Royal College of Physicians.

Students who wished to prepare for the qualifying examinations for the LSA and the MRCS were now required to take courses and be in hospital attendance for both licenses. That is, they were required to be at the hospital, shadowing the hospital clinicians, a certain number of hours every day. The shortest possible time to qualify for the MRCS was twenty-two months, and for the LSA, thirty-one months. However, Snow was able to take the surgical examination after only eighteen months and the apothecary examination just six months after that, so it is presumed that some of the courses he took earlier at the then unaccredited Newcastle medical school must have been accepted for qualification.

For the dual qualification, students were required to take courses in all the same subjects Snow had studied at the Newcastle medical school, with the addition of courses in forensic (investigative and legal) medicine, midwifery and diseases of women and children, and dissection. However, their education was largely self-directed. Sir James Paget, the physician who tried and failed to help Lewes's son Thornie, commented in his memoirs, "For the great majority of students, and for myself at first, work at that time had to be self-determined and nearly all self-guided: it was very little helped by either the teachers or the means of study."[11] John Snow took an

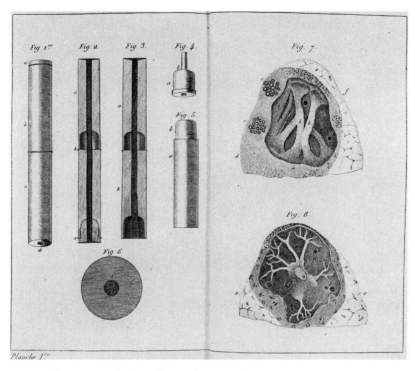

Laënnec stethoscope, 1826. © Wellcome Library, London.

oral examination on May 2, 1838, at the Royal College of Surgeons, ranking seventh in a field of 114 successful candidates, and the apothecaries' examination in October 1838, scoring eighth out of ten candidates.

Snow now moved to new lodgings at Frith Street where he set up practice. After a few years, he decided to take the next step up in medical qualifications and earn a bachelor of medicine degree. He passed examinations for this degree in November 1843, having studied for it at the University of London. Only a year later, he passed exams (now both written and oral) for the doctor of medicine, or MD, degree. This was the highest qualification for a medical man at the time and meant that he would now be formally titled "Dr. Snow." As Dr. Snow, he was qualified for a post as lecturer at a London hospital, and he managed to obtain a position as lecturer in forensic medicine at the Aldersgate Street School in 1846. But such was the competition in the London medical world that the school lost out to St. Bartholomew's and closed at the end of the 1848–49 session. Snow returned to full-time practice in London.

John Snow would doubtless have remained an obscure figure in Victorian medical history, despite his pioneering role in tracing the transmission of

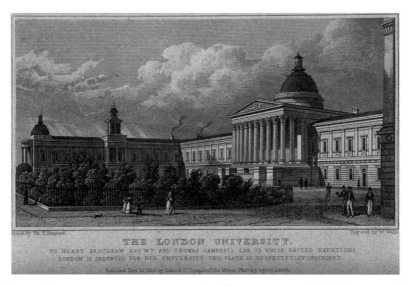

"The London University," 1828. Drawn by Thomas Hosmer Shephard, engraved by W. Wallis. © Wellcome Library, London.

cholera, had not an American dentist, William Morton, initiated the use of ether as anesthesia in 1846. Reading about anesthesia in the burgeoning medical journal literature of the day, Snow began to experiment with the use of both ether and chloroform and became well enough known for this practice that he was called in to administer anesthesia to Queen Victoria for the birth of two of her children (see chapter 8). He also began to publish accounts of his experiments and discoveries. Most of Snow's over 100 publications are now available on the website "The John Snow Archive and Research Companion."[12]

Snow's health had been "indifferent from his student days," and he died of a stroke in 1858 at the age of forty-five. But his career as a medical practitioner, beginning with an apprenticeship to a surgeon-apothecary in provincial England and culminating with the MD degree from the University of London, exemplifies the diverse and extensive range of medical education available in this transitional period when medical practice changed from medicine based on the doctor's interaction with his patient to medicine based on hospital practice and scientific investigation. Although apprenticeship continued to be common until the 1840s, hospital-based education of doctors became dominant in the latter half of the century.

Nevertheless, in 1858, when the Medical Act was passed, the medical profession was still "a hybrid agglomeration of learned, university-educated physicians, surgeons in transition from an old craft to a new 'science,' and apothecaries who claimed the practical skills of physic and surgery while drug sales wedded them to trade."[13] The act created a General Medical Council (GMC) which registered all qualified practitioners annually, but did not specify whether they were physicians, surgeons, or apothecaries, nor did it impose national license requirements. Licenses continued to be granted by local corporations as well as the more prestigious ones in London. Although the act abolished such obvious anomalies as the Archbishop of Canterbury's right to grant medical licenses at will, it did not fully protect licensed practitioners from the unlicensed quacks. It was still possible for anyone to hang up a shingle and claim to be an apothecary or a surgeon, or a practitioner of one of those other forms of alternative medical practice such as hydropathy, homeopathy, or mesmerism. Only when the Medical Act Amendment Act was passed in 1886 did the medical profession in England become unified and governed by national standards.

THE STRUGGLE FOR CONTROL: THE PATIENT'S PERSPECTIVE

Butcher is very ill tonight, he was took middling last night and is worse today and Dr Giles has been up, he spits blood so.[14]

Joseph Turrill, a market gardener in Oxfordshire, kept a diary from March 1862 to June 1867. Along with details of weather, of which vegetables and fruits were ripening, and of business details, he makes frequent mention of illnesses in the community. Outbreaks of cholera, measles, scarlatina, and smallpox are noted, along with the cattle plague. Historian Anne Hardy comments that he appears to have had quite a specific framework of reference for health. "Illness" was severe and required a doctor, meaning perhaps even a physician, or a surgeon-apothecary. Feeling "middling" meant a condition of more or less discomfort, such as having some diarrhea, but did not require a doctor or even cessation of work. "Sickness" was somewhere in between, perhaps severe enough to force stopping work, even to call a doctor, perhaps not. But Turrill does not appear preoccupied with illness, certainly not with the state of his own health.[15]

On the other hand, it has been argued that more upper-class Victorians were almost obsessed with their own health. They complained of dyspepsia (indigestion), sleeplessness, headaches, melancholy, and many other symptoms that their doctors typically found very hard to cure.[16] An entire culture of invalidism emerged, with many Victorians identifying themselves as invalids and producing a large literature of works about both the miseries and the opportunities afforded by a state of chronic ill health. Harriet Martineau's *Life in the Sick-Room*, first published in 1844, is an example of such a work. It was extremely popular and sold out in less than two months. Many famous writers, such as Elizabeth Barrett Browning, Charles Darwin,

Alfred Tennyson, and Robert Louis Stevenson, were publicly acknowledged as invalids. But ordinary people considered themselves, and were considered by others, invalids as well. "What small community cannot array a host of invalids? What family is without one or more?" was asked by the *Christian Examiner* in its 1845 review of Martineau's book.[17]

In the face of chronic illness that conventional practitioners seemed unable to alleviate, let alone to cure, many Victorians turned to alternative forms of medicine such as hydropathy, homeopathy, and mesmerism. Hydropathy, or water treatment, was a favorite of many middle-class Victorians, who frequented spas where they drank copious amounts of spring waters, bathed in them, engaged in various forms of healthful exercise, and also consulted spa physicians who were happy to advise them, for a fee, on ways to improve their health. This was also the era when homeopathy became very popular. Developed by Samuel Hahnemann, homeopathy advocated the Law of Similars, or like being cured by like, as in the use of hot compresses for burns and cowpox vaccination against smallpox, and also the Law of Infinitesimals, or that the smaller the dose, the more efficacious the medicine. Robert Browning swore by it, while his wife Elizabeth preferred the opiates recommended by her physicians. Laudanum, a mixture of opium and alcohol, was one of the most common medicines of the Victorian age and could be easily obtained without a prescription.

Harriet Martineau was convinced she had been cured of a four-year period of severe illness, including being able to reduce and finally cease the use of opiates, by mesmerism, sometimes called animal magnetism. In an *Athenaeum* article, she described how, after the well-known mesmerist Spencer Hall had twice tried passing his hands over her and induced a delightful trance in which she ceased to feel pain, she asked her maid to try to replicate the mesmeric effects. The maid complied, with equally successful results, producing "twilight and phosphoric lights" and then "a delicious sensation of ease" that removed all pain and distress.[18] During the 1840s, attempts were also made to induce anesthesia with mesmerism, but these lost credibility with the introduction of ether anesthesia in 1847.

Although the experience of illness was pervasive in Victorian society, the incidence of illness varied according to several factors. One was where you lived: when GRO statistics were first analyzed in 1860, it was learned that people who lived in cities were much less healthy than those who lived in the country. But the figures also showed that those who lived in the north of England died sooner than those who lived in the south. Later, it was realized that those who lived on the western side of the country, where industry was concentrated, were less healthy and had shorter life spans than those who lived on the eastern side. The most significant difference was that of social class: statistics showed that upper classes had less illness and lived longer than lower classes.[19] Infants were in a class by themselves: Anthony S. Wohl speaks of the Victorian era as "the massacre of the innocents."[20] Recorded infant mortality was extremely high throughout the nineteenth century, remaining constant at around 153 per thousand, not including thousands of unrecorded stillbirths. By comparison, the figure in England as of 2007 averaged five per thousand.

The experience of illness also differed according to *when* you lived. Before the nineteenth century, practitioners relied so much on the patient's report of his or her illness that it was not uncommon to treat patients via correspondence. But early in the nineteenth century, doctors began to rely more on measurement of bodily signs, as with the newly invented stethoscope (1819), and less on the patient's account. Nicholas Jewson has characterized this change as one in which medical practice moved from "Bedside Medicine" to "Hospital Medicine," and then later in the century to "Laboratory Medicine."[21] In bedside medicine the practitioner diagnosed the patient's illness largely on the basis of what the patient told him about it, as there was little other evidence available, while in hospital medicine, in which clinicians began to see large numbers of patients in hospitals, the focus shifted from the sick person to the case, or the disease condition. With the increasing use of the microscope and the identification of disease-causing bacilli such as the tubercle bacillus (1882) in the late nineteenth century, laboratory medicine became more important and medical focus shifted even further away from the patient, as the physician-scientist became more impressed by laboratory studies and less by the patient's feelings.

More recent historical studies, however, suggest that medical practice continued to be dominated by bedside or home-based medicine for the more privileged classes in England even after the practitioner's education had come to be largely hospital based. One important difference between middle- or upper-class patients and poor or working-class patients was that only the poorer classes were hospitalized. Hospitals were feared, rightly, as places where patients with internal complaints would die of "hospital fever" (contagious diseases), while surgical patients would die of "hospital gangrene" (wound gangrene). Like the puerperal fever which killed so many women who gave birth in hospitals, these were hospital-acquired infections spread by the contaminated hands or clothing of doctors, or simply by bacteria present everywhere in the air and on patients' bodies. Ignaz P. Semmelweis, working in the University of Vienna obstetric clinic in the late 1840s, recognized that puerperal fever was transmitted to women patients by the hands of doctors and medical students coming from the autopsy room. He proved that the incidence of the fever could be drastically cut by instituting routine hand-washing with a chlorine solution. But most of his colleagues were unimpressed by his theory and completely convinced that he was wrong about "wound fever," or postsurgical infection, having the same cause.[22] Not until Joseph Lister demonstrated in the 1860s that hospital infections could be prevented by the lavish use of carbolic acid as an antiseptic did hospitals gradually become safer. Aseptic technique, in which the operating room, surgeon, nurses, and other attendants and the patient were thoroughly cleaned and instruments sterilized in order to remove bacteria before surgery, followed shortly after. Prior to the development of these infection-preventing techniques, those who could afford treatment at home had the doctor come to them.

It is likely, therefore, not only that bedside medicine continued for the more privileged classes throughout the century but also that doctors cultivated a good bedside manner, and even appearance, particularly among more affluent patients. "Dr. H. L. Thomas, who was a popular practitioner with the middle classes in London during the first half of the nineteenth century was praised for having had an elegant appearance. He habitually wore the 'black dress-coat, waistcoat and trousers, black silk stockings and pumps, and a spotless white cravat' of the traditional physician. Moreover, he was said to be 'perfect in the sickroom; cool, attentive, and kind.'"[23] Later in the century, advice books such as *The Physician Himself* (1882) and *The Young Practitioner* (1890) were written to instruct the new practitioner on how to adopt a pleasing professional presence. They gave advice not only on how to develop "Professional Tact" but "Business Sagacity."[24]

Physicians, who saw themselves as a professional elite, catered to the wealthy. As there were relatively few physicians in proportion to surgeons and apothecaries (only about one in five by midcentury), the middle and upper classes in the provinces did not necessarily consult physicians. Also, like Lady Chettam in *Middlemarch*, some of those who could afford to consult a physician preferred a practitioner of inferior class status, so that the patient could inform the doctor about the characteristics of her constitution and dictate the treatment she desired. In short, those of higher-class status were unlikely to experience their status as a patient as simply that of a case, even if the hospital-trained practitioner was silently thinking of the patient that way (but prudently keeping it to himself).

Working-class people maintained some control over their medical treatment by joining "friendly societies," which paid fees to both hospitals and doctors to cover the care of members. For example, at the Westminster Hospital where Snow put in his required period of hospital attendance, hospital physicians diagnosed and prescribed for working-class people who came to the clinics, most often as accident victims. People with complaints considered chronic, or incurable, were not admitted to the hospital, but they could be admitted as outpatients and would be examined by hospital clinicians and receive drugs in the dispensary. If they were dissatisfied with their treatment, they could return a second day and be seen by a different physician.

But the experience of being a patient was very different for the poor. The New Poor Law, passed in 1834, was intended to discourage pauperism.

It mandated the merging of several parishes into a union system, and the building of unions or workhouses where those who requested relief were to be subjected to strict discipline. Whereas, under the old Poor Law, individual parishes might appoint a medical man to treat the poor of that parish, the New Poor Law created medical districts which in rural areas might be impossibly large for a single medical officer to manage.[25] Parishes sometimes selected a practitioner according to how much he charged, which often meant they chose an unqualified practitioner. The General Medical Order of 1842 attempted to remedy some of these abuses by legislating "a maximum medical district of 15,000 acres for a single medical officer" and insisting on a double qualification in both medicine and surgery. But as late as the 1860s, medical districts of up to 100,000 acres could be found, and medical officers selected because they were well qualified might hand off most of their work to an unqualified or poorly qualified assistant.[26]

In addition, it was found that as many as three-quarters of the poor who required relief were actually sick: workhouses became largely infirmaries. Paupers in these workhouse infirmaries were paid to care for other paupers, so that nursing care was often unskilled and ignorant. Meanwhile, the enormous size of many medical districts meant not only that medical officers were unable to get to the homes of the sick poor but also that the sick poor had difficulty getting to the practitioner's office.

Unscrupulous medical officers in such districts might serve only paying patients themselves, while hiring an unqualified assistant to care for the poor. One historian suggests as a guess that one in every fourth or fifth surgical practice employed such an assistant in mid-nineteenth-century Britain.[27] One such unqualified assistant, Alexander Blyth, kept a diary that provides an instructive contrast with Snow's assistantship in the 1830s. Blyth got his job through a London agent who simply took down his name after seeing some testimonials. With that, he got an indoor position in a busy practice run by the Ceely brothers in Aylesbury, Buckinghamshire, in the 1860s. The Ceely brothers claimed that they were disappointed that Blyth had attended no medical lectures, so they reduced his starting pay to £40 per annum for the first six months, and £45 after that. It was very hard work; Blyth found that he had succeeded two other short-lived assistants. Although the practice included such famous and wealthy patients as Benjamin Disraeli, the Duke of Buckingham, and Lord Carrington, Blyth saw only the poorer patients. His daily schedule began at 8:00 A.M. in the dispensary, continued with house calls on the poor in the afternoon, and ended after a return to the dispensary in the evening. His take on his patients was that they were "a lot of wretched sick paupers in the union, or in the back slums, or any other dirty stinking place that generates disease."[28] One can only wonder how they felt about him.

Although doctors had, for the most part, become better educated and more qualified by the end of the Victorian era, standards in the medical profession were still unevenly enforced. Patients, in turn, could receive very different treatment depending on their ability to pay. Frances Power Cobbe noted, "As medical officers in parishes and unions, factory and prison surgeons, public vaccinators, medical officers of health, inspectors of nuisances, and very commonly as coroners, the doctors are daily assuming authority."[29] Yet she excoriated them for their monetary motives, and also for their "double" treachery to women, on whom they enforced the Contagious Diseases Acts (which held prostitutes responsible for the spread of venereal disease), yet whom they had excluded from the medical profession.[30] Major changes for both doctors and patients were, however, already happening or were to happen in the near future. Women were in fact beginning to enter the profession: the 1881 Census noted twenty-five female practitioners (see chapter 8). In 1886 Parliament passed the third act regulating medical education and practice in Britain, the Medical Act Amendment Act. In 1911 the National Insurance Act would be passed, offering medical insurance to workers, but not to their dependents. Most women and all children, the elderly, and the self-employed were not covered.[31] The act was, nevertheless, the first step toward a national insurance plan that would insure treatment by qualified medical practitioners to all.

THE STRUGGLE TO CONTROL INFECTION: INSIDE VICTORIAN HOSPITALS

Prof. then dressed it with the spray, then put on chloride of zinc and moved the arm to and fro. The pain was indescribable. I never felt such excruciating pain before. I also felt the arm quite loose from my body. The pain caused me almost to faint.

Prof. said to the students: "Gentlemen, I have a great fear of putrefaction setting in and you all know its outcome. Thus I will look anxiously for the second day or third day between hope and fear. I hope the chloride of zinc will preserve it but it is only an experiment. However we will see if spared."[32]

Margaret Mathewson describes her experience in the Royal Infirmary in Edinburgh with the famed surgeon Joseph Lister, with whom she sought treatment for a tubercular shoulder joint in 1877. Louis Pasteur had proved that putrefaction was caused by airborne bacteria, rather than being a chemical process in which bacteria were spontaneously generated. After reading Pasteur's work, published in 1861, Lister had developed the process of antisepsis. He began with carbolic acid as antiseptic agent, but went on to test other agents as well. As a result of his own publication on antiseptic technique, Lister was appointed professor of surgery at the University of Edinburgh in 1869. Mathewson kept a diary about her experiences in the hospital there, a rare document that gives us a live account of what it was like to have an operation in a Victorian hospital.

Her diary leaves no doubt that by this time patients were treated as cases from which medical students could learn. She describes how "Prof. Lister, Dr. Cheyne and about 40 students came downstairs, and into our ward." She was told to undress, and the "Professor" then told the students that "this is a case of consumption [tuberculosis] of the lungs but is providentially turned from the lungs to the shoulder joint. There it has formed a circumficial [circumferential] abscess. Also here is another glandular abscess on the collar bone which makes this a very interesting case for us all."[33] Mathewson describes how she was called "to be lectured on" and was put into a dark room to wait, only to be told after two hours that she was not wanted

Joseph Lister, 1st Baron Lister (1827–1912), surgeon, c. 1895. © Wellcome Library, London.

that day as there were so many others. Next day she again sat for two hours in the "dark hole" and was again told there were too many others ahead of her. While she was waiting, dinner was served in the ward, so she didn't get any. Finally, on the third day she was called again, and this time went into the "big theatre," where she was "lectured on before about 40 gentlemen and all the lecture was in English so I had the benefit of it too." The professor asked the same questions and explained the case as before.[34]

In a later lecture in the theater, the professor invited her to "turn your back on these gentlemen" and look at the blackboard. There she saw a diagram of her much swollen arm, along with an arm in its "natural state," and "special marks where it had to be operated on." She almost fainted, as it was clear the operation was going to be much more serious than she had hoped. When the time came for the operation, she was taken into the theater by Dr. Cheyne, where she was met by Professor Lister, who "bowed and smiled." She returned the bow, then climbed up on to the table, around which four gentlemen were sitting. Cheyne laid a towel saturated with chloroform on her face and told her to "breathe away." When she came to, she found herself in a bed in a strange ward, extremely sick from the anesthetic and in severe pain from the operation. It was at this point that Lister demonstrated her case to the students and his fear of putrefaction or bacterial infection and its known outcome, which was death in nearly all cases. But Mathewson was one of the lucky ones: when the bandages were taken off, Lister found neither color nor smell and commented that the chloride of zinc had preserved the wound entirely from putrefaction. She was discharged from the hospital after eight months and returned to her home in Shetland. Only three years later, however, she died, most likely of tuberculosis. She was thirty-two years old.[35]

Mathewson exemplifies hospital medicine as outlined by Jewson. The relationship between a patient and her doctor had changed from that of bedside medicine, typical in the eighteenth century, in which the doctor listened carefully to the patient's description of her symptoms and based his treatment on it, to hospital medicine, in which the doctor ascertained the patient's condition by examination and based his treatment on his own diagnosis and his specialized knowledge. The patient was assigned to a "passive and uncritical role . . . his main function being to endure and to wait."[36] The hospital was central to this change in the relation between patients and practitioners.

Hospitals were originally founded primarily for the care and treatment of the sick poor. But during the nineteenth century, hospitals were transformed from places where sick people went because they had no other recourse, and where they were tended by a Poor Law medical officer and most often nursed by other paupers, to places where medical students were trained and patients treated by physicians and surgeons who were most interested in producing new medical knowledge. Middle- and even upper-class patients began to seek admission to hospitals. But doctors increasingly wielded a new authority based on knowledge of science, and the patient was subordinated to this new knowledge. By the turn of the century, laboratory medicine was emerging along with the modernized Victorian hospital, sanitary and spacious with its high-ceilinged pavilion wards, to offer patients the benefit of knowledge gained in the scientific realm. Diphtheria antitoxin, produced in laboratories from the blood serum of horses, became the first agent capable of actually curing an existing disease in 1892. These dramatic changes in medical practice, not always appreciated by patients, were made possible by changes in the design and function of hospitals.

An Appeal on Behalf of the Intended Hospital at Huddersfield, written about 1825 by a Dr. William Turnbull who had been awarded an MD from the University of Edinburgh in 1814, demonstrates how nineteenth-century hospitals were founded on motives as much practical as philanthropic. Turnbull writes that, as the poor are unable to afford medical advice, they often are driven into debt by sickness, and from there into "a sort of moral despair" which deprives them of independence of spirit and makes them willing to leave their debts unpaid and to rely on the parish for support. Thus, providing a hospital where they could be treated would not only render their cure "short and easy" but also obviously save the parish money in the long run. But, Dr. Turnbull adds, "The instruction which such establishments afford those persons who are destined to practice the various branches of the healing art . . . ultimately becomes advantageous to all ranks of society." A hospital would represent not only a worthy charitable venture for the relief of the sick poor, and be a cheaper method than just letting them become more and more dependent on the rest of the parish. It would also afford an invaluable resource for instruction to those who would become medical practitioners.[37]

Since the poor are currently employed in trade and manufactures which are housed in "crowded and ill ventilated" quarters, Turnbull goes on to say, "the constitutions of the people are generally weak and prone to disease." Trade and manufacturing lead to an increase in both prosperity for some and "misery and misfortune" for others. The need for medical care is bound to not only continue but increase. "The wail of the widow and the cry of the orphan still vibrate on the ear." Turnbull's appeal for the new hospital, planned to have some twenty beds and also to treat outpatients, resonates with the intensifying medical and surgical needs produced by the rapid industrialization of England in the early nineteenth century.

In fact, a building accident had occurred in Huddersfield in April 1825, killing sixteen people and seriously injuring others.[38] *Rules and Regulations of the Huddersfield and Upper Agbrigg Infirmary, 1834* documents how a tight class system was formed in such institutions. The rules stipulated "that no patient be admitted without a recommendation, except in cases of accident or great emergency; and a certain number of beds shall be reserved for such cases as will not admit of delay. That Governors, recommending patients from distant places, be desired to send their cases drawn up by some Physician, Surgeon, or Apothecary, (post-paid,) to which an answer shall be returned, whether and when they may be admitted: but the Board shall be at liberty to reject such patients, if their cases appear to have been misrepresented, or their circumstances such as to enable them to provide for their own cure."[39] In addition, no person who was able to pay for medical aid could be admitted as either an inpatient or an outpatient. No apprentices or domestic servants could be admitted as inpatients, except for "capital operations," and in that case, their master or mistress was to pay ten shillings and sixpence per week for their subsistence. Soldiers could not be admitted as inpatients unless an officer was willing to pay one shilling per day for subsistence.

Obviously, such rules were designed to insure that no malingerers could get into the hospital and receive free room and board. The fare offered in such hospitals was probably substantial, though not what we would call especially nutritious or vitamin rich. Mathewson recorded of her 1877 hospital stay that patients received a breakfast of porridge and milk, followed by coffee and bread. Dinner consisted of a first course of soup and bread, followed by potatoes and meat. At 4:30 P.M., tea was served, with bread and butter. And at 7:30 P.M., a supper of bread and milk was provided.[40] In workhouse infirmaries after the institution of the New Poor Law in 1834, however, the food was deliberately limited to the cheapest and coarsest fare possible, in order to discourage all but the most desperate poor from applying for admission. Medical officers sometimes prescribed additional fruit and vegetables as medicine for inmates.

The Huddersfield hospital rules and regulations also made it very clear that inpatients were to be subjected to a discipline not unlike that of a prison. Patients could not leave the hospital without a practitioner's permission, on pain of expulsion. They were required to remain in their own ward and not to enter any other. Cursing, swearing, and "rude and indecent behavior" were not permitted. In addition, the rules stipulated that "there be no playing at cards or any other game within the limits of the Infirmary; nor any smoking, without leave from a Physician or Surgeon, first signified to the Apothecary: neither shall spirituous [sic] liquors, nor any provisions, be introduced by the patients or their friends. That such patients as are able, be employed in nursing the other patients, washing and ironing the linen, cleaning the wards or any other work, but not without leave of the Physician or Surgeon."[41] Even half a century later, Mathewson had to remind herself that she was not in a prison: "Though it does look bleak and dreary yet it is a hospital and not a prison and I am here for no crime."[42] Mathewson also found herself abruptly moved from one ward to another and, when the hospital became more crowded, was required to share her bed with another patient, despite the fact that this caused such discomfort in her still-healing shoulder as to interfere with her sleep.

The Huddersfield hospital was typically very choosy about what kind of patient could be admitted:

> That no woman advanced in pregnancy, no child under six years, (except in particular cases, as fractures, cutting for the stone, amputations, couching [cataract surgery], or where some other surgical operations may be required,) or persons disordered in their senses, subject to epileptic fits, suspected to have the smallpox, measles, itch, or other infectious distemper, having habitual ulcers, syphilis, (except when required by the faculty,) or those suspected to be in a consumption, or in an incurable or dying state, be admitted as in-patients.[43]

Hospitals for such specialized purposes as treatment of children, childbirth, mental illness, and infectious conditions were built in increasing numbers throughout the century, however. George Eliot's fictional surgeon, Lydgate, is engaged in setting up a fever hospital that would have a special ward for cholera patients. Over the course of the Victorian era, hospitals were transformed from institutions for care of the sick poor to places where the working classes felt they had a right to admission and free medical care, and where patients who could afford to pay were admitted to special hospital wings with private rooms. Florence Nightingale, who was convinced that infections were caused by bad air, advocated the pavilion design for hospital wards in order to facilitate the free circulation of air. Hospital wards were to be at least fifteen or sixteen feet high, and no more than thirty feet wide, with large windows on opposite walls, so that sunlight and fresh air could be plentiful.[44]

In 1894, hospitals in London began treating diphtheria cases with the newly produced antitoxin. Until this time, diphtheria patients had only been admitted to hospitals so that a tracheotomy (making a surgical opening in the trachea or windpipe) could be performed to prevent suffocation from the thick gray membranes that grew inside the throat. Most hospitals did not even admit diphtheria patients until the 1880s or later. The diphtheria antitoxin serum had first been developed by a German scientist, Emil von Behring, in 1890. But it was not until Emile Roux, a French physician who had conducted more extensive trials of the serum in the Hôpital des Enfants Malades in Paris, published his reports that English hospitals began to use the serum. It was with this development that English hospitals could be said to have entered the age of laboratory medicine. Ironically, the new disease that kills George Eliot's fictional surgeon was also the first disease to be treatable, and usually curable, with an agent specific to that disease and first produced in the laboratory.

2

Cholera

He had come at last, Baalzebub, god of flies, and of what flies are bred from; to visit his self-blinded worshippers, and bestow on them his own Cross of the Legion of Dishonor. He had come suddenly, capriciously, sportively, as he sometimes comes; as he had come to Newcastle the summer before, while yet the rest of England was untouched. He had wandered all but harmless about the West-country that summer; as if his maw had been full glutted five years before, when he sat for many a week upon the Dartmoor hills, amid the dull brown haze, and sunburnt bents, and dried-up water-courses of white dusty granite, looking far and wide over the plague-struck land, and listening to the dead-bell booming all day long in Tavistock churchyard. But he was come at last, with appetite more fierce than ever, and had darted aside to seize on Aberalva, and not to let it go till he had sucked his fill.[1]

Charles Kingsley, Victorian clergyman and writer of many popular novels, images the disease of cholera as Baalzebub, "the god of flies, and of what flies are bred from," i.e., sewage and polluted water. In *Two Years Ago* (1857), he describes the third epidemic of cholera in Great Britain, which began in 1853, only four years after the preceding one of 1848–49. Baalzebub (the name, often translated as "lord of the flies," is taken from a Philistine god) bestows on "self-blinded worshippers," or those who believed the disease was a visitation sent by God to punish the sinful and that they therefore should do nothing to help the afflicted, the "Cross of the Legion of Dishonor." Cholera came "capriciously," even "sportively," for it spread in baffling patterns. It hit in one village or city district and not another, even one house on a street but not its next-door neighbor. Sometimes it took a whole family and sometimes only one member, or felled a healthy young man while sparing his sickly old father. Although the poor were known to be far more severely affected, the middle classes and the rich did not escape the dreadful, vampiric disease, which drained bodily fluids so rapidly that victims literally turned blue and died in an agony of cramps and spasms within a few days or even hours.

The first epidemic of what became known as "Asiatic cholera" struck Great Britain in 1831. The disease, which in previous centuries had been known only in India, was to appear again in Britain in 1848–49, 1853–54, and 1866–67 as pandemics swirled around the globe. Having known more than a century of plague-free history, the British responded to cholera's rapid approach across Europe to the shores of Britain with terror-stricken language and exaggerated statistics. The *Quarterly Review* called it "one of the most terrible pestilences which have ever desolated the earth" and claimed that it had killed fifty million in fourteen years. "If this malady should really take root and spread in these islands, it is impossible to calculate the horror even of its probably financial results alone."[2]

Although the *Quarterly Review* writer's thoughts turned to financial consequences first, probably the most terrifying aspect of the "horror" of cholera lay in its "foreign, Eastern origin—it had crossed God's 'moat' which was supposed to protect England from invasion."[3] A "choleraphobia" emerged from fears, as one doctor was to put it later, that "the cholera was something outlandish, unknown, monstrous [*sic*]; its tremendous ravages, so long foreseen and feared, so little to be explained, its insidious march over whole continents, its apparent defiance of all the known and conventional precautions against the spread of epidemic disease, invested it with a mystery and a terror which thoroughly took hold of the public mind, and seemed to recall the memory of the great epidemics of the middle ages."[4] The spread of this shock disease from the dark territory of colonial India obsessed the British public. As parliamentarian and historian Thomas Babington Macaulay wrote to his sister: "The great topic now . . . is not, as you perhaps fancy, Reform, but cholera. There is a great panic, as great a panic as I can remember, particularly in the City."[5]

Cholera proved to be of unique significance in the history of nineteenth-century medicine. As the first epidemic disease to strike the British Isles in over a century (the last epidemic, bubonic plague, or the Black Death, had ravaged London in 1664–65), it not only produced public panic but also fueled rapid (or at least more rapid) development of plans to improve public health and sanitation. Cholera was and is a "disease of society," as historian Asa Briggs puts it: it thrives in densely populated areas, and it travels where crowds of people travel.[6] In the nineteenth century, the explosive growth of cities resulting from industrialization was a major factor in producing the pandemics of cholera. (While the difference between *pandemic* and *epidemic* is always somewhat ambiguous, the first term generally refers to an outbreak of infectious disease that spreads across many countries or even around the world, while the second refers to outbreaks in more localized areas, such as particular nations, regions, or cities. *Endemic,* on the other hand, refers to an infectious disease that is nearly always present, though sometimes to a greater extent than at others.)

Cholera pandemics in the nineteenth century were also unique in that efforts to combat epidemics in localized areas eventually led to control not only of cholera but also of other epidemic disease. The Victorian physician John Snow brilliantly tracked the cause of the terrible Broad Street epidemic of cholera in 1854 to a single London pump, and then documented by his pioneering epidemiology his hypothesis that cholera was spread chiefly by contaminated drinking water.[7] British health authorities had been persuaded of the contagious character of the disease long before Robert Koch identified its exact cause in 1883: a bacterium to be known as *Vibrio cholerae.* Although cholera was not eradicated, it could be controlled.

But cholera had even more far-reaching effects than the understanding and control of this epidemic disease. The repeated epidemics exposed not only the filthy conditions in which the urban and rural poor of Britain lived but also the submerged connections between this domestic filth and the diseases, real and figurative, of colonialism and capitalism. As cholera maps and tables showed the numbers and locations of the sick, the fluidity of boundaries between rich and poor in Britain became visible. John Snow's tireless shoeleather epidemiology (he conducted his investigations by walking house to house in London) demonstrated that the modern city was one body interconnected by an invisible circulatory system of water pipes and sewage drains. Upper- and lower-class British citizens drank the same water and suffered the same disease. This alien invader was a key factor in the British nation's recognition that protecting the health of some could only be accomplished by protecting the health of all.

CHOLERA GOES GLOBAL

In August 1818, the secretary to the Madras Medical Board wrote a detailed description of the terrifying symptoms of cholera (see sidebar). Finding himself in the midst of the first Indian epidemic of cholera in the nineteenth century (1817–24), the secretary evidently felt a responsibility to record what was to him a new disease. But the disease had already become pandemic, moving into Southeast Asia via the small subequatorial country of Mauritius. Cholera had been observed by the Portuguese on the west coast of India in the

It commences with a sense of heat in the epigastrium and slight watery purg-
ings accompanied by a great languor and depression of spirits, with a dimin-
ished temperature of the surface of the body. The uneasiness at stomach and
watery purging with a most remarkable prostration of strength increase rapidly; spasms are felt in the extremities, the pulse becomes very small and languid, and unless these symptoms are arrested by medicine, the vomiting and
purging of a glary nearly colourless matter becomes more urgent—the cramp
extends from the feet and legs to the muscles of the abdomen, thorax and
arms—affecting those of a robust habit and in whom the attack is severe,
with most excruciating pains, and exhausting the vital energies so rapidly that
the patient in six or eight hours loses his pulse at the wrist; his body is
bedewed with a cold clammy sweat, the eyes, dull and heavy, are covered with
a film, occasionally suffused with blood and insensible to the stimulus of
light, and in this state of the disease he is often afflicted with deafness, the
breathing becomes greatly affected, and is sometimes performed . . . with
much labor and a sort of grunting—the tongue is generally white, sometimes
but seldom parched.

During this awful and rapid progress of symptoms the countenance . . .
becomes collapsed, the eye sinks, the patient has occasionally the appearance
of being comatose and is roused for a few moments with difficulty, the
extremities become cold and the circulation gradually dies away.

In the progress of the disease the patient complains of great, and in some
instances, insatiable thirst, having a strong desire for cold fluids—the secretion
as well as the excretion of bile would appear to be entirely suppressed—the
burning uneasiness in the stomach extends to the whole alimentary canal, and a
total want of urine is observed in all the worse cases of disease.

In this severe epidemic, death has hitherto been observed to ensue from
ten to twenty-four hours from the commencement of the attack.[8]

sixteenth century, and ancient Indian records indicate the disease had been
known in that country since 400 BCE.[9] But it was not until the early nineteenth
century that the disease suddenly migrated from Bengal on the east coast of
India, where it was endemic, to the west coast, and subsequently to other
Asian countries. In a second path of contagion, the disease spread up the
Persian Gulf to Baghdad and as far north as Astrakhan in the Russian Empire.
But in this first nineteenth-century cholera pandemic, the disease did not
spread into Europe or the Americas.

Why did an ancient disease found only in India suddenly become the
cause of global pandemics in the nineteenth century? Evidence suggests that

a local disease was transformed into a global one first by a British military campaign. In 1817, as part of the expansion of British rule in India that had begun in 1798, the Marquess of Hastings marched his troops across India from Bengal to Bombay (now Mumbai).[10] As David Arnold points out in his study of medicine and epidemic disease in nineteenth-century India, it has become so customary to employ military metaphors such as "attacks" and "invasions" to epidemic diseases, or to their "conquest" by science, that "one could easily overlook the literal correspondence between cholera and military power in colonial India."[11] Cholera, which had already decimated Hastings's troops in Calcutta, arrived in western India in July and August 1818, coinciding closely with the British defeat of the peshwa of Pune (a hill station south of Bombay).[12] Soldiers, always vulnerable to epidemic disease because of primitive hygiene arrangements, crowding, fatigue, and inadequate water and food supplies, carried cholera with them, spreading it throughout India as the British consolidated their conquest of the country. Once in Bombay, a major shipping port, the disease was spread by commercial shipping as well as by further troop movements.

Commercial shipping became both much more extensive and, with the advent of oceangoing steamships in 1838, much more rapid in the nineteenth century. The development of railway systems (in India some five thousand miles had been laid down by 1870) also speeded the transit of people, and with them cholera.[13] Both Hindu and Muslim pilgrimages to major shrines, which had caused outbreaks in various parts of India when people traveled mostly by foot, attracted more pilgrims and moved them, and cholera, farther and faster by means of the railway. But military campaigns in the nineteenth century have come under particular scrutiny as vectors of epidemics and pandemics because this was the era in which imperialist ideologies vastly extended the scope of colonial conquest. Especially in the case of the Asiatic cholera that invaded Britain in 1831, crossing God's moat or the English Channel, it no longer seems far-fetched to propose that, although the disease originated in India, the pandemic form of it originated with the British military campaign to subjugate India.

TURNING BLUE: CHOLERA ENTERS BRITAIN

The next major outbreak of cholera in India after 1817 occurred in 1826. It seemed to be the result of Hindu pilgrimage to the northern city of Hurdwar (now Hardiwar). But commercial trade carried it farther north this time, and it moved inside the boundaries of the Russian Empire via Persia and Afghanistan. When the disease appeared in Moscow in 1830, the British realized, as R. J. Morris puts it, "that cholera was no longer just a problem for the East India administration."[14] In 1831, pushed along by a Russian military campaign in Poland, the disease moved through northern Europe.

By August 1831 it was in Berlin and Vienna, and it reached Hamburg in October. From there it skipped across the English Channel to Sunderland, a port and shipbuilding center on the northeast coast of England and just a few hours by ship from Hamburg.

At first the inhabitants of Sunderland didn't recognize the disease. The town had tried to prepare for the disease by forming a Board of Health and inviting a military surgeon, James Butler Kell, to join the board. Kell had actually seen cases of cholera in Mauritius when stationed there with his regiment in 1819–20 and 1829. But members of the medical profession in the town were divided by social class and did not communicate much with each other or with Kell. As a surgeon, Kell was considered much below the social status of the town physicians.[15] Moreover, town surgeons considered themselves above Kell because he was a military surgeon. Consequently, Kell had difficulty learning about sick people whose illness might have been cholera, while the town physicians, surgeons, and apothecaries who attended such people were unsure how to diagnose the disease. Even when they suspected it, Sunderland doctors were reluctant to admit that the dread Asiatic cholera was actually in their midst.

In its early stages, cholera was in fact difficult to differentiate from such ordinary afflictions as summer diarrhea. Only the severity of the illness and the rapidity with which it developed into a life-threatening condition would arouse the doctor's suspicions that what he was seeing might be something worse. But one characteristic of this intestinal illness could clinch the diagnosis, if the medical man knew enough to recognize it: victims became so severely dehydrated so fast, they would literally turn blue. Lips, nails, and eventually the whole body took on a bluish-gray cast as vomiting and the characteristic "rice-water" (mostly colorless but filled with small white specks) diarrhea drained bodily fluids. Perhaps in deliberate reference to the now bygone Black Death, the new disease was spoken of as "the blue terror."[16]

Besides having difficulty in diagnosing the disease and being unwilling to communicate with other doctors or health authorities, doctors were in complete ignorance at this time as to how the disease was spread. Two opposing theories prevailed: in one, the disease was contagious and was spread from person to person, though by what agent no one knew (bacteria had not yet been discovered); in the other, the disease was not contagious from person to person but was generated by miasmas—foul effluvia rising from sewage or water polluted by sewage—and hence could be spread by flies, which were also believed to be generated by foul waters. If the disease was contagious, then quarantine of sick people and their families should be an effective measure against it. But wherever quarantine was tried, stiff opposition rose against it because it halted trade and imposed a particularly heavy economic burden on the working poor. In Sunderland, for example, ships were

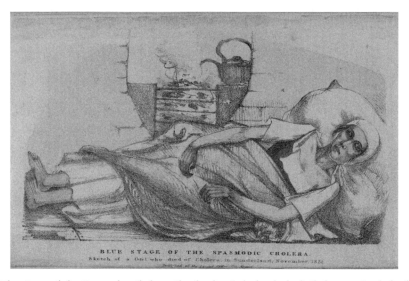

"Blue Stage of the Spasmodic Cholera. Sketch of a Girl who died of Cholera, in Sunderland, November, 1831." *Lancet,* February 4, 1832. © Wellcome Library, London.

quarantined and their cargoes could not be unloaded, thus depriving dock-workers of their livelihood. Those who owned shares in ships, including several local surgeons, also lost money, as did numerous small tradesmen.[17] Quarantines thus tended to arouse violent protest, even riots.

But riots during this epidemic in Britain were chiefly aimed at the medical profession, whose members were suspected of stealing the dead bodies of cholera victims, or even of hastening their deaths, in order to secure the bodies for dissection. This fear had been greatly heightened by the Burke and Hare scandal in Edinburgh that took place only a few years earlier. Because each student at the Edinburgh medical school required three bodies on which to practice during the sixteen-month course in anatomy and surgery, and because only the bodies of convicted murderers could legally be used for dissection, grave-robbing became a lucrative business. But William Burke and William Hare took the business of supplying bodies to medical schools one step further: in 1827 and 1828 they murdered at least sixteen people by suffocation or some other method that left no visible marks of violence and sold the bodies to the Edinburgh medical school. This practice became known as "burking," and many riots during the first cholera epidemic were fueled by fears of the poor that the very doctors who were supposed to be helping them were actually engaged in killing them off in order to get the bodies for dissection. In 1831, just as the cholera epidemic was beginning to take hold, no fewer than three gangs of burkers were arrested in London, so the fears of the poor, who were sometimes forcibly carried to fever hospitals, were not entirely unjustified.[18]

The capricious manner in which cholera spread also made it hard to decide whether the disease was contagious or environmental. What was not known at the time was that cholera is usually only weakly infectious. As John Snow was later to realize, the disease can be contracted only by swallowing what he called the "cholera poison," i.e., the organism, *Vibrio cholerae*, that causes the disease. And once swallowed, that organism must survive stomach acids in order to reach the favorable climate of the intestines, where it embeds itself in the wall of the intestine and is thus able to survive long enough to produce illness. Hence, though a number of people might have drunk from the same contaminated water source or eaten from the same pile of contaminated apples, only some of them would come down with the disease. And only about half of those who contracted the disease would die of it.[19]

Outside the favorable climate of the human body, the *Vibrio cholerae* must have even more favorable environments to survive long enough to find its way back to another human body. Food and water must be contaminated by sewage to become carriers of the disease, as it spreads person to person by the fecal to oral route. While it can live for as long as sixteen days in apples and some other fruits, and up to fourteen days in water, it lives only eight hours in beer or wine. In winter, when Victorians craved hot drinks such as tea and so boiled most of the water they drank, cholera attacks declined. Thus, although cholera spread from Sunderland to the whole of northeast England, to Edinburgh, Glasgow, and the lowlands of Scotland, and then south to London during the winter months of November through February, the progress of the disease notably slowed as the cold continued, and by May London was declared free of the disease.[20] But as the weather warmed again, new cases began to appear, and the epidemic peaked during the months of July, August, and September 1832. By November 1832, it was virtually over.

In fact, not only is cholera only weakly effective as an epidemic agent, but the number of people who died in Britain in this and later epidemics was small in relation to the numbers dying from such endemic diseases as smallpox, tuberculosis, and syphilis and other fevers such as typhus, typhoid, and yellow fever. Even in the worst epidemic (1848–49), cholera killed only slightly more people than typhus, a disease carried by the body louse.[21] About 32,000 people out of a total population of 16.5 million died in the epidemic of 1831–32. Almost twice as many, 62,000, died in the epidemic of 1848–49, another 20,000 in 1853–54, and about 14,000 in 1866–67.[22]

Why then did the 1831 cholera epidemic cause such panic? First, of course, the almost incredible rapidity of its onset and the appalling nature of the symptoms (which sometimes caused victims to collapse and die in the street) were extremely shocking. People died, as Kingsley put it in *Two Years Ago*, "wild with disgusting agony." Someone who had been perfectly healthy in the morning could be dead by nightfall. But second, many historians have pointed out that cholera in the nineteenth century was similar to AIDS in the twentieth: it was a disease new to the British and to all the world except India, and it was quickly surrounded by rumors of unsavory origins. It was considered a filth disease, believed to occur chiefly in crowded and unhygienic living conditions, such as those of the poor or the common foot soldier. And like AIDS, cholera was blamed on its victims. People believed it was the "vicious habits" of the poor—drunkenness, prostitution, lack of religion—that made them subject to this new disease from the unknown and alien East. To succumb to cholera, then, carried innuendoes of immorality. Cholera, like AIDS, was socially construed as a disease that struck mostly people who had brought it on themselves by their "immoral" behavior.[23]

"THE CHOLERA IS RAGING ABOUT NEW CROSS"

In August 1849, Elizabeth Barrett Browning wrote her sister Arabella in great alarm from Florence, where she and her husband Robert and their baby son were living: "I am very, very uneasy about the cholera— Increasing it is, instead of diminishing." Her sister's persistence in not only walking through the open streets of London but "joining in crowded associations on hot evenings" made Barrett Browning fear that she was in grave danger of contracting cholera. "Where it prevails," she wrote, "the authorities have often found it necessary to prevent assemblages of people even in the open air: & in close rooms there must be a more positive degree of danger. Oh *do* get out of town, all of you, as fast as you can— I am not easy indeed."[24]

Barrett Browning's letter was written towards the end of the second cholera epidemic to hit Britain. The poet's alarm for her sister was justified, for this was by far the most severe of the four cholera epidemics in nineteenth-century Britain: reaching England in 1848, again striking in the port of Sunderland first, it killed almost twice the number of the first epidemic.[25] It also hit London much harder than had the first epidemic, thus raising Barrett Browning's fears for both her own family, most of whom lived in inner London, and her husband Robert's, who then lived in a part of London known as New Cross.

Barrett Browning's letter also demonstrates the prevailing belief that cholera was spread by breathing in bad air, not only from miasma but perhaps even from the air surrounding a cholera victim. People believed they could catch cholera by breathing in the stench emitted from sewage drains or cesspools, or from the effluvia rising from the badly polluted Thames River, or even from graveyards crowded with the bodies of cholera victims. Barrett Browning accordingly feared that walking about in the streets (which were likely to be full of the disgusting smell of open sewage drains) could cause cholera, but being in hot and crowded rooms might also expose one to the disease.

Although cholera is not transmitted by gases from cesspools or cemeteries, efforts made to clean up the city by improving its sewage and drainage systems and purifying its water supplies were eventually to prove effective in controlling the disease in London, even before its actual cause was known. As cholera moved across Europe, much of which was taken up with the revolutionary political movements of 1848, its specter hastened the passage of the Public Health Act of 1848 in Britain. This act set up a General Board of Health as recommended by Edwin Chadwick, a clergyman who played a leading role in attempts both to reduce poverty and to improve public health. Although this board had only advisory powers and was not in itself very effective, over the following years more such legislation calling for various sanitation practices was passed, such that by the time of the Public Health Act of 1875, Britain had the most comprehensive system of public health and sanitation measures in the world.[26]

Meanwhile, as the daily mortality tolls published in the *Times* rose at a frightening rate, physicians rushed to find treatments for the disease. Although the Central Board of Health in London had made recommendations for treatment of cholera patients, every apothecary, surgeon, or physician felt free to devise his own treatment. By far the most common treatment was opium, or a form of it known as laudanum. The report of a coroner's inquest into the death of a seaman explains why:

The Coroner.—Just describe to the jury how the case was.

Witness.—Deceased was in a state of great depression. He was passing rice-water sort of stools every minute, and reached [i.e., retched] a kind of bilious matter. He was in very great pain, and the cramps were awful. He rolled himself about the deck. There was also a blueness on the skin.

The Coroner.—Did you administer the laudanum in the proportions as recommended by the medical Board of Health?

Witness.—I gave deceased 40 drops of laudanum for the first two half hours, and repeated the dose afterwards every hour.

The coroner here referred to the circular issued by the Board of Health, and observed that it was very desirable a copy should be sent to every medical man, as it was most important that a treatment which was recommended by men of the highest medical science should be known by every practitioner.[27]

Opium or laudanum might ease the severe pain of the cramps, and it also was known to slow or even stop peristalsis, thus possibly functioning as an anti-diarrheal remedy. But the second most common remedy, calomel, a powerful laxative, was often given in combination with laudanum in the belief that by further stimulating purging, it would hasten the expulsion of the poison thought to cause cholera. The two medicines might well have canceled each other out. All sorts of other treatments were tried, including blood transfusion, electricity applied with a "galvanic machine," heat or packing the patient in blankets, cold applied by giving the patient a "frigorific mixture" by enema, and that favorite remedy, doses of brandy.[28]

What is today considered an effective treatment for cholera, intravenous injection of saline fluid (water with a proportion of salt equivalent to that which occurs naturally in the blood), was actually proposed during the 1831–32 epidemic by William Brooke O'Shaughnessy, whose experiments had shown that the blood was depleted of salts by the extreme diarrhea of cholera.[29] When Thomas Latta, a physician living near Edinburgh, decided to try the method, however, several patients died after an initial improvement, and although he was able to report some successful outcomes, they required such extensive injections (one patient was given more than twenty pints of saline fluid) that other physicians were unconvinced the method was safe and did not attempt it.[30] John Snow was later to recommend the method, because he felt it was reasonable to try to replace fluid and salts lost, but his recommendation was not well received either.

Another treatment tried for the first time in this second cholera epidemic was the use of the new anesthetic agent chloroform. It may have been this aspect of the 1848–49 epidemic that attracted Snow's interest in the disease, for the young doctor had been experimenting with the use of chloroform for many different purposes, including easing the pain of childbirth.[31] By 1853 he was well enough known for this practice that he was called in to administer chloroform to Queen Victoria in the delivery of her eighth child.[32] But it was in August 1849 that he published a pamphlet, *On the Mode of Communication of Cholera*, in which he argued that cholera was a waterborne disease.[33] Another physician, William Budd, announced in September 1849 that he had identified the nature of this waterborne organism as being "of the fungus tribe." Although Budd was wrong about cholera being a fungus, his conclusions about how to prevent the spread of the disease were just as accurate as if he had correctly identified the organism. He recommended that all discharges from the sick be treated with disinfectants. But even more importantly, he recognized that drinking water, already established as "the principal channel through which this poison finds its way into the human body" by Snow's researches, must be supplied "from healthy quarters, or from sources beyond the reach of contamination," or if this was not possible, that the water should be boiled. He mentioned particularly the practice of ship crews in the Thames of simply drawing up their drinking water from the river, a practice undoubtedly connected with the fact that ships had proven to be "great instruments" of the diffusion of cholera.[34]

"A DROP OF WATER"

The most terrible outbreak of cholera which ever occurred in this kingdom, is probably that which took place in Broad Street, Golden Square, and the adjoining streets, a few weeks ago. Within two hundred and fifty yards of the spot where Cambridge Street joins Broad Street, there were upwards of five hundred fatal attacks of cholera in ten days. The mortality in this limited area probably equals any that was ever caused in this country, even by the plague; and it was much more sudden, as the greater number of cases terminated in a few hours.[35]

In his second edition of *On the Mode of Communication of Cholera*, published in January 1855, John Snow vividly describes what became known as the Broad Street outbreak. Although cholera seemed to have largely disappeared from Britain after the terrifying epidemic of 1848–49, in 1853 cases began to be reported again. This epidemic, the third, was to claim a far lower mortality (about twenty thousand) than the second. But it was during this epidemic that the sudden and devastating Broad Street outbreak took place in August and September of 1854 right in the neighborhood of Snow's residence on Sackville Street.[36] Snow had begun investigating the water supply of the city during the 1848–49 epidemic, for he already suspected that cholera was transmitted primarily through water contaminated with sewage. But as cholera cases in the Golden Square area mushroomed, he focused his attention on the water supply there. As he later wrote, he almost immediately "suspected some contamination of the water of the much-frequented street-pump in Broad Street," even though the water at first appeared to have very little impurity visible to the naked eye.[37] He requested a list from the General Register Office of deaths from cholera for the week ending on September 2 in the subdistricts of Golden Square, Berwick Street, and St. Ann's. As most had occurred during the last three days of the week, he concluded that this outbreak had actually begun on Thursday, August 31. And he continues, "On proceeding to the spot, I found that nearly all the deaths had taken place within a short distance of the pump," and he further discovered that of those more distant from the pump, most of the families told him they drank the water from the Broad Street pump because they preferred its taste, even though it was farther away. Snow accordingly had an interview with the Board of Guardians of St. James parish, on Thursday, September 7, and, "in consequence of what I said, the handle of the pump was removed on the following day." Deaths from cholera had already begun to decline, probably because so many people had fled the neighborhood, but after the closing of the pump-well, deaths declined to almost nothing and the outbreak was clearly over. As Snow noted, it had lasted only about ten days, but killed more than five hundred people.

Two or three weeks later, Snow returned to his investigations of this outbreak, and now found that, because the taste of the water from this pump was so much liked, it had been used in local dining rooms (restaurants), coffee shops and pubs (bars). Snow found that it was even "sold in various little shops, with a teaspoonful of effervescing powder in it, under the name of sherbet." Thus he concluded that people who didn't think they had drunk of the Broad Street pump water might nevertheless have done so. His investigations at various businesses and institutions in the neighborhood also showed that those who had a different supply of water had had very few cases of cholera. Workers in the local brewery, who were allowed to drink all the beer they wanted and so usually drank no water, had not come down with cholera. A workhouse, or institution where paupers were housed, had had only five cases of cholera out of 535 inmates, despite the fact that the workhouse was located in the midst of the epidemic area. The workhouse turned out to have its own pump-well, in addition to water supplied by the Grand Junction Water Works.

"Monster Soup commonly called Thames water, being a correct representation of that precious stuff doled out to us!!! . . ." Etching by W. Heath, 1828. © Wellcome Library, London.

Snow also heard of a case which he regarded as "the most conclusive of all in proving the connection between the Broad Street pump and the outbreak of cholera." A widow, age fifty-nine, died of cholera in the West End, at a distance from Broad Street, on September 2.

> I was informed by this lady's son that she had not been in the neighborhood of Broad Street for many months. A cart went from Broad Street to West End every day, and it was the custom to take out a large bottle of the water from the pump in Broad Street, as she preferred it. The water was taken on Thursday, 31st August, and she drank of it in the evening, and also on Friday. She was seized with cholera on the evening of the latter day, and died on Saturday. . . . A niece, who was on a visit to this lady, also drank of the water; she returned to her residence, in a high and healthy part of Islington, was attacked with cholera, and died also.[38]

Snow was aware that cholera attacks had begun to diminish before the pump handle was removed, which he believed was because such a large proportion of the population had either died or fled within the first two or three days. He remained convinced, however, that the Broad Street well was the source of the outbreak. What he did not know was how the well had been contaminated, and whether it still was. Moreover, most people were still not persuaded that cholera was caused by polluted water, let alone that this particular well where the water was known to have such a good taste could possibly have been the source of whatever it was that caused cholera. Henry Whitehead, a curate at St. James, heard of Snow's theory when he served with him and five other medical men, one other clergyman, and eight vestrymen on the Cholera Inquiry Committee that was set up to investigate possible causes for the outbreak. "But," as Whitehead later wrote, "scarcely any one seriously believed in his theory."[39] Whitehead in fact confidently asserted his belief that a careful investigation would disprove Snow's hypothesis.

Later, Snow sent Whitehead a copy of the second edition of *On the Mode of Communication of Cholera*, and Whitehead found that Snow attributed the outbreak to special contamination of the well "from the evacuations of cholera patients, which he conjectured must have reached the well from the sewer or a cesspool."[40] But, Whitehead reasoned, if the well was contaminated by a sewer, then the outbreak should have continued much longer, as cholera excretions seeping into the well from a leaking sewer pipe should have increased with the increase in cholera cases. And, "as for cesspools, I at that time supposed they had mostly been abolished."[41]

Whitehead knew both the area and its residents extremely well, part of his duties as curate being the visiting of parishioners in their homes, especially in times of illness or death. Indeed, on the morning of Friday,

September 1, 1854, he was asked to visit a house in which he found four persons who, having been seized with cholera during the night, were already in a state of collapse. On leaving this house, whichever way he turned, he found similar scenes, and when he ran into his "brother curate" and a scripture-reader from St. James, they had both had the same shocking experiences. Whitehead spent the entire day visiting houses in which people had been attacked by cholera, and he later sadly reported that, of all the people he had visited that day, only one recovered.[42] A yellow flag was hung on Berwick Street to warn the people of the sudden outbreak of cholera in the neighborhood. The weather had been stiflingly hot (the thermometer had climbed to 98.5 degrees Fahrenheit the previous day) and cholera cases had been increasing in nearby areas of London.[43] Florence Nightingale, who was to leave for the Crimea in two months to help care for the soldiers, was laboring night and day in Middlesex Hospital, caring for cholera patients there. But no one expected cholera in the neighborhood of the Broad Street pump, as there had never been many cases of it there in earlier epidemics.[44]

The Cholera Inquiry Committee expected to find some atmospheric cause for the sudden outbreak. They accordingly investigated such matters as "elevation of site, nature of soil and subsoil, surface and ground plan, streets and courts, density and character of population, internal economy of houses, cesspools, house-drains, and sewerage," but though they "found much to lament or condemn . . . we could not find . . . any satisfactory explanation" of the sudden appearance of cholera and its almost equally sudden disappearance.[45] Whitehead also expected that common beliefs about cholera, such as that fear of the disease, or failure to keep one's house clean, or being intemperate (drunk), made a person more likely to succumb to the disease, would be proved true. But in fact he found the opposite: the mostly elderly and infirm inmates of the workhouse had been much afraid of the disease, but suffered very little from it; three houses that had been specially commended by the parish for cleanliness were almost the only houses in one street that had been visited by the disease, one of them losing no fewer than twelve of its inhabitants, and in general, he had to conclude, "There was no ground in this outbreak for saying that the intemperate suffered more than the temperate, the poor than the rich, the weak than the strong."[46]

On the other hand, Whitehead's inquiries confirmed to an almost startling extent Snow's suspicion of the Broad Street pump. Among those who had come down with cholera, even people who lived much closer to another pump, Whitehead found that all had been in the habit of sending to the Broad Street pump for their water, as they liked the water so much. Many London pump-wells, in fact, were almost universally disdained, because water from them had such a disagreeable odor—a rather obvious connection to the poorly maintained and haphazardly organized sewer system. But the Broad Street water appeared to be clean, almost sparkling.

Whitehead's inquiries eventually came down to the question, "What after all was the matter with the well?"[47] Examination of the area around the well now turned up a cesspool in front of the house next to the well, its brickwork in a "disreputable state." The main drain of the house (which led to the sewer) also had "decayed" brickwork. And in close proximity to both drain and cesspool "stood the Broad Street well," which now proved to be quite obviously contaminated by the contents of the cesspool and drain.

Whitehead had, in fact, decided to investigate the ground near the well because he had uncovered what turned out to be the "index case," or the first case of the outbreak: on the registrar's returns it had been noted that a five-month-old baby girl had died at 40 Broad Street, the house next to the well, on September 2, after an attack of diarrhea beginning *"four days previous to death."*[48] Whitehead italicized this phrase, because he realized that, if the attacks had begun on August 31, they might well have followed on the child's attack of August 28. Hastening to the house, Whitehead questioned the child's mother and found that she had first soaked the baby's "napkins" (diapers) in a pail of water, and then had dumped the pail into the cesspool in front of the house. The baby's diarrhea had stopped on August 30, though she did not die until September 2. Whitehead thought it was easy to see, if the contaminated water had stopped being dumped into the cesspool on August 30, the shallow well might easily have cleared itself after a few days, especially as cholera patients drank the water in prodigious amounts, "some as much as four gallons a day!"[49]

The curate's inquiries had, to his own surprise, confirmed the physician's hypothesis. And although closing down the Broad Street pump had not stopped this particular outbreak, it almost certainly prevented another. The baby's father, Thomas Lewis, came down with cholera on September 8—the day the pump handle had been removed—and his wife began pouring the water in which she had soaked his bed linens into the cesspool.

Snow had come by his hypothesis that cholera was chiefly spread by impure water through not only his own experience but extensive research in the medical literature of the day. In his second edition of *On the Mode of Communication of Cholera*, he lays out evidence from both sources in a dramatically clear and persuasive manner. Remembering his own experience as an apothecary's apprentice when only eighteen years old, sent to care for miners during the 1831–32 epidemic, he observes that "the mining population of Great Britain have suffered more from cholera than persons in any other occupation," and points out that "there are no privies in the coal pits," and that workmen worked such long hours they were obliged to take their food with them. He quoted a letter received from a relative of his concerning these appalling working conditions: "Our colliers descend at five o'clock in the morning, to be ready for work at six, and leave the pit from one to half-past three. The average time spent in the pit is eight to nine hours. The pitmen all take down with them a supply of food, which consists of cake, with the addition, in some cases, of meat; and all have a bottle, containing about a quart of 'drink.' I fear that our colliers are no better than others as regards cleanliness. The pit is one huge privy, and of course the men always take their victuals with unwashed hands."[50]

Snow pointedly comments: "It is very evident that, when a pitman is attacked with cholera whilst at work, the disease has facilities for spreading among his fellow laborers such as occur in no other occupation. That the men are occasionally attacked whilst at work I know, from having seen them brought up from some of the coal pits in Northumberland, in the winter of 1831–2, after having had profuse discharges from the stomach and bowels, and when fast approaching to a state of collapse."[51]

Snow had traced out the connections between ingesting water or food contaminated by sewage and outbreaks of cholera. In his 1855 book on cholera, he reasoned that, as the disease "invariably commences with the affection of the alimentary canal," then the "morbid material producing cholera . . . must, in fact, be swallowed." Although he did not know what this morbid material was, he realized that it must have the property of reproducing itself once inside the body and that the incubation period, or time between when the "morbid poison" entered the system and when the illness began, must be only twenty-four to forty-eight hours with cholera. This was why, he thought, "cholera sometimes spreads with a rapidity unknown in other diseases."[52]

He further explains that it was not just because the poor were dirty, let alone immoral, that cholera spread so rapidly among them, but because they had to live in "crowded conditions," as when one or more poor families might all live in just one room. The working classes, he noted, "often have to take their meals in the sick room: hence the thousands of instances in which, amongst this class of the population, a case of cholera in one member of the family is followed by other cases; whilst medical men and others, who merely visit the patients, generally escape."[53] Cholera spread in the same way among institutionalized pauper children, who might sleep two or three in a bed and vomit over each other.

Just as his experience as an eighteen-year-old apprentice sent to care for miners indicated that cholera was spread person to person by something ingested, Snow's own decision at that time to adopt the vegetarian regimen of John Frank Newton, which emphasized the necessity of drinking only pure (i.e., filtered) water, and even then as little of it as possible, probably contributed to his suspicion of water as source of the "cholera poison."[54] But he also recognized in his initial investigation of the great epidemic of 1848–49, which, unlike the 1831–32 epidemic, took such an enormous toll in London, that the water supply of London was much worse in 1849 than it had been in 1832. This was due, he noted, not only to the increase of population in the city, but to "the abolition of cesspools and the almost universal adoption of water closets in their stead."[55] This meant that sewage was routed through the sewage system and dumped into the Thames River, from whence it was pumped up by water companies and delivered to London residents for drinking water. The water was often so odious that it was common for kitchen sinks to stink of sewage. One can easily see why London residents who had access to the Broad Street pump, where the water appeared clear and clean, preferred that for their drinking water.

After the Broad Street outbreak was over, Snow went back to the "grand experiment" he had been studying before. In a second investigation, even more important than the first but less well known, Snow demonstrated conclusively his hypothesis that cholera was waterborne. After the 1848–49 epidemic, Parliament passed the Metropolitan Water Act in 1852. This act required water companies not to take their water from the Thames below Teddington Lock, meaning that they had to take their water from the river upstream of the city, where it was not fouled by the city's sewage system. But the Metropolitan Water Act gave water companies until 1855 to move their water intake systems to the new, safer location. Two of the water companies, the Lambeth Water Company and the Southwark and Vauxhall Water Company, ran parallel pipelines down the same streets in London, but Lambeth had relocated its water works upstream in 1852, while Southwark and Vauxhall did not comply with the parliamentary act until 1855. Snow realized that these two companies thus furnished "natural" materials for a "grand experiment." He began a massive inquiry (he soon had to accept help from other investigators) to discover from which water company the households of cholera victims had bought their water. He was able to prove that households who bought their water from the Southwark and Vauxhall Water Company had more than fourteen times the death rate of households buying their water from the Lambeth Water Company, even though the houses were on the same street and shared the same air and miasma. This study brilliantly pinpointed the source of contagion as drinking water, and specifically as drinking water contaminated by sewage. Reformers began to campaign for the water companies to install filtering systems, and Snow recommended boiling drinking water. Even popular magazines began "preaching the gospel of clean water."[56]

Meanwhile, an Italian doctor and microscopist, Filippo Pacini, actually identified the cholera organism in 1854 when cholera hit Florence. But when Pacini announced that he had found a unique organism in the feces of cholera victims, he was ignored by the Italian medical community, which preferred to believe in the miasma theory of the illness.[57] Pacini's discovery was not recognized until the German scientist Robert Koch presented what he believed was the first discovery of the *Vibrio cholerae* in 1884 to the Berlin Cholera Commission, which informed him of Pacini's priority. Koch,

FARADAY GIVING HIS CARD TO FATHER THAMES;
And we hope the Dirty Fellow will consult the learned Professor.

"Faraday Giving His Card to Father Thames; and we hope the Dirty Fellow will consult the Learned Professor." *Punch*, 1855. © Wellcome Library, London.

however, has been almost universally accredited with the discovery and continues to be so today.

When British soldiers were sent to the Crimea in 1854, they found cholera there before them, brought by French and German soldiers. (This was the only known time cholera traveled eastward in the Mediterranean, and it is characteristic that the vector for its movement here also was a military campaign.) In the Crimean War theater, as in Britain, measures based on the mistaken belief that cholera was environmental, or spread by bad air, were nevertheless effective in controlling the disease. Florence Nightingale did not believe in the contagion theory. In her *Notes on Nursing: What It Is, and What It Is Not*, published in 1859, a few years after the Crimean War, she noted: "First rule of nursing, to keep the air within as pure as the air without."[58] Scarlet fever (and other fevers), she insisted, ought not to be ascribed to contagion, but to foul air. She warned that the sickroom ought not to be made into a sewer, and that slop-pots should have lids, because of the danger from "effluvia from excreta."[59] Although neither bad air nor effluvia actually caused cholera and her concern for cleanliness of the hospital environment did not stop deaths from cholera (nurses as well as soldiers and officers died of it), the sanitation measures she instituted undoubtedly did help to keep the incidence down.

THE LAST CHOLERA EPIDEMIC IN BRITAIN

The last cholera epidemic to strike Britain differed from the others in that it came from Egypt rather than from European ports. Although it began, like all the others, in Bengal, India, this time it spread to the port of Aden on the Red Sea, and thence to Egypt, where over sixty thousand people died in the months of June and July 1865 alone.[60] British-administered railways in India and in Egypt greatly facilitated the spread of cholera, and British shipping carried the disease back from Egyptian ports to Great Britain. As historian J. N. Hays notes, "Changes in transportation infrastructure, which so dramatically transformed world disease environments, were part of the dynamic Western industrial economy's expansion into the world."[61]

But by this time in Britain, public health measures were becoming so much more effective that deaths were limited to about fourteen thousand in this epidemic (1866–67). When cholera broke out in the East End of London, for example, public health authorities immediately suspected the water supply in that area, and they successfully traced this outbreak to one water company's reservoirs, which had become contaminated by the nearby River Lea. And although cholera epidemics continued in other parts of the world throughout the nineteenth and twentieth centuries (and continue to this day), Britain has never had another. In 1884, as mentioned above, Robert Koch discovered the cholera bacillus, and this time the discovery was recognized. But it was still the implementation of public health measures that made the difference between high and low mortality rates: in the Indian epidemic of 1937, some 236,143 Indian civilians died, but not a single British or Indian soldier in the Indian army.[62]

Although cholera was not the only contagious fever disease present in Britain in the nineteenth century, it was unique in many respects: its direct connection with British imperial campaigns in India, its newness in the rest of the world, including Britain, and the major discoveries that this disease inspired in understanding how epidemic disease was transmitted and how it could be controlled. Although cholera epidemics continue today (according to the World Health Organization, we are now in the midst of the seventh cholera pandemic, which began in 1961),[63] in Britain these epidemics were unique to the nineteenth century and were the almost inevitable product of the expansion of British imperialism, commerce, and urban development.

3

Tuberculosis

My dear Sir

When I wrote in such haste to Dr Epps, disease was making rapid strides, nor has it lingered since, the galloping consumption has merited its name—neither physician nor medicine are needed more. Tuesday night and morning saw the last hours, the last agonies, proudly endured till the end. Yesterday Emily Jane Brontë died in the arms of those who loved her.

Thus the strange dispensation is completed—it is incomprehensible as yet to mortal intelligence. The last thre[e] months—ever since my brother's death seem to us like a long, terrible dream. We look for support to God—and thus far he mercifully enables us to maintain our self-control in the midst of affliction whose bitterness none could have calculated on

Believe me yours sincerely
C Brontë
Wednesday[1]

Only a few short months before Emily Brontë's death on December 19, 1848, her brother Branwell had died of consumption on September 24. Anne Brontë would die of consumption just a few months later, on May 28, 1849. The two oldest sisters in the family, Maria and Elizabeth, had died of consumption nearly twenty-five years earlier, on May 6 and June 15, 1825.[2] Charlotte herself would die of consumption on March 31, 1855. Charlotte lived the longest: she died a few weeks before her thirty-ninth birthday.

The Brontë family history is among the tragic instances in Victorian England known as "familial phthisis" (pronounced tee-sis), a terrible susceptibility to consumption (tuberculosis) seen in the members of a single family that seemed to prove that the disease or a predisposition to it was inherited. Although in some countries, such as Italy, consumption had long been feared as contagious and sufferers were expelled as quickly as possible, in other countries, such as France and England, the disease was thought to be contracted only by those who were already susceptible to it, usually through family inheritance. Both theories have turned out to be correct, although to differing degrees. It is now established that tuberculosis is contagious, as it is known to be caused by a bacillus easily spread through sputum droplets in the air around infected individuals and even in dust carrying dried particles of sputum. But it is also known that only a certain proportion of those exposed to the disease will become ill. Others will wall off the bacterium and either never become ill or only develop the illness at some point when their normal immunity has been lowered, as in old age or after infection with a disease that lowers immunity, such as HIV. The capacity to wall off the bacterium on first encounter is most probably an indication of generally robust health, rather than an inherited immunity, but recent work in genetics suggests an inherited susceptibility to the disease may exist, though it is probably uncommon.[3] The fact remains, however, that during the nineteenth century, tuberculosis became the single greatest killer among the infectious diseases, taking a far larger toll than all the epidemics of cholera combined. Entire families could be wiped out by tuberculosis, just as with cholera.

In all other respects, tuberculosis could not have presented a greater contrast to cholera. Far from being a new epidemic disease, never seen before, it had been known among Europeans since the time of the ancient Greeks. In seventeenth-century England, John Bunyan had written in *The Life and Death of Mr. Badman* (1680), "The captain of all these men of death that came against him to take him away, was the Consumption, for it was that that brought him down to the grave." Unlike cholera, with its shockingly violent, agonizing, and sudden death, tuberculosis was mythologized as the "beautiful death" and associated with poetic and artistic talent that first burned feverishly and then peacefully passed from earthly sorrows to heavenly visions. For some time during the early nineteenth century, it was actually fashionable to have the look of a consumptive: to be extremely thin, languid, and pale. And unlike cholera, which migrated out of India in the nineteenth century and for the first time infected Europeans and inhabitants of other parts of the globe, tuberculosis was spread by European colonizers of the eighteenth and nineteenth centuries among Africans, American Indians, and other populations previously free of the disease.

Tuberculosis also differed from cholera in that, although the rise of this infectious disease to its worst epidemic heights seemed to have logically followed on industrialization and the accompanying increase in urban populations living in crowded, unhygienic conditions, tuberculosis mysteriously declined in England and Wales during the nineteenth century. Although historians differ on precisely when the decline began, it was certainly no later than the 1870s, well before Robert Koch's 1882 identification of the bacillus that caused the disease, and decades before any effective treatments were known. In 1976 Thomas McKeown presented the radical thesis that the decline in tuberculosis mortality in England had actually begun in the eighteenth century, and that this decline was due primarily to an improved standard of living, especially improved nutrition, rather than to any public health measures undertaken in the nineteenth century in better housing, cleaner water, safer food handling, and better sewage and waste disposal.[4] However, his thesis has since been challenged by historians who note that the disease did not decline in nineteenth-century France at the same rate as in England and Germany, yet question whether the French were more poorly nourished than the English or the Germans.[5] Historians also point to McKeown's argument that tuberculosis was declining in the eighteenth century as especially dubious, as registration of the cause of death did not begin in England and Wales until 1837.

Greta Jones notes that although tuberculosis is an ancient disease, we speak of a tuberculosis epidemic when mortality rates begin to climb. Such epidemics are now thought to have a long, slow curve, lasting over several generations and perhaps requiring fifty to seventy-five years for an epidemic to peak. The great merit of McKeown's work is its demonstration that we should turn our attention from the admittedly triumphal history of nineteenth-century medicine, in which a small number of brilliant scientists evolved germ theory, to the less celebrated achievements of public health, sanitation, and labor regulation measures that may actually have turned the tide before the discovery of *Mycobacterium tuberculosis*.[6]

FROM PHTHISIS TO CONSUMPTION

The history of what we now call tuberculosis is a shape-shifting and name-changing history, for the very concept of infectious disease as we know it, that is, as illness caused by a single infectious agent despite varying symptoms, did not exist in ancient cultures. Nor did it develop in any logical or predictable fashion in any modern culture. We can trace changes in the conception of the disease by looking at different names for it in Western medical history and reflecting on the function of those names as metaphors for whole systems of thought about the body in health and in sickness. The oldest accounts of the disease, appearing in ancient Hindu as well as Greek and Roman writings, describe a wasting disease of the lungs, and the name applied to it was "phthisis," or the Greek term for wasting.[7] Disease as the Greeks were able to diagnose it was simply a collection of characteristic symptoms, the most striking of which in this case was the sufferer's wasting away. Oddly enough, from a twenty-first-century perspective, the treatment for such wasting was bloodletting. But the Greek conception of the body was that it was filled with fluids (called humors), and that if these fluids got out of balance, the result was illness. If a person became ill with a febrile disease, that is, was hot and feverish, it followed that he or she had too much blood. Hence, the proper treatment was bloodletting. The other most common treatments were emetics, to induce vomiting, and purgatives to relieve the bowel of its excess.[8] This might not seem relevant to tuberculosis in the Victorian era unless one knows that, just as the term phthisis continued to be used, particularly in medical literature, throughout the nineteenth century, so the treatments associated with the ancient Greek conception of health and disease continued to be used, despite new knowledge of the body that should have caused doctors to cease to adhere to the archaic medical tradition. Bloodletting continued to be used in cases of phthisis and other diseases well into the nineteenth century. And emetics and purgatives were the first line of treatment for diseases both major and minor until after antibiotics came into general use in the mid-twentieth century.

The history of scrofula, an infection of the lymph glands in the neck now known to be a form of tuberculosis, is a case in point in which the changing meanings of the disease are reflected in its name. In the medieval period scrofula seems to have become a very common disease.[9] The nodes in the neck glands were painless but the disease caused disfigurement, sometimes to a hideous degree, as swollen and ulcerated glands distorted the face. The term "scrofula" comes from Latin and means "sow," a female pig. Whether the name originated in what was perceived as a piglike appearance of the neck and head or because the disease was associated with living in dirt is not known. But it is known that the disease was called the "King's Evil," and it was believed that the touch of a king could cure it. Edward the Confessor, king of England in the eleventh century, was the first English monarch to claim this power, long ascribed to the kings of France. Not until the Renaissance, when physicians first began to dissect bodies to search for the signs of disease and the cause of death, and the bodies of scrofula victims proved to have the same kind of nodules found in those who had died of phthisis, was it even possible to conceive that scrofula and phthisis might be the same ailment in different forms. Despite such anatomical evidence, however, scrofula continued to be considered a different affliction and to offer the potential of a miraculous cure by a royal touch. So uncounted thousands sought the "King's Touch" over the centuries. Samuel Johnson was touched by Queen Anne in 1712 for his scrofula and, doubtless like many others, was not cured, but the practice continued.

In their classic study of tuberculosis, *The White Plague: Tuberculosis, Man, and Society*, René and Jean Dubos state that approximately half of the English population had scrofula in the nineteenth century.[10] In institutional populations, such as a workhouse for paupers, practically all of the children were apt to develop the disease, even though only a few had been diagnosed with it on admission. (Ironically, it is now known that, while scrofula in adults usually is tuberculous, in children it is usually caused by a nontubercular bacterium.)[11] By this time scrofula was definitely associated with poverty and dirt, and even worse. During the eighteenth century, the disease had come to be associated with sexual excess, especially onanism (masturbation), and by the nineteenth century, "scrofulous" referred not only to the appearance of a scrofula sufferer but to morally corrupt literature, as in a "scrofulous French novel."[12] Scrofulous children, especially, were suspected of having an "hereditary . . . syphilitic taint."[13] It is speculated that the reason the Reverend Patrick Brontë wore a huge stock that completely covered his throat throughout his life was to hide the swollen nodes of scrofula.[14] Given the changing connotations of scrofula, it is perhaps no wonder that a member of the clergy might wish to disguise signs of the disease, if in fact he actually had it.

From the sixteenth century onwards, European physicians postulated theories about phthisis based on their observations of living patients or of dissected bodies, but their interpretations were shaped not only by the classic Greek and Latin medical tradition but also by national differences in those interpretations. The Florentine physician and poet Girolamo Fracastoro (Fracastorius), famous today for his long poem about syphilis, proposed in 1546 a theory of contagion in which disease was spread by the transmission of what he called "seeds" from one person to another, by direct contact or on soiled clothing or through the air. His theory was remarkably close to germ theory as developed in the nineteenth century. This theory was applied to phthisis or tuberculosis and was at first accepted throughout Europe. But later, physicians in northern Europe adopted the opposite theory that the disease, or a predisposition to it, was inherited, and that it was not spread by contact with those who had the disease. This geographical division in theorizing phthisis as contagious or hereditary continued until almost the twentieth century, with countries in southern Europe treating phthisis as contagious while northern European countries treated it as hereditary or noncontagious.

By 1660 the term "consumption" had come into general usage in England in connection with "phthisical decline," apparently to describe the manner in which the body seemed to be consumed by fever.[15] This new name, with its common English meaning as opposed to the term derived from the learned medical language of Greek, signaled the beginning of a new metaphorization or social construction of the disease. In eighteenth-century England it was increasingly associated with a certain kind of individual constitution: the sufferer was now identified as a "consumptive." Physicians debated whether the disease of consumption had any relation to the consumption of material goods, held to have reached alarming and excessive levels in this new consumer culture, ever more richly supplied by goods imported from colonies. The wasting condition of consumption might result from overindulgence in food and drink, or overheated houses, or even by overindulgence in fashion, as the latest and newest fashions involved dressing in cotton materials, surely not warm enough for the English climate. Hence, some advocated a strict regimen of dietary abstinence, eating no flesh and drinking no alcohol. Others argued that it was precisely a pernicious adherence to dietary delicacies and a "languishing" lifestyle that was causing the increase in disease, particularly consumption, and advocated a return to a hearty diet with plenty of meat and milk.[16]

During approximately the same period from the late seventeenth century through the early eighteenth, a number of observations were made that might have led physicians away from the concept of consumption as a disease associated with a particular inherited constitution and toward one characterized by a particular kind of internal lesions. In his *Opera Medica* (1679), Franciscus de la Boe Sylvius, a professor of medicine at the University of Leyden (Holland), coined the term "tubercle" to denote nodules found in the lungs of people who had died of phthisis. He further noted that he had found these nodules in other organs of the body, and that they could progress into ulcers or cavities. Just a decade later, in *Phthisiologia* (1689), English physician Richard Morton suggested that all such tubercles, including those of scrofula, might have some relation to phthisis or consumption. In 1702 John Jacob Manget described tiny tubercles disseminated throughout the body as looking like millet seed, a form of tuberculosis that continues to be called miliary tuberculosis.[17] Despite these indications of a common origin, tuberculous infections of different organ systems continued to be considered different diseases, and pulmonary tuberculosis continued to be either phthisis or consumption, a wasting disease suffered by an individual who had inherited a particular constitution.

In 1720, the English physician Benjamin Marten published *A New Theory of Consumption, more especially of a Phthisis or Consumption of the Lungs*, in which he articulated a theory even closer to germ theory than that of Fracastoro: "The Original and Essential Cause . . . may possibly be some certain Species of *Animalculae* or wonderfully minute living creatures that, by their peculiar Shape or disagreeable Parts are inimicable to our Nature; but, however, capable of subsisting in our Juices and Vessels."[18] However, his theory was ignored and his book disappeared from sight, not turning up again until 1911, long after Koch's discovery of the bacillus that causes tuberculosis.

Although there are few reliable figures, most historians believe that tuberculosis began to increase in European urban populations during the late seventeenth century and to have continued this increase until sometime in the second half of the nineteenth century, though there were significant variations between nations.[19] Around the turn of the nineteenth century a number of different physicians registered their alarm at the seriousness and extent of the disease. Two English physicians, Thomas Beddoes in 1799 and William Heberden in 1802, wrote that pulmonary consumption was by far the most deadly disease. Thomas Young, in his *Historical and Practical Treatise on Consumptive Diseases* (1815), claimed that pulmonary consumption killed off one-quarter of the inhabitants of Europe. In eastern cities of the United States, it was estimated that the annual tuberculosis rate was as high as 400 per 100,000 population.[20] J. N. Hays estimates that the peak tuberculosis mortality exceeded 300 deaths per 100,000 population during the nineteenth century.[21] Jacalyn Duffin puts the estimate in Britain even higher, at 500–600 deaths per 100,000 population.[22]

The actual mortality rate from tuberculosis at this time and throughout the nineteenth century, however, is impossible to determine with complete accuracy. Not only were such nontuberculous lung conditions as lung abscesses and bronchitis misdiagnosed as pulmonary consumption, but many nonpulmonary forms of tuberculosis were not recognized as such. In addition to scrofula, there were lupus vulgaris, or tuberculous infection of the skin; Pott's disease, or tuberculous infection of the spine or other bones or joints; tubercular meningitis, sometimes called "brain fever" and invariably fatal; and tabes mesenterica, or tuberculous infection of the abdominal lymph nodes, a condition especially liable to attack infants.[23] Tuberculosis, in fact, can affect almost any organ or organ system in the body, and in the nineteenth century many of these tuberculous infections could not be diagnosed and might not even be suspected as the cause of death. Even the much-studied pulmonary tuberculosis can take many forms, varying from asymptomatic infection to galloping consumption, the acute form that could follow after a lengthy period of milder illness. The disease could also go into spontaneous remission, with periodic recurrences of greater or lesser virulence. Patrick Brontë developed an "inflammation of the lungs" at the age of fifty-three, the first serious illness of his life, in June 1830.[24] This was after his oldest two daughters had died of consumption but many years before the rest of his children died of the disease. Patrick had recurrent bouts of "bronchitis" for the rest of his life, but far outlived his children, dying at the age of eighty-nine after developing convulsions and lapsing into unconsciousness. He had had two previous strokes.[25] His death certificate cited the cause of death as "chronic bronchitis." He may have had pulmonary tuberculosis, as he may have had scrofula, but he was never diagnosed with either of these conditions.[26]

FROM CONSUMPTION TO TUBERCULOSIS

It was not until the nineteenth century that physicians began to change their conception of consumption as a particular disease characterized by certain visible symptoms, especially wasting or consumption of the body, to that of a group of diseases all characterized by the internal lesions that Sylvius had named tubercles. By 1839, enough evidence of this had been gathered so that a physician in Zurich, Johann Lukas Schönlein, could suggest that all conditions known to be associated with tubercles should be called "tuberculosis."[27] Duffin points out that this name change denotes a major conceptual shift from symptom-based diagnosis to lesion-based terminology: that is, from diagnosis based on the classification of symptoms and known as "nosology," to diagnosis based on pathological anatomy, or anatomical changes, most of which could be observed only during autopsy, associated with illness.[28] But the term tuberculosis at this time had no reference to the tuberculosis bacillus, to any notion that the disease was caused by bacteria, or even that it was contagious. It simply denoted the new understanding that victims of consumption and of some other wasting diseases had tuberculous lesions in their lungs or elsewhere in their bodies. In England, as in France and most of northern Europe, physicians continued to base their diagnoses of consumption on the characteristic symptoms of pulmonary consumption and to believe that those who contracted the disease were constitutionally predisposed to it.

The ability to recognize that a person's illness might be caused by unsuspected internal tubercles or lesions began to develop with the French physician J. N. Corvisart's translation of a work by an Austrian physician, Leopold von Auenbrugger, that had been published some forty-five years earlier, in 1761. Auenbrugger had invented the method of percussion, or tapping on the body, to detect chest diseases. He had learned as a boy how to determine whether his father's wine casks were full or empty by tapping on them and listening to differences in sound. Tapping on the chest wall could similarly determine whether there was fluid collected around the lungs, as in pneumonia. However, although his method was taught in a few German medical schools, it otherwise went unnoticed until Corvisart translated it into French in 1808 with a lengthy commentary, four times as long as the original, of his own.[29]

Corvisart developed the method to a point where he could diagnose many conditions of the heart and lungs that physicians had previously been unable to distinguish on the basis of visible or audible symptoms. One of his students, Gaspard Laurent Bayle, recorded detailed histories of illnesses in living patients, then performed some nine hundred autopsies. This exhaustive comparison of clinical and pathological histories showed him that those who had pulmonary consumption might have tubercles not only in their lungs but in other places in their bodies, and also that the tubercles might be of apparently different kinds. The prevailing medical belief in the hereditary nature of pulmonary consumption, however, led him to the conclusion that the reason some patients with tubercles elsewhere than in the lungs had nevertheless shown clinical signs of pulmonary consumption was that these individuals had a "diathesis" or inherited predisposition to consumption. And, puzzled by the different appearance of tubercles in different stages of development (they could be nodes, abscesses, infiltrations, or cavities, for example), he also decided that tuberculosis of the lungs was not one but six diseases, of which pulmonary consumption was only one. Bayle died of consumption himself, an unfortunately common fate of those who worked with either living patients with tuberculosis or their dead bodies.[30]

But another student of Corvisart's, René Théophile Hyacinthe Laënnec, reached the opposite conclusion: that tubercles in all stages and in all parts of the body were aspects, indeed proof, of a single disease. In 1804 he delivered a lecture setting out this revolutionary thesis. But since he, like most other French (and English) physicians, still believed that the disease developed only in those with a predisposition to it, his unification of tuberculosis did not imply that the disease was contagious. Laënnec was, according to David S. Barnes, a proponent of "essentialist" medicine: that is, in common with other French physicians, he believed that disease in general, and especially tuberculosis, was part of a person's essence. Those with a constitutional predisposition would simply develop the disease from internal causes, although external factors might increase the individual's vulnerability. Moreover, Laënnec and his colleagues believed in psychogenic factors such as "profound sorrows" and "bitter regrets," especially when these emotions were aroused by such immoral behaviors as masturbation or sexual excess, as important contributing causes to the development of tuberculosis in an already susceptible individual.[31]

Laënnec's invention of the stethoscope, and of the method of auscultation (see chapter 1), allowed the diagnosis of consumption to be made with far more precision than ever before. His treatise on auscultation was translated into English in 1840 by the eminent London physician John Forbes, although Forbes didn't think very highly of this new French instrument. But even those physicians who did make use of the stethoscope and developed skill in auscultation were still unable to treat the sufferer any more effectively than before. And Laënnec himself died of pulmonary tuberculosis in August 1826.

In 1825, Pierre Charles Alexandre Louis analyzed some two thousand cases of tuberculosis by correlating the frequency of various symptoms, age

T. CHARTRAN

LAENNEC

A l'Hôpital Necker, ausculte un phtisique (1816).

D'après l'estampe originale éditée par M. Barnot, 34, rue de l'Échiquier, Paris.

Frontispiece, Laënnec, *Traité de L'Auscultation Mediate* . . . 1826. Painting by Theobald Chartran, 1816. © Wellcome Library, London.

and sex of sufferers, and the outcomes of treatments, most notably bloodletting. He put these figures in numerical tables and proved, among other things, that bloodletting was of no use in cases of phthisis or most other diseases.[32] His method was called "numerical medicine" and is one of the foundations of evidence-based medicine today.[33]

It was not until 1865, when Jean-Antoine Villemin presented to the French Academy of Medicine his discovery that phthisis could be transmitted from an infected animal to a healthy one, that the first strong evidence of the contagious nature of tuberculosis was produced. Villemin not only repeatedly and successfully inoculated different animals with tuberculosis but also proved that whatever caused the disease was contained in the sputum of consumptives. He made a further advance in proving the likelihood that diseases characterized by tubercles such as scrofula were caused by the same agent as pulmonary consumption by using material from a scrofulous gland to produce symptoms of tuberculosis in guinea pigs and rabbits. Louis Pasteur had previously discovered anaerobic (non-oxygen-consuming) bacteria in 1861, and Villemin's experiments established the existence of some kind of causative germ in tuberculosis. He published his work in 1868, but the notion of contagion was so resisted that many English physicians never even heard about his work.

Among those who apparently knew nothing of Villemin's groundbreaking work was the English physician William Budd, who had worked with John Snow to prove the contagious nature of cholera and to attempt to discover the causative agent (Budd thought he had proved it was caused by a fungus). Ever since 1856, Budd had been thinking about the curiously high rate of "phthisis or tubercle" among blacks who had worked on British ships. Many were sent to Clifton and Bristol, where Budd worked, for treatment. "The idea that phthisis is a self-propagated zymotic (infectious, as in a fermenting process) disease, and that all the leading phenomena of its distribution may be explained by supposing that it is disseminated through society by specific germs contained in the tuberculous matter cast off by persons already suffering from the disease, first came into my mind, unbidden, so to speak, while I was walking on the Observatory hill at Clifton, in the second week of August, 1856," wrote Budd in a memo that he sent to a friend who later, at his request, submitted it to the medical journal *Lancet*.

In this memo Budd noted that wherever aborigines who had been free of phthisis had come into contact with Europeans, the disease had soon become widespread among them and so fatal as to threaten their extermination. He mentions the late Dr. Rush of Philadelphia, who had noticed that phthisis had been unknown among American Indians when America was first discovered by Europeans, but that now it is "very fatal" to them. But his star evidence is that of Africa and Africans.

Budd's theory that Europeans with their diseases could endanger whole racial groups who, though considered primitive, were typically free of European afflictions, today seems remarkably progressive. But it's probable that he did not publish his views until so long after the idea had first occurred to him because he feared negative reaction and perhaps even ridicule from English colleagues who were almost universally in favor of hereditary predisposition and scoffed at any notion of contagion. His theory, like that of the fungus he thought he had identified as the cause of cholera, was a little wide of the mark, as he believed that his views on tubercle might apply to cancer as well.

But by the decade of the 1860s, germ theory was everywhere on the verge of being demonstrated. Louis Pasteur's work on fermentation proved

It is well known that negroes are peculiarly liable to phthisis.

Now, everywhere along the African seaboard where the blacks have come into constant and intimate relations with the whites, phthisis causes a large mortality among them. In the interior, where intercourse with the whites has been limited to casual contact with a few great travelers or other adventurous visitors, there is reason to believe that phthisis does not exist. Dr. Livingstone and other African travelers have given me the most positive assurances on this point.[34]

that the process was the work of living microorganisms. In 1863 he invented "pasteurization," heating fluids (most importantly, milk) to a temperature that would kill such microorganisms.[35] Also in the 1860s, surgeon Joseph Lister applied Pasteur's theory to the problem of wound infections, using the disinfectant carbolic acid to kill germs and prevent wound infection. His successful prevention of infection in an open fracture of a boy's leg (open fractures, in which the broken bone protrudes through the skin, had almost inevitably killed by infection) through use of disinfectants was published in the *Lancet* in 1867, the same year in which Budd published his thoughts about transmission of phthisis by Europeans to peoples previously free of it.[36]

New announcements concerning germ theory now began to come fast and furiously. In 1874 Pasteur discovered that surgical instruments could be sterilized by placing them in boiling water. In 1876 Koch identified the anthrax bacillus, and in 1881 Pasteur devised a vaccine for anthrax. Then in March 1882 Koch first saw the tuberculosis bacillus, *Mycobacterium tuberculosis*; that is, he had developed a new staining method that made it visible. He read a paper, "On the Aetiology of Tubercular Disease," to the Physiological Society in Berlin on March 24, 1882, and published it on April 10. Very shortly after, also in April 1882, another German, K. H. Baumgartner, published his evidence of the same discovery. And also in April 1882, William Thomson of Melbourne, Australia, published his *Germ Theory of Disease*. Thomson had been arguing since 1876 that consumption in his country was caused by the arrival of "phthisics" who infected others because their breath contained a disease-causing microorganism. He explained the higher death rate in women as caused by their employment as domestic servants who inhaled dust contaminated by dried sputum while working indoors.[37]

Only Koch's discovery was promulgated in the British press, and even his impressive work did not meet with immediate acceptance by the medical profession. Many continued to insist on the "seed and soil" metaphor: both the seed, or bacillus, and the soil—a body predisposed to receive it by a tubercular constitution, poor general health, or some other chest disease—were necessary in order for the active illness to develop.[38] To some extent, of course, this was correct. Physicians also worried that, if tuberculosis were contagious, then a "phthisisophobia" might develop, and those with the disease might be treated like lepers.[39] And unfortunately, this too was to prove true. Tuberculosis was now socially constructed as a deadly illness caused by an invisible agent that could be spread by such behaviors as coughing, let alone spitting, and by dust, contaminated milk, and even meat. If tuberculosis were contagious, then those who had the disease could no longer be viewed as proudly enduring sufferers in charge of their fate, like Emily Brontë, but people whose existence endangered others and whose lives should be under the control of public health authorities.

THE NIGHT-SIDE OF LIFE: METAPHORS AND REALITIES OF TUBERCULOSIS

Susan Sontag writes brilliantly about the fantasies inspired by tuberculosis, this "night-side of life," in the nineteenth century. Contrasting it with cancer, the disease more commonly metaphorized in the twentieth century, she writes that tuberculosis was "thought to produce spells of euphoria, increased appetite, exacerbated sexual desire." It was a disease of time that "speeds up life, highlights it, spiritualizes it." It was thought to be relatively painless, and to culminate in "almost symptomless, unfrightened, beatific deaths." "The dying tubercular," she comments, "is pictured as made more beautiful and more soulful," in contrast with the cancer patient pictured as dying in fear and agony.[40]

All of this was true, particularly in the era from the late eighteenth century through to the mid-nineteenth century. Writing about Emily Shore, who died of consumption in 1839 at the age of nineteen, Barbara T. Gates notes that "during the romantic period and just afterward, tuberculosis was believed to bestow heightened awareness, creativity and intensified intellectual powers."[41] Ancient Greek physicians had been struck by the determined hope of recovery and feverish urge for accomplishment, which they called *spes phthisica*, seen even in patients whose disease was obviously advanced. But around the time of the Romantic era, the myth was so pervasive that consumption was thought to have an almost mystical capacity to produce artistic talent. "Is it possible genius is only scrofula?" Elizabeth Barrett Browning heard someone say, and Théophile Gautier is widely quoted as saying that, "When I was young, I could not have accepted as a lyrical poet anyone weighing more than ninety-nine pounds."[42]

John Keats, who died of consumption at the age of twenty-six—after having nursed his mother, ill with an undiagnosed wasting disease, and then his brother Tom, who died at age nineteen of consumption—is a frequently cited example of the association between genius and tuberculosis. Both the course of his disease and the various treatments he endured were characteristic at the time. Having trained as a surgeon-apothecary, he recognized his spitting up of bright red blood as a symptom of the disease that would kill him. Because he suffered frequent pulmonary hemorrhages, his doctors bled him frequently. They also kept him on a starvation diet, classic treatment for consumption at that time; some physicians believed it to be a disease of excess consumption of alcohol, meat, and rich foods in general. He was also sent on a trip to Italy, in search of a warmer climate, where bleedings and the torture of an even more limited diet (a single anchovy and a bit of bread!) were made even harder to bear by his Italian landlady's refusal to help as she, like all Italians, rightly believed that the disease was contagious. He died in Italy in February 1821, and an autopsy showed his lungs to be almost entirely destroyed.[43]

Emily Shore, entirely unknown until her sisters produced edited versions of her journal in 1891 and 1898, was believed by her family to possess the genius characteristic of those young people ill with consumption. Although it was more common for male sufferers to be advised to travel for their health, she too traveled to a warmer climate (Madeira), and she too lived only a short while after her arrival. But her experience with consumption differs from Keats's significantly in other ways. As Maria Frawley points out, women received "conflicting cultural messages about intellectual work and health." On the one hand, they were warned that competing with men intellectually was unnatural for women and would be destructive to their health. But on the other, they were also warned against idleness.[44] This conflict is represented in Shore's journal as she criticizes herself for "a very idle week," but then also criticizes her brain, grown "muddy and rusty with disuse."[45]

Shore's medical treatment also differed dramatically from Keats's, for she greatly mistrusted doctors and, like Emily Brontë, refused to consult one. Probably because of this, she apparently did not have to suffer bloodletting, and she ate what she desired, including delicacies such as gifts of fruit from friends. She diagnosed herself, based on the characteristic symptoms of consumption:

What is indicated by all these symptoms—this constant shortness of breath, this most harassing hard cough, this perpetual expectoration, now tinged with blood, this quick pulse, this painfully craving appetite, which a very little satisfies even to disgust, these restless, feverish nights, continual palpitations of the heart, and deep, circumscribed flushes? Is it consumption really come at last, after so many threatenings?[46]

Although Keats's and Shore's illness and death from consumption repeat the classic picture of pulmonary tuberculosis as known at the time, it is certain that many other sufferers died of other forms of tuberculosis that were not recognized as such. Charlotte Yonge gives an extremely realistic picture of what was probably tuberculosis of the hip in her popular novel published at the time of the Crimean War, *The Heir of Redclyffe* (1853):

> Charles was at this time nineteen, and for the last ten years had been afflicted with a disease in the hip-joint, which, in spite of the most anxious care, caused him frequent and severe suffering, and had occasioned such a contraction of the limb as to cripple him completely, while his general health was so much affected as to render him an object of constant anxiety. His mother had always been his most devoted and indefatigable nurse, giving up everything for his sake, and watching him night and day. His father attended to his least caprice, and his sisters were, of course, his slaves; so that he was the undisputed sovereign of the whole family.[47]

Charles lives with his affliction to the end of the narrative (though the other two male protagonists both die of an unnamed fever), but suffers repeated exacerbations of his disease, with fever and pain. He will be an invalid to the end of his life, yet the disease will not kill him, and it will not be recorded in the registrar of causes of death as tuberculosis. Today, this disease is known as osteoarticular tuberculosis, a condition in which the tuberculosis bacillus directly infects the bone or joints. Charles's affliction of the hip joint, beginning at age nine, is especially characteristic of the disease as it affects children, for in children the joints are more richly supplied with blood and therefore more vulnerable to infection carried in the blood. Although now rare in industrialized countries, the disease is still common in developing countries. The "limping child" can be treated with appropriate antibiotic drugs today, if indeed the child is diagnosed as having a tuberculous infection.[48] But in Victorian England, this crippling childhood illness was unrecognized as having any connection with consumption.

George Henry Lewes's son, Thornton or "Thornie," wrote to his father and to "Mutter," that is, the novelist George Eliot, in October 1868 from South Africa where he and his brother had gone as colonists, saying that he had suddenly come down with startling symptoms:

> The fact is this, that what with this stone in the kidney and other internal complications, for there is something serious besides the stone, I am gradually wasting away. I eat almost nothing, nothing but delicacies tempt me, and those we can't afford. I can't do a stroke of work of any sort, I can hardly stoop to touch the ground, I can't sit up for half

an hour, all I can do is lie down, then get up and walk about for half an hour, then lie down again. Every evening about sundown when the paroxysms come on, I can hardly turn myself over, and if I want to sit up, I must push myself up with my hands, from my shoulder blades downwards I am powerless: and I have a sort of shooting compression of the chest, which makes breathing difficult, and makes me shout with pain. And as this lasts usually for 2 to 3 hours, and sometimes there is more or less pain all night long, so that I can get no sleep, and sometimes I have slight attacks in the day time—you can fancy that my life is not a pleasant one.[49]

Thornie arrived home unexpectedly early, in May 1869. His emaciated appearance was so shocking that when his older brother Charles first saw him, Charles fainted. For the next five months, Eliot and Lewes nursed Thornie in their London home. Though they hired a nurse to help, they did much of the nursing themselves. Thornie spent much of his time lying flat on the living room floor, as this was the one position in which he felt some relief from the incessant pain. The pain was so great that Lewes often was up four times in a night to administer morphia. Although such eminent London physicians as Sir James Paget and Sir Henry Holland were called in, they were baffled: they could form no idea as to the nature of Thornie's disease. On October 19, 1869, Thornton Lewes died of what had first been described in the eighteenth century by Sir Percival Pott, and is called Pott's disease, but is now commonly recognized as tuberculosis of the spine.[50]

Physician John Snow's death, though the immediate result of a stroke, may have been caused by an earlier infection with tuberculosis. On autopsy, his kidneys were found to be "shrunken, granular, and encysted" and to be marked by "scar tissue from old bouts of tuberculosis."[51] Diseased kidneys can bring on hypertension (high blood pressure), and longstanding hypertension can cause a stroke.

In England and Wales, and also in Scotland though somewhat more slowly there, mortality from tuberculosis (recognized cases, that is) began to decline in the 1870s.[52] It is highly probable that, as infections diagnosed as tuberculous declined, so also did those that were not recognized as such. But after the infectious nature of tuberculosis as established by Koch's discovery of the bacillus came gradually to be accepted, attitudes toward consumptives began to change also. In 1888, the new journal published by the Society of Medical Officers of Health, *Public Health*, announced that "the doctrine of the contagion of phthisis and tubercle generally must be preached from the house-tops until the knowledge . . . has filtered down to the people."[53] Evidence that tuberculosis was extremely contagious was becoming more and more disturbing. Even minute quantities of infective material taken from the walls of rooms occupied by consumptives could cause tuberculosis in guinea pigs. Yet the thought of what would happen if the disease was advertised as contagious was also very disturbing. Right after the *Lancet* had announced Koch's discovery, William Dale wrote that he could not imagine "a more lamentable thing than that the public at large should get the idea that phthisis is contagious . . . for seeing the disease is so widespread, and seizes young, delicate and helpless girls and women chiefly . . . [it is] a barbarous and unwarrantable thing to raise the question in the public mind in connexion with it, and on evidence which I believe to be utterly worthless."[54] Many medical men were opposed to the idea that notification of cases should be required, for fear that there would be a public scare. And indeed, there was something of a public scare: it became difficult for those with any sort of chest disease to be hired as domestic workers, and opposition to consumption hospitals was strong.

By 1900 the disease was virtually defined as a disease of poverty, spread by the unhygienic habits of the poor. In an American nursing text, Ellen N. LaMotte's *The Tuberculosis Nurse: Her Functions and Qualifications* (1915), tuberculosis was called principally a disease of the poor, particularly afflicting "those who are mentally and morally poor, and lack intelligence, will power, and self control."[55] In the United States, racism was fueled by the new fear of tuberculosis. John Bessner Huber, in his *Consumption, Its Relation to Man and His Civilization, Its Prevention and Cure* (1906), wrote that the Negro's small lung capacity and deficient brain capacity made him less resistant to tuberculosis.[56]

Nevertheless, in England public health measures continued to be taken that further contributed to the decline in mortality from tuberculosis long before the discovery of the BCG (Bacillus Calmette Guérin) vaccine in 1923 (never much used in either Britain or the United States, though it was in France and other European countries, as well as in Canada) or the first antibiotic to be effective against the disease, streptomycin, in 1944. In 1908, Poor Law officers were required to report cases of tuberculosis, and by 1913, all cases of the disease had to be reported.

It would be good to be able to record that tuberculosis is now one of the bygone diseases of the Victorian era, like smallpox. But the tuberculosis bacillus, like other bacilli, is able to mutate in resistance to antibiotics. In 2001, about nine million new cases of tuberculosis occurred throughout the world. Deaths between 1998 and 2001 ranged from 1.5 to 2 million per year. Although the incidence has declined dramatically in developed countries such as Britain and the United States, we are today faced with MDR, multidrug-resistant, and XDR, extremely drug-resistant, tuberculosis. Tuberculosis is again today perhaps the most dangerous disease on the globe.[57]

4

Syphilis

"It is a peculiar and horrible sensation; and I cannot give you an adequate idea of it," he said: "it is as though the marrow in my bones were transformed into something animated—into blind-worms, writhing, biting, and stinging incessantly"—and he shuddered, as did I also, at the revolting comparison.[1]

In *Passages from the Diary of a Late Physician*, a novel serialized in *Blackwood's Magazine* between 1830 and 1837, Samuel Warren describes the horrifying symptoms and eventual death of a man from what is clearly implied to be syphilis, though never named as such. Warren, who was also a physician, calls his patient "an abandoned profligate, a systematic debauchee, an irreclaimable reprobate," and also "a glaring tower of guilt." The chapter titled "A Man About Town" narrates a cautionary tale about the tortures endured by this upper-class man, making it explicit that he has no one to blame but himself.[2] The Honorable St. John Henry Effingstone suffers agonizing pain in his bones, a creeping paralysis, nightmarish hallucinations, and the actual rotting of his flesh, which creates an "effluvium" so sickening that a nurse faints and even the doctor can scarcely stand to be in the same room with the patient. Ultimately he dies a lonely death in his rented lodgings, unable to return home in the final week of his illness as he had planned because he has deteriorated so drastically in both mental and physical condition.

The novel, which was sufficiently popular to run through five hardcover editions in the nineteenth century after its serial run, is unusual in its graphic description of the symptoms of syphilis. In Victorian England, the "secret disease" was almost wholly excluded from literary works, and if it was alluded to, the author did so in an obscure manner, rarely describing bodily manifestations of the disease and never explicitly naming it. Yet syphilis and other venereal diseases were prevalent in both civilian and military populations. The French-trained venereologist William Acton reported in 1846 that nearly half the surgical outpatients (venereal disease was considered the province of surgeons) of St. Bartholomew's Hospital in London had venereal complaints, and he also pointed out that syphilis was especially deadly for infants under one year of age, who accounted for 30 out of every 53 deaths from the disease in London. In the 1860s it was reported that one in three patients in the army was afflicted with venereal disease, and one in eleven in the navy. Although statistics on syphilis and other venereal diseases in the nineteenth century must be recognized as at best biased and incomplete, it is evident that syphilis was endemic in Victorian England, and it is thought to have been especially prevalent among middle- and upper-class men and among the transient working poor.[3] Contemporary estimates suggested that at least 10 percent of the population of large cities was infected with syphilis.[4] The peculiar terror of syphilis lay not only in its ghastly symptoms but in the hidden and undetectable nature of its progress. The disease is invisible during its latent stages, yet works incurable damage on various organ systems while the victims believe that they are cured, or that their symptoms are due to some other condition. Meanwhile, the active but unseen infection could sicken unsuspecting wives and cause the death of infants in the womb or after birth. What was not known about syphilis in the nineteenth century would have been as frightening as what was known.

Yet it was also during the nineteenth century that major advances in knowledge about syphilis were made: first, that it was not simply the same disease, though a later stage, as gonorrhea (a sexually transmitted disease characterized by discharge from the urethra or vagina); and second, that syphilis itself occurred in three stages, separated by latent periods during which the infected person might appear perfectly healthy. Prior to the nineteenth century, it was commonly believed that syphilis, or the "pox," was a later stage of gonorrhea, or the "clap," and that if a man (or a woman) who had the clap was treated, the pox could be prevented. By the end of the nineteenth century, however, with the rise of the new science of bacteriology, gonorrhea had been identified as a bacterial infection, and early in the twentieth century the specific bacterium that causes syphilis, *Treponema pallidum*, was also identified.

As a disease known to be sexually transmitted, syphilis was always a guilt disease: either it was one's own fault or somebody else's. Warren's early nineteenth-century portrait of the debauched syphilitic male, naming him as "a glaring tower of guilt," is typical. Throughout most of the Victorian era, however, syphilis was blamed on prostitutes, imaging them as a kind of

womb of infection and implying that syphilis was a product of the degenerate female body. In Dante Gabriel Rossetti's poem "Jenny," which the poet
began writing in 1848 but did not publish until 1870, the speaker describes
a prostitute in imagery which identifies her as the source of contagion and
himself, her client, as a distanced, impervious observer, a scholar who reads
her like a book.

> For is there hue or shape defin'd
> In Jenny's desecrated mind?
> Where all contagious currents meet,
> A Lethe of the middle street?[5]

The speaker's attitude toward Jenny precisely reflects common Victorian
attitudes towards both prostitutes and venereal disease. Physicians and public health authorities became increasingly convinced that the female body
was itself the source of contagion and could even spontaneously generate
venereal disease. A series of laws called the Contagious Diseases Acts were
passed in 1864, 1866, and 1869. These acts permitted surveillance of prostitutes in selected naval ports and garrison towns and mandated the prostitutes' submission to gynecological examinations and to compulsory
treatment in a "lock" hospital (hospital for the treatment of venereal diseases) if they were found to be infected with syphilis or any other kind of
venereal disease, such as gonorrhea or chancroid (a localized genital infection). Meanwhile, an 1857 report of the Royal Commission on the Health
of the Army had called for discontinuing genital examination of soldiers on
the grounds that it destroyed their self-respect and wasn't medically effective anyway.

Although similar, and in fact more severe, programs for surveillance and
control of prostitutes were enacted all over Europe and in the British colonies in the nineteenth century, in England the Contagious Diseases Acts led
to a powerful feminist campaign, called by one dismayed member of Parliament "the revolt of the women," and in 1886 the acts were repealed. Thus,
ironically, a disease that was blamed on women, while men were pitied as
innocent victims, ultimately empowered Victorian women in their struggle
for civil rights and equality.

In the same period, the *fin de siècle* or closing decades of the nineteenth
century, the delusionary theories that led scientists to identify attributes of
the prostitute's body (such as the shape of an ear) as signs of degeneracy
produced fears that certain types of men might also exemplify racial degeneracy. The new field of sexology focused on male sexual deviance, and
it was now the deviant male body that was suspected of harboring syphilis
and other shameful diseases. Robert Louis Stevenson's *Strange Case of
Dr. Jekyll and Mr. Hyde* (1886) may be read as representing fears that modern,

civilized (white) man had a dark side that could suddenly degenerate into a racialized, criminal type with a suspiciously syphilitic appearance. "New Woman" novels, written by women who considered themselves independent of the traditional notions of femininity imaged by the aging queen, depicted married men as guilty of infecting their innocent wives and unborn infants when they returned to the marital bed carrying their loathsome secret disease with them.

Following the discovery by Fritz Schaudinn and Erich Hoffmann in 1905 of a method that made the pale and fragile, spiral-shaped *Treponema pallidum* visible under the microscope, August von Wassermann discovered a blood test for syphilis in 1906. In 1910, Paul Ehrlich identified an arsenical compound (arsphenamine), called Salvarsan, that was an effective though difficult-to-use treatment for syphilis. But it was not until the advent of antibiotics, when it was found that a single injection of penicillin could cure the disease, that hopes were raised for the eradication of syphilis once and for all. Syphilis has not been eradicated, however: on the contrary, the WHO estimates that 12 million new cases of venereal syphilis occurred in 1999, mostly in developing countries, but the number of cases in Europe and North America has also increased in recent years.[6] In 1981 the even more terrifying sexually transmitted disease AIDS appeared. The emergence of AIDS brought new intensity to the history of that other sexual disease which, when it broke on human awareness in July 1495, seemed to many to be the worst disease ever known.

BLAMING THE OTHER NATION

In 1497, the Scottish Privy Council ordered all syphilitics into banishment on the island of Inchkeith near Leith. A few months before, the town council of Aberdeen had ordered that "light" women desist from "their vices and syne of venerie" in order to protect others from the new disease of syphilis and threatened to brand with a hot iron, as well as banish from the town, all those who did not.[7] These are early instances of blaming the disease of syphilis on the "other," in this case what was to become pervasive in the Victorian era, the other woman. But when syphilis appeared in Europe, it was first blamed on the other nation.

In July 1495, a strange and horrifying disease broke out among the soldiers fighting for the French king, Charles VIII, in Fornovo, Italy. (Charles had invaded northern Italy the previous year to claim what he believed to be his rights to the Kingdom of Naples.) The disease caused not only sores on the genitals but fever, pain and swelling in the arms, legs, and feet, and a rash of acorn-sized pustules all over the body that, in addition to giving off a powerful stench, was excruciatingly painful. The sufferer's body seemed to be rotting away. Alexandri Benedicti, a Venetian physician present in

Fornovo, wrote that he saw sufferers who had lost their eyes, hands, noses, or feet and commented that "the entire body is so repulsive to look at and the suffering is so great, especially at night, that this sickness is even more horrifying than incurable leprosy or elephantiasis, and it can be fatal."[8] At this time it was not recognized that the disease had more than one stage.

The disease spread with appalling speed. It appeared elsewhere in Italy in 1495, in France, Switzerland, and Germany by 1496, and in England and Scotland by 1497. Every European country had it by 1500, and it was even reported in China by 1505. It was obvious that the disease was spread by sexual contact, as the sores always appeared first on the genitals, but people also believed that it was caused by an unfortunate conjunction of the stars or that it heralded the end of the world: apocalyptic prophecies abounded before 1500, the end of the fifteenth century. Girolamo Fracastoro, physician and poet, in 1530 wrote a long poem in which a shepherd named Siphilus [sic] is punished with the disease because he worshipped his king instead of the sun god. But in 1546, Fracastoro published a theory of contagion remarkably close to nineteenth-century bacteriological theory, proposing that this disease, and others such as phthisis or tuberculosis, was spread by tiny living particles that could multiply inside the body and be spread directly from person to person or in the air or on infected clothing (see chapter 3). In the case of the new disease, as it was spread by sexual contact, Fracastoro warned young men not to succumb to the "attractions of love."

As the new disease appeared in one nation, it was blamed on some other nation. While the Neapolitans called it the "French disease," the French called it the "Neapolitan disease." Since some of Charles' soldiers were Spanish, it was also called the "Spanish disease," and since some of these Spanish soldiers were supposed to have sailed with Columbus to the New World, some blamed it on the "Indians," meaning Native Americans. When the disease appeared in India after Vasco da Gama had sailed to that country, it was called the "Portuguese Scorre" (sore). The disease was also blamed on internal "others," especially Jews and women. Still other names cropped up: the "great" or the "grand" pox, to distinguish it from smallpox, and the "foul" disease, probably not just because of its foul symptoms but because of its association with illicit sex. The disease appeared to be almost literally the wages of sin.

Medicine at this time was based on the classic Greek and Roman literature which was thought to encompass all knowledge. According to Hippocrates and Galen, all diseases arose from an internal disturbance of the humoral system, the fluids thought to make up the individual's constitution. But new diseases, such as the Black Death and syphilis, clearly came from outside the body. Even more disturbing, no description of a disease like the French (or the Neapolitan, the Spanish, etc.) disease could be found in the

Fracastoro warns the shepherd Syphilus and the hunter Ilceus against yielding to "attractions of love." Engraving by Jan Sedaler I after Christopher Schwartz, 1588/1595. © Wellcome Library, London.

ancient Greek and Roman literature. Gonorrhea was described not only in Greek and Roman literature but in the Bible, and the theory that syphilis must simply be a later stage of gonorrhea appeared at this time. However, if this was so, it was still clear that this was a far worse form of gonorrhea than had ever been seen before.

It is nevertheless possible that syphilis was not a new disease, but that it was first described at this time as a separate entity that came from somewhere outside the body. Fracastoro described several other diseases—measles, bubonic plague, phthisis, leprosy, typhus, and others—for the first time now also.[9] Two theories as to the origin of syphilis persist to this day, known as the unitary treponema theory and the Columbian theory. In the unitary treponema theory, syphilis is one of four diseases caused by *Treponema* spirochete bacteria: the nonvenereal diseases of yaws (a disease of the skin and bones, probably originating in Africa), pinta (a skin disease originating in the Caribbean island of Hispaniola and in Central America), bejel (an Old World disease found mainly in children), and the venereal disease syphilis. In this theory, the venereal disease syphilis might simply have mutated from one of the other nonvenereal forms of *Treponema* spiro-chetes.[10] In the Columbian theory, syphilis was a New World disease contracted by sexual encounters between Native Americans and the soldiers who sailed with Columbus, and thereafter spread all over the virgin soil of Europe by the soldiers. Recent work by historians on the spread of European diseases (such as smallpox and measles) to the similarly virgin soil of the Americas in the sixteenth century lends credence to the possibility that syphilis might simply have traveled the other way.

However, in the sixteenth century most physicians thought syphilis was a new disease. So treatments with new substances, such as guaiacum wood, a wood that came from the New World, or the newly discovered element mercury were thought likely to be most effective. Such new treatments were still based on humoral theory, for as syphilis was thought to produce an excess of phlegm, treatments that caused salivation and sweating would force the patient to expel the excess phlegm. Mercury, which caused extreme salivation, was commonly combined with various means of sweating the patient, such as placing him or her in a box heated by a stove or confining the patient to a bed piled high with blankets.

Peter Lowe, a Glasgow surgeon, published *An Easy, Certaine and Perfect Method, to Cure and Prevent the Spanish Sickness* in 1596. Lowe was unusual in his opinion that prostitutes were less likely to spread the disease because, according to humoral theory, they were not emotionally involved in their work and were therefore "less hot and do not pass on the venom." However, his treatment was entirely usual: he advocated the administration of mercury pills for thirty or forty days, combined with enemas, purging, and sweating. Patients' willingness to accept such torturous treatment testifies to the agonizing nature of syphilis at this time, despite the fact that the disease appeared to have moderated somewhat since its first appearance in 1495.[11]

PROFITING FROM SYPHILIS

From the late seventeenth to the early eighteenth century in England, changes begin to appear in the writings of medical practitioners that indicate their sense of entering a new age of modern medicine. This was particularly evident in works that dealt with syphilis and venereal disease. For one thing, like many medical texts of the time, these texts were now written in English, plain English, for the common reader, rather than the learned language of Latin for the privileged communication of one scholarly physician with others. For another, many began with a survey of current beliefs about the origin of the pox. Since these had been in circulation for only two hundred years, medical writers felt that syphilis was a prime indication that the ancients hadn't known everything. They were confident that new discoveries about how to treat this new disease were being made every day. Works such as John Marten's *Treatise of all the Degrees and Symptoms of the Venereal Disease in Both Sexes* (1704) and *Gonosologium Novum, or a New System of All the Secret Infirmities and Diseases* (1708) and Daniel Turner's *Syphilis, A Practical Dissertation on the Venereal Disease* (1717) were all based on the now common belief that gonorrhea and syphilis, or the clap and the pox, were two stages of the same disease and that if the clap was not treated, it would develop into the more feared pox. Multiple opportunities for profit-making were thus spawned by venereal disease in eighteenth-century England, as new cures could be advertised, along with new specialists.

Surgeons were thought to be the proper kind of doctor to treat venereal disease, as they treated all external problems, such as diseases of the skin, eyes, and teeth. However, because there was no formal system of education, registration, or licensing for any of the commonly recognized categories of medical practitioners at this time (physicians, surgeons, apothecaries, and midwives), practically anyone could practice medicine (see chapter 1). Most surgeons, like midwives, had learned their trade through an apprenticeship. This situation, together with the growing incidence of what Marten called the "secret infirmities and diseases," appears to have provided a unique opportunity in medicine for women.

Handbills advertising London practitioners and their treatments, estimated dates 1660–1715, document a significant number of women practitioners in the new field of venereology.[12] The handbills, which repeatedly refer to patients' desire for privacy, even secrecy, while being treated for the pox, testify to the shame felt by those afflicted with venereal disease. Sufferers were advised that the practitioner's office could be entered by a back door or were given instructions for finding the office after dark. In addition, male practitioners often advertised that those of the female sex who had "any private Distemper" could be accommodated by the practitioner's wife. For example, one self-termed physician who offered to treat the "Foul Disease" with complete secrecy also promised the same service to women because "His Wife likewise for the more modest Accommodation of the Female Sex (being well skill'd in all Distempers incident to Women) gives her attendance."[13] A married woman might also continue her husband's practice after his death. One such woman advertised her ability to continue treatment of the secret disease by a practitioner of the appropriate sex, despite her husband's demise: "If any Gentleman has any Distemper not fit to be discourst of to a Woman, he may speak to my Son, who hath practis'd Physick above twenty years with good success. He hath great experience in curing any Venerial and all other Distempers."[14]

As treatment with mercury—which, in addition to being extremely unpleasant (producing extreme salivation, loss of teeth and hair, and pain in the teeth and bones), also required a four to six weeks' confinement—would make the nature of the sufferer's illness obvious to others, many patients sought some other form of treatment. Advertisements proliferated for other gentler and less visible forms of treatment, such as vegetable-based mixtures or the Montpellier (a French university) mercurial treatment that did not require confinement. Venereologists also advertised their willingness to send treatments by messenger or by mail. Some even employed retail agents, such as booksellers, at whose shops the embarrassed pox sufferer could pick up a treatment without arousing suspicion of his or her affliction.

Not all treatments in the eighteenth century were motivated by the desire for profits, however, as various institutions now offered free care. In 1746 the Lock Hospital, a private charitable hospital dedicated solely to the treatment of patients with venereal diseases, was founded in London. Prior to its founding, the royal (public) hospitals of St. Bartholomew and St. Thomas maintained "foul wards" to which the poor could apply for admission. In the face of an increasing incidence of syphilis, St. Bart's, as the hospital was called, developed the policy of sending excess foul patients to "outhouses" formerly used to house lepers. One of these, known as the Lock, was used for foul men and the other, the Kingsland, for foul women. (The term "lock" derives from the French word *loques*, referring to the lint rags and bandages used for lepers.) St. Thomas's considered building an "outhouse or spittlehouse" for foul patients but never realized this goal: patients with syphilis or other venereal diseases, if they were among the lucky few to be admitted, were sent to the foul wards.[15]

By the mid-eighteenth century, a distinction was increasingly made in institutional settings between innocent and culpable victims. In 1755 a special ward was built in the London Lock Hospital for married women. In 1766 children began to be treated as well, as sexual attacks were made on children as young as two, many as the consequence of the belief that intercourse with a virgin could cure syphilis.[16] It was also increasingly recognized that children could be born with syphilis, or that they could contract it from an infected wet nurse, and also that a syphilitic infant could infect a wet nurse. In France the world's first hospital for sick children opened in Paris in 1802, but infants born with syphilis were immediately transferred from it to a venereal hospital at Vaugirard. Here they were treated by suckling wet nurses who had syphilis themselves and were being treated with mercury.[17]

In 1787, a separate institution from the London Lock Hospital, the Lock Asylum, was founded in London. Its purpose was the moral and social reform of women who had been cured of syphilis and other venereal diseases. Although the Lock Hospital accepted both men and women for treatment, only women were admitted to the Lock Asylum. In order to be admitted, they had to apply immediately upon discharge from the Lock Hospital, and they had to be seen as likely to become a "sincere penitent" during the stay at the asylum. Here they were subjected to a disciplinary regimen, including required attendance at services in the Lock chapel.[18] This was the first of many "penitentiaries" to be founded for prostitutes in England, and the beginning of an increasing prejudice that the female body was in itself the source of venereal disease.

BLAMING THE OTHER WOMAN

> Like a rose shut in a book
> In which pure women may not look,
> For its base pages claim control
> To crush the flower within the soul;
> Where through each dead rose-leaf that clings,
> Pale as transparent Psyche-wings,
> To the vile text, are traced such things
> As might make lady's cheek indeed
> More than a living rose to read;
> So nought save foolish foulness may
> Watch with hard eyes the sure decay;
> And so the life-blood of this rose,
> Puddled with shameful knowledge, flows
> Through leaves no chaste hand may unclose.[19]

Rossetti's prostitute is a "vile text," a book in which "pure women may not look." Exploiting the traditional literary symbolism of the rose as metaphor for the female genitalia, he describes this rose as "puddled with shameful knowledge." Later in the poem, the speaker heaps more imagery of pollution on the prostitute, describing her dream of "the magic purse" as a "grim web, how clogged with shriveled flies!" As "purse" was an obscene term for the female genitalia, as well as a reference to the purse in which Jenny's clients would place money, he here refers to her vagina as a web clogged with "shriveled flies," which might be either a derisive image for her clients or a reference to the semen of many men, thought to be capable of spontaneously producing disease when mingled in the womb of a prostitute. The poet echoes the kind of language used in some medical texts that, as one critic comments, read like "perverse pornography."[20] N. D. Falck, MD, in his 1772 *A Treatise on Venereal Disease*, had described the "common whore" as having "art, deceit, treachery, and mischief . . . with which like a spider's web, she catches the imprudent profligate, and entangles him 'till he is ruined of worth, health, peace, and even life itself.'"[21] The poem, like the medical text, places the origin of venereal disease in the body of the prostitute.

Although this notion of the prostitute's body as the source of disease was not new to the Victorian era, it reached new extremes in nineteenth-century England. Both popular and medical literature represented women as divided between the "pure" and the "fallen." Those who were pure were believed to be innocent of any knowledge at all about female (or male) sexuality. Indeed, Acton, who had studied with the eminent French venereologist Philippe Ricord, made the famous statement that many females "never feel any sexual excitement whatever."[22] But the prostitute was held to be a veritable sewer in which all sorts of diseases bred. Medical and public health authorities alike pinned the blame for what they believed was an epidemic of the terrible scourge, syphilis, on one sex: the female. Men, it was thought, could be protected from venereal disease if the prostitutes from whom they sought the necessary relief of their sexual urges could be cleaned up. But because knowledge of all venereal diseases was itself a fog of confusions and contradictions at this time, ill-sorted beliefs about the disease-producing nature of all women's bodies arose alongside those that scapegoated prostitutes.

The "unicity" theory of John Hunter, the well-known Scottish surgeon who lived and practiced in eighteenth-century London with his brother William, professor of anatomy at the Royal Academy of the Arts, still prevailed at the beginning of the nineteenth century. This was the old theory that gonorrhea and syphilis were just different stages of the same disease. Hunter's book *On the Venereal Disease* (1786) continued to be cited as the authoritative work on the subject by French as well as British physicians during the first decades of the nineteenth century.

But the work of Ricord at the Hôpital des Vénériens (hospital for those suffering from venereal disease), where he was appointed surgeon to wet nurses, conclusively disproved Hunter's unicity theory.[23] Ricord was admired as a brilliant lecturer and attracted many students from abroad, Acton being one of them. But what made his work ultimately persuasive to others was his reliance on experimentation rather than mere observation. Ricord performed self-inoculations on some 2,500 hospital inmates.[24] That is, he took material from a patient's syphilitic chancre (skin ulcer) or gonorrheal discharge or lesion and reinoculated it somewhere else on the patient's body. What this proved was that only the syphilitic chancre would produce another syphilitic chancre; gonorrhea, as it turned out, could not be self-inoculated. Ricord's conclusion was that gonorrhea had no cause, as it was simply a local irritation, but that there was a "fatal poison" that produced syphilis, which he now called the "syphilitic virus."[25] But he (wrongly) concluded that the secondary stage of syphilis, characterized by a rash, inflammation of the bones and other organ systems, and tumors, was a different disease from primary syphilis, and also that the disease was not contagious in this stage. Finally, Ricord identified a third, or tertiary, stage of syphilis, often appearing after a lengthy latent period during which the patient was asymptomatic. Ricord noted syphilitic tubercles of the brain, tooth decay, and certain other not clearly defined "internal affections" as characteristic of this stage. Ricord's major work, *Traité pratique sur les maladies vénériens*, appeared in 1838 and was translated into English in 1858.

In Ricord's opinion, mercury was useful as a treatment only in the secondary stage of syphilis. He did not believe it useful at all in the treatment of gonorrhea, in which was still included a variety of conditions that caused vaginal discharge in women. It is not known whether mercury was of some benefit in treating syphilis, but it most certainly was not for gonorrhea, and as the effects of mercury treatment could be as bad as the effects of syphilis, leading to chronic ill health and even death, Ricord's work probably saved a lot of lives, not to mention a lot of misery. In 1858, Nathan Knepfler described the horrific effects of mercury treatment: "The mouth feels unusually hot . . . ; the gums are swollen, red, and tender, ulcers make their appearance and spread in all directions; the saliva is thick and stringy, and has that peculiar, offensive odor characteristic of mercurial disease; the tongue is swollen and stiff, and there is some fever. . . . The disease progressing, it destroys every part that it touches, until the lips, the cheeks, and even the bones have been eaten away. . . . The teeth . . . become loose and rot, perhaps fall out; or worse still, the upper and lower jaw-bones exfoliate and rot out sometimes . . . and the poor object lingers out a doleful existence during life. . . . This happens when mercury performs a *cure*!"[26] Although actuarial tables from the early twentieth century, when mercury was still being prescribed, indicate that untreated syphilitics had mortality rates lower than those supposedly cured through treatment with mercury, some evidence indicates that mercury may have had some antibacterial effectiveness.[27] Some Victorian practitioners believed that treatment of syphilitic parents with mercury, however unpleasant mercurial treatment was, might have the great benefit of preventing transmission of the disease to offspring.[28]

Ricord, whom Oliver Wendell Holmes described as the "Voltaire of pelvic literature," believed that sexual incontinence was universal and inevitable

---

"Do you wish to contract clap? This is the way. Take a pale, lymphatic woman, blond rather than brunette, and as leucorrhoeic as possible, dine with her; begin with oysters and continue with asparagus, drink of a good many dry white wines and champagne, coffee, liqueur. All this is well. Dance after your dinner and make your partner dance. Warm yourself up, and drink a good deal during the evening. When night comes, conduct yourself bravely; two or three acts of intercourse are not too much, more are still better. On waking do not fail to take a long warm bath and to make an injection. If you do not get the clap, it is because God protects you."[29]

among men.[30] And since he thought the body could be "acclimatized" to gonorrhea, he actually advised men to get themselves a case of the "clap." Ricord had no idea that gonorrhea could affect the internal reproductive organs in women, producing a serious and painful condition, pelvic inflammatory disease (PID), that could lead to sterility. He thought gonorrhea was only a local infection in women, often so mild as not to be noticed, while in men it was a serious disease, though not, of course, as serious as syphilis.

Ricord strongly advocated the use of the speculum, a new instrument that allowed doctors to look into the vagina and see symptoms not visible on manual pelvic examination. However, many women simply refused examination with the speculum.[31] In England, there was a particularly horrified reaction to the speculum. When disciples of Ricord, such as Acton, attempted to introduce its use, they were attacked in articles in medical journals such as the *Lancet* or the *British Medical Journal*, decrying the shocking immorality of imposing such examination on virtuous women. It was even claimed that women's minds were poisoned by the experience and that they had become addicted to speculum examination and had deteriorated into "uterine hypochondriacs."[32]

During this period of much new but still incomplete and often inaccurate research on syphilis, attention was increasingly focused on prostitutes as the source of the disease. In 1836, Alexandre Parent-Duchâtelet published his study of Parisian prostitutes, *De la prostitution dans la ville de Paris* [On prostitution in the city of Paris]. Based on a study of twelve thousand prostitutes over a fifteen-year period, the work had a strong impact in Victorian England. Venereal disease of all kinds seemed to the authorities to be increasing in England, particularly in the military, at an alarming rate. Meanwhile, penitentiaries for prostitutes were being founded by various charitable organizations, especially the new Anglican sisterhoods, as well as civic authorities. More lock hospitals, many of which at first admitted only female patients and subjected them to a disciplinary regimen, were opened in Glasgow (1805), Newcastle (1813), Manchester (1819), Liverpool (1834), Leeds (1842), Bristol (1870), and Birmingham (1881).[33] In Glasgow, there was vigorous opposition to the founding of a lock hospital, on the grounds that syphilis was God's punishment for sexually promiscuous women, so they should not be treated. Agreement was finally reached with the provision that the hospital would not be constructed without an accompanying penitentiary or "magdalene home."[34]

In his *Complete and Practical Treatise on the Venereal Diseases* (1841), Acton repeated all kinds of ancient myths about the source of venereal disease as "foul women," "leprous women," or "unclean wombs." This work held that venereal disease was principally transmitted through the vagina.[35] In 1857, Acton published his *Prostitution, Considered in its Moral, Social and Sanitary Aspects, in London and other Large Cities.* Written to promote some kind of regulation of prostitutes, though not, the author insisted, anything like "the system of prostitution-management practiced by the police of continental States," *Prostitution* argued for the treatment of venereal disease in prostitutes for the good of the nation.[36] Commenting that "the streets of London are an open book," his chapter "The Modern Harlot's Progress" takes up a position surprisingly similar to that of Rossetti's distanced and judgmental speaker in the poem "Jenny."[37]

> Descend a step to the promiscuous category, and trace the harlot to whom a tavern-bar was congenial instead of repulsive on her first appearance there—say at sixteen or eighteen years of age. At thirty and at forty you will find her (if she rises in the scale) the loudest of the loud, in the utmost blaze of finery, looked on as "first-rate company" by aspiring gents, surrounded by a knot of "gentlemen" who applaud her rampant nonsense, and wondering, hotel-sick, country men of business, whose footsteps stray at night to where she keeps her foolish court. She is a sort of white-washed sepulchre, fair to the eye, but full of inner rottenness—a mercenary human tigress.[38]

The Crimean War (1854–56), during which the incidence of venereal disease among soldiers was found to be scandalously high, pushed the British

"Syphilis." Painting by Richard Cooper, 1910. © Wellcome Library, London.

conviction that prostitutes were the cause of disease to a further peak. In 1862 Florence Nightingale, who had supervised the care of wounded and sick soldiers in the Crimea, organized a Sanitary Commission on the subject of venereal disease in the army.[39] Nightingale did not believe that prostitutes should be regulated as a means of cutting down on venereal disease in the army. But by this time, the idea that control of prostitutes was the key to keeping men (especially military men) healthy had become generally accepted.

The first Contagious Diseases Act was passed in July 1864. It provided for compulsory examination of a woman suspected of being a prostitute and for her detention in a lock hospital for up to three months if she was found to be diseased in eleven garrison towns and ports in the south of England and Ireland.[40] The bill passed with little notice. In 1866 a renewal bill was presented. It called for mandatory fortnightly inspection of prostitutes for up to a year, and detention in a lock hospital for six months if they were found to be diseased. Although the first bill had actually been acted upon in only four of the eleven designated towns, this one increased the number to twelve. Again, the bill passed with little debate.

But in 1867, enthusiasm for the extension of the acts to the entire civilian population in Britain led to the foundation of an "Extensionist Association." A select committee was formed to consider the proposition. The medical practitioners who testified before this committee still manifested all sorts of confusions, even sheer nonsense, such as whether syphilis might be due to the "poisonous influences of an unhealthy female," whether women spontaneously generated "soft sores" or chancroid, and whether "impure intercourse" was the likely cause of gonorrhea. Most doctors were opposed to the use of such heroic measures as mercury treatment or treatment with escharotics, substances used to burn off sores or growths. Nevertheless, some doctors urged their use for prostitutes, in what seems an obvious desire for painful and punitive treatment for this particular group of syphilitics.[41] In 1869, the third Contagious Diseases Act was passed, this time allowing for the detention of prostitutes in a lock hospital for up to nine months. Six more districts were added, bringing the total number to eighteen.

But the passage of this act saw the beginning of opposition. The passage of the Reform Act of 1867, which gave the vote to a portion of working-class men for the first time, enabled political activism for this population. It was also a time of political activism for women. Women's suffrage societies had been formed in the hope of extending the franchise to women, and although this did not happen, a major advance was made for women in 1870 with the passage of the Married Women's Property Act. (This act allowed married women to become the legal owners of their own earnings and also of some inherited property, both of which had previously been the legal property of the husband.)

Although the first group founded to oppose the Contagious Diseases Acts, the National Association for the Repeal of the Contagious Diseases Acts (NA), initially excluded women, membership was soon offered to them. However, a separate female association, the Ladies' National Association (LNA), was founded in 1869. Josephine Butler, a powerful feminist leader who had been especially active in "rescue work," that is, rescue of prostitutes from police prosecution, was asked to lead the LNA. Butler, although born to the upper classes herself, always identified strongly with the working classes. In her rescue work, she often took poor and sick women into her own home. The repeal movement saw the unlikely coalition of middle-class women, motivated especially by women's causes, and working-class men, motivated in part by the obvious class discrimination of the Contagious Diseases Acts, which not only targeted working-class women almost exclusively but also legitimated male vice, especially in working-class men such as soldiers and sailors. Both groups were united in a hatred of "profligate aristocrats."[42] One of the first acts of the LNA was to issue a Ladies' Manifesto that denounced the acts as blatant class and sex discrimination that not only deprived poor women of their constitutional rights but also officially sanctioned male vice.

Hearing women speak in public on such matters as prostitution and venereal disease, even on gynecological examinations, was a new experience for the British public. Some applauded their efforts: the *Spectator* praised them as providing a "new ideal of women's intellectual courage and capacity of political life." But others reacted violently against them: the *Saturday Review* called them the "shrieking sisterhood."[43] Women themselves were by no means united in their support of the repeal campaign. Even the strong feminist Frances Power Cobbe wrote to a friend that she was most anxious women should not "get mixed up in this controversy which must do *us* harm & in which I feel perfectly persuaded we can do no good."[44]

Other women, however, sought to rescue prostitutes from their representation as "vile text" and source of contagion, as weavers of grim webs, designed to catch and ruin unwary men. Augusta Webster, one of many women writers who took the fallen woman as their subject, opens her poem "A Castaway" with a prostitute reading her own book, her "poor little diary." In this book she reads her "simple thoughts" and "good resolves," to "study French, read Modern History, darn stockings, go to church, take soup to someone, and go out for tea." This young woman had obviously intended to lead a virtuous life, had had "the young girl's hazed and golden dreams / That veil the Future from her." Although poverty had driven her to the life she now leads, she knows herself a very different kind of woman than the one Rossetti pictures:

And what is that? My looking-glass
Answers it passably; a woman sure,
No fiend, no slimy thing out of the pools,
A woman with a ripe and smiling lip
That has no venom in its touch I think.[45]

In 1886, the Contagious Diseases Acts were repealed in Britain. Although prostitutes continued to be the target of anti-syphilis campaigns, another type of gendering of venereal disease was now under way: the deviant male, diagnosed as either the cause or the product of racial degeneration.

BLAMING THE "HUSBAND-FIEND"

In a short story by Arthur Conan Doyle, "The Third Generation," a very frightened young man of twenty-one consults a doctor about a lesion that has suddenly appeared on his shin. After looking at the shin lesion, the doctor asks to see the young man's teeth, and then to examine his eyes. Mentioning the term "interstitial keratitis," he pronounces the young man's doom: "In broad terms, I may say that you have a constitutional and hereditary taint."[46] When the young man tells him that he is to be married on Tuesday, the doctor informs him bluntly that the marriage must not take place. In short, he has hereditary syphilis and he could pass "the poison" on to his children. The young man, horrified at the prospect of breaking the engagement and thus putting such a public affront on his fiancée, leaves the doctor's office and throws himself beneath the wheels of a heavy, two-horse dray. He dies while being carried to the hospital.

The story, written in 1894, has been analyzed by literary critics as illustrating the diagnosis of congenital syphilis by the presence of two of the characteristics of "Hutchinson's triad": interstitial keratitis, or inflammation of the cornea, and notched incisor teeth. The third symptom, deafness, is not evident, but as the young man has another common symptom of congenital syphilis, a skin lesion on the shin, the doctor is sure of the diagnosis, and very sure that the young man must not marry for many years.

Doyle, who had an MD from Edinburgh (1885), wrote his thesis on tertiary syphilis and would have been acquainted with Hutchinson's triad, the combination of three symptoms identified by the English physician Jonathan Hutchinson as diagnostic of congenital or hereditary syphilitic infection, even if they appeared as late as the sufferer's twenties or thirties. The story has been understood as meaning that the young man has acquired syphilis because his grandfather, a "foul old dandy," had infected his grandmother, who then passed the disease to his father through placental transmission during pregnancy. The young man's father, described as having led an "innocent life" but as having always been afflicted with skin lesions of various sorts, had infected his mother, who had then passed the disease to the young man through placental transmission during her pregnancy. This understanding of how syphilis might be transmitted to the third, or even the fourth, generation although only the original paternal figure might have acquired the disease through sinful sex, is still compatible with theories of the inheritance of syphilis today, though it would doubtless be considered an unlikely story. But "The Third Generation" more probably represents the late nineteenth-century belief that syphilis could be transmitted to offspring directly through the father's sperm.[47] The mother might not be infected at all, or she might be infected by the already poisoned fetus. Alfred Fournier, leading venereologist of the time, believed in this theory of direct paternal transmission through the semen.

Fournier, who had studied with Ricord, did extensive research on syphilis that both demonstrated that tertiary syphilis was far more destructive than had hitherto been suspected and contributed to fears about congenital syphilis as not only more prevalent but as productive of congenital defects worse than had been imagined. He identified tabes dorsalis—an infection of the spinal cord resulting in stabbing pains in the trunk and legs, unsteady gait, incontinence, and impotence—as a manifestation of tertiary syphilis in 1876. He attempted throughout the last years of the century to persuade other venereologists that general motor paralysis of the insane (GPI), a combination of partial but generalized paralysis and insanity, was also a late consequence of syphilis, although there was much resistance to this idea (now known to be correct).[48]

Fournier's research on congenital or hereditary syphilis led to an increasing emphasis on men, particularly middle-class men, as the source of syphilis in the unborn and in succeeding generations of the original sinner. Fournier became convinced, as were Hutchinson and other venereologists of the time, that syphilis could be transmitted by an infected man's sperm at the moment it united with the woman's "germ" or ovum. (It is now known that the fetus can be infected only through the placenta or by contact with a syphilitic lesion at the time of birth.) His work publicized the pathetic "little old man" appearance of the syphilitic newborn (so described, regardless of the infant's sex) and fed fears that succeeding generations of syphilitics would lead to racial degeneration. In 1904 he wrote:

> It emerges from recent research that syphilis can, because of its hereditary consequences, debase and corrupt the species by producing inferior, decadent, dystrophic and deficient beings. Yes, deficient; they can be physically deficient . . . , or they can be mentally deficient, being, according to the degree of their intellectual debasement, retarded, simple-minded, unbalanced, insane, imbecilic or idiotic.[49]

Such work shifted emphasis in venereology from the supposedly disease-producing female body to the male body as carrier of inherent degeneracy. Popular literature shifted from representing women as divided between the pure and the polluted to the Jekyll and Hyde figure of the divided man, appearing respectable but concealing a Frankensteinian monstrosity within.[50] Henrik Ibsen's play *Ghosts* (first produced in 1889), presented in London to horrified audiences and critics, is another instance of the male deviance now blamed for the horrors of syphilis: an innocent young man discovers himself to have a fatal disease and eventually learns from his mother that he acquired it from his apparently honorable but secretly dissolute father. The young man subsequently kills himself.

Blackwood's Magazine now commented on how "the Husband-Fiend is trotted out so often in fiction and in drama, that one wonders how the demon manages still to command a premium in the marriage-market."[51] "New Woman" novels, such as Sarah Grand's sensational and very popular *The Heavenly Twins* (1893), took up the plight of the innocent wife who discovers too late that the man she has married is a moral leper. Grand's heroine Evadne refuses to consummate her marriage, fearing infection with a disease she cannot name.[52]

Advice literature written by both doctors and women writers warned of the horrifying possibility of giving birth to a syphilitic infant (see sidebar). Fournier, in *Syphilis and Marriage* (1880, translated into English 1881) urged readers, "Think of the unhappy infant, who in place of being the 'dear baby,' upon which the hopes and dreams of the young wife have centered, and whose advent the family have expected with so much delight, is to all nothing but an object of horror and disgust."[53] Yet many doctors

Another class of disease worth noting, one that is liable to take possession of marriageable young men, is of such a private nature as makes it unfit to refer to with any fullness. It can take such severe forms, after marriage, that not only may a wife be affected from her husband, but the children born of the marriage may suffer to a serious extent; in other words, certain private diseases of the father, that have been contracted before marriage, can be transmitted in hideous and loathsome forms to his children. It is very difficult to convey a sufficient amount of information to the reader concerning such diseases, to be of use, without running the risk of communicating indecent information; but the subject is one of such importance that one would not feel to be doing proper justice to the main subject if it were left unreferred to altogether. It will perhaps be sufficient to mention that such private diseases as are denoted result from impure and illicit intercourse before marriage.[54]

continued the old tradition of collaboration with husbands in concealing venereal disease from their wives, as they still believed that gonorrhea was an insignificant and temporary affliction for women, while the prevailing medical dogma about syphilis was that the man should simply wait a few years until he was (supposedly) cured before marrying.

POST-VICTORIAN SYPHILIS: CONTINUING TO BLAME THE OTHER

The Victorian era ended, then, with darkened views of syphilis and its potential for degeneration of the species, now as the "hideous progeny" of "Husband-Fiends." These bleak views fueled eugenics movements, in turn propelled by Darwinian doctrines.[55] Although both the cause of syphilis and the means of diagnosing it even in the complete absence of symptoms (the Wasserman blood test) were to be discovered within the first few years of the new century, and an effective treatment, Salvarsan, in 1910, neither syphilis nor its damage to populations identified as the other were to be eradicated. Prostitutes were described as "Treponema machine-guns" during World War I, and the "clean-looking" girl was named on military posters as someone to be suspected.[56] From 1932 to 1972, the U.S. Public Health Service conducted the infamous Tuskegee study of syphilis in black men, half of whom were not informed that they were not being treated for their disease, even though penicillin, the ultimate magic bullet, was available from the 1940s on.[57] As Allan Brandt states, no magic bullet or treatment designed to target and destroy a particular microorganism is sufficient to end a disease, because "medicine is not just affected by social, economic, and political variables—it is embedded in them."[58] There could be no better demonstration of this than the history of syphilis in Victorian England.

5

Smallpox

"Now, Charley, when she knows I am ill, she will try to make her way into the room. Keep her out, Charley, if you love me truly, to the last! Charley, if you let her in but once, only to look upon me for one moment as I lie here, I shall die."

"I never will! I never will!" she promised me.

"I believe it, my dear Charley. And now come and sit beside me for a little while, and touch me with your hand. For I cannot see you, Charley; I am blind."[1]

Esther Summerson, heroine of Charles Dickens's novel *Bleak House* (1853), warns her thirteen-year-old maidservant, Charley, not to let her dear friend and fellow ward of court Ada into her sickroom. Esther has caught what she calls "the contagion" from Charley, whom she has nursed tenderly throughout the young girl's illness. Because Esther is aware of how very contagious this terrible illness is, she would not allow her "darling" Ada to come anywhere near her while she was nursing Charley. She would not even look out the window into the garden below when Ada called up to her from there, but remained behind the curtain. She now threatens Charley with the worst threat she can command, her own death, if Charley allows Ada anywhere near her during her illness with the contagion. Only Charley can be with her and nurse her, because Charley has already had the illness and is therefore immune to it. Esther now confesses to Charley that she has become blind. Although she not only recovers from the illness but later regains her sight, she discovers she has suffered the loss of her looks.

When she finally finds a mirror (all mirrors have been removed from her room during her illness), she sadly recognizes that she is very much changed: "O very, very much. . . . I had never been a beauty, and had never thought myself one; but I had been very different from this. It was all gone now."[2]

What is Esther's disease? Dickens does not name it (he does not name any of the illnesses described in *Bleak House*). Esther's awareness of the extreme degree of contagiousness of her illness and Charley's, the blindness she suffers during her illness, and her discovery that, although she has not lost her beautiful hair, her facial appearance is very much changed for the worse, all point to smallpox. But today's readers of Dickens' brilliant novel are puzzled by this retrospective diagnosis. Why wouldn't Esther have been vaccinated against smallpox, since it had been proved more than half a century earlier that this dread disease could be prevented by vaccination with the far milder disease of cowpox? Most twenty-first-century readers of Victorian novels have never even heard of a smallpox epidemic, let alone seen a case of it, because smallpox was eradicated from the globe by a worldwide campaign of vaccination that ended in 1979, as the last case of naturally acquired smallpox had occurred in 1977. Many readers today, in fact, have never been vaccinated themselves, and the history of vaccination and of the disease it eventually conquered has faded from common knowledge. Surely, it is assumed, a middle-class heroine like Esther Summerson would have been vaccinated and could never have actually caught smallpox. Even if she had nursed a servant who had caught the disease, doubtless because a poor family might be less likely to have had their children vaccinated, Esther would not have caught it.

None of these seemingly reasonable assumptions about smallpox in nineteenth-century England, however, are correct. Smallpox was endemic throughout the nineteenth century everywhere in the world. Britain suffered several major epidemics during this time as well. Vaccination was not universal, nor did it infallibly protect against smallpox. Middle- and upper-class people were not necessarily more likely to have been vaccinated than poor people. Esther Summerson's illness is a very realistic representation of smallpox as experienced in Victorian England.

In the same year *Bleak House* was published, Britain passed the Compulsory Vaccination Act of 1853, making vaccination compulsory for all infants before four months of age. Vaccination had been available ever since English physician Edward Jenner (1749–1823) had tried out the process on an eight-year-old boy in 1796, but it had been neither free nor compulsory in Britain. In 1840 a vaccination act was passed that made vaccination free as administered by Poor Law medical officers. (The New Poor Law Amendment Act of 1834 attempted to restrict relief for the poor to those willing to enter union workhouses, which were run on a harsh and disciplinary regimen. Dickens vividly represents workhouse life in his 1838 novel *Oliver Twist*.) Many of the working poor felt degraded by having to get their free infant vaccination as if they were paupers accepting relief. The much older though riskier practice of inoculation or variolation, in which matter taken from actual smallpox pustules was inserted into incisions, continued to be preferred by many. Rather than being administered by Poor Law medical officers, inoculation was generally performed in the nineteenth century by local people or traveling inoculators. Though they often lacked much, if anything, in the way of medical education, they were usually familiar folk who did not insult their clients. Unfortunately, those who had been inoculated, though they usually suffered only a mild case of smallpox themselves, could infect others with smallpox in its naturally virulent form. Inoculees could therefore greatly worsen an existing epidemic in their attempts to protect themselves from it.

The less risky process of infant vaccination with cowpox was complicated by the difficulty of obtaining sufficient lymph (matter from cowpox pustules) from cows or calves. The procedure was therefore commonly administered arm-to-arm. That is, a baby who had been vaccinated was brought back after eight days, matter was taken from that baby's vaccination and inserted into several incisions made in the arm of the waiting infant, a process not only painful but that sometimes resulted in the transmission of other blood-borne diseases such as syphilis. Not until the late 1860s was administrative machinery put in place to force the public to comply with the 1853 Compulsory Vaccination Act, and it typically prosecuted the working classes, who fought back with vigorous and sometimes violent antivaccination campaigns. Middle- and upper-class families could have their infants vaccinated by their doctors—or not, if they so chose. In addition, the fact that vaccination did not supply lifelong protection but needed to be repeated at intervals was not widely known or accepted.

The history of smallpox in Victorian England is a history of social and political struggles, for methods of preventing the disease always entailed risks and sacrifices, and it was never easy to see which risks were the greatest or whose sacrifices the most justifiable. Few people understood why or how deliberately infecting a healthy child with an animal disease could confer immunity against a human disease. Confusion and anxieties about contagion, about crossing animal–human boundaries, and above all, about the government's right to control the individual's body led to mass protests against vaccination. Smallpox became a classroom for an education in just how complex and difficult a task it is to teach people how to stamp out a disease, even after the knowledge of how to do that has become available.

AN EQUAL OPPORTUNITY DISEASE

In December 1694, Queen Mary II of England came down with an illness at first thought to be the measles, but one of her physicians soon told her she had smallpox. As the nineteenth-century historian Thomas Macaulay wrote: "She received the intimation of her danger with true greatness of soul. She gave orders that every lady of her bedchamber, every maid of honor, nay, every menial servant who had not had the smallpox should instantly leave Kensington House. She locked herself up during a short time in her closet, burned some papers, arranged others, and calmly awaited her fate."[3] Despite the best care that could be given, the queen died on December 28. Looking back from his position in Victorian England after the introduction of vaccination, Macaulay wrote, "That disease, over which science has since achieved a succession of glorious and beneficent victories, was then the most terrible of all the ministers of death."[4]

King William III had already suffered losses from smallpox. His father had died of the disease the week before William was born, and his mother died of it when he was ten years old. He had had a very severe case of the disease himself, but had survived it. As Queen Mary had died before she had any children and King William never remarried, he was succeeded after his death eight years later by Mary's sister Anne. However, Anne's only child, the eleven-year-old Duke of Gloucester, had died of smallpox two years before his mother became queen. Queen Anne endured eighteen pregnancies, but all of the infants were stillborn or died in infancy. Smallpox thus ended the royal Stuart line in Britain, and the English throne was turned over to a distant relative, George I of the House of Hanover.

No one was safe from smallpox. The "speckled monster" had been killing rich and poor, princes and peasants alike everywhere in the world for thousands of years. Donald R. Hopkins's *The Greatest Killer: Smallpox in History* (2002) includes a seven-page chronology of the disease that cites such startling figures as the death of 50,000 people in Paris circa 1438, two million Aztecs in 1576, nine-tenths of the Native American population along the Massachusetts coast in 1617–19, 30,000 Brazilian Indians in 1660, 18,000 of the total population of 50,000 Icelanders in 1707, and so on. And these almost incomprehensible numbers of deaths from smallpox among whole populations are punctuated everywhere with the deaths of entire royal families in numerous countries all over the globe, causing momentous changes in national histories. Had smallpox not killed Queen Mary II, for example, there never would have been a Victorian Age in British history, for the nineteen-year-old Queen Victoria crowned in 1837 was a descendant of the House of Hanover.

Smallpox knew neither class, national, nor racial difference. The disease had been around at least since the first century BCE, when a description of smallpox and of the worship of a goddess of smallpox was recorded in India. Egyptian mummies from this period bear evidence of smallpox-like scars. Where it did not kill, survivors were left with disfiguring scars and often lost their hair, eyebrows, and eyelashes. Many were also left blind by the disease, thus permanently disabled, and male survivors might be left with reduced fertility.[5]

Until the seventeenth century, however, smallpox was thought of as mostly a children's disease in Britain and in Europe. But something changed in the seventeenth century, and the disease seemed suddenly much more virulent than before. After an incubation period of a week to twelve days, during which the victim did not seem ill, the characteristic symptoms of high fever, backache, and headache, and sometimes convulsions and delirium, would appear. Some sufferers had nightmarish dreams for as long as three or four days. After this period, the victim would actually feel a little better as the rash of flat reddish spots began to appear. But then the spots would turn into pustules and, as Hopkins puts it, "the miserable, aching victim was transformed into a hideous, swollen monster."[6] The severity of the illness was determined by the kind and density of the pustules: where they remained separate, though raised and swollen, about 20–40 percent of adult victims died; where the pustules became confluent (ran together), mortality rates were higher, perhaps 60–70 percent. In the most severe form of the disease, the rash was accompanied by bleeding, both internal and external. This was known as "black" or hemorrhagic smallpox and was almost invariably fatal.[7]

Victims were contagious for a period of about three weeks, from just before the rash appeared (thus, often before the disease had been recognized for what it was) until all of the scabs from the pustules had dropped off. As the disease spreads not only by contact with the patient but also by breathing the same air, sometimes even in another part of the same house, it was extremely contagious. Dickens' heroine Esther Summerson is not being overcautious when she refuses to lean out the window and talk to Ada in the garden below: it is possible the disease could have been passed to Ada in that manner.

The dead bodies of victims were contagious, as were the clothing and even the shrouds that covered them. Corpses were hurriedly sealed in closed caskets, lest infection spread among the mourners. Clothing, bed linens, even

As late as 1970, a single case of undiagnosed smallpox in a hospital in Meschede, West Germany, caused 17 other cases of smallpox in the same building, though none of these other cases had had any contact with the original case. Smoke tests later proved that infection had occurred through a pattern of air currents moving away from the patient's room.[8]

dust, could also carry the contagion from dried pustules, called fomites, for months. This fact was well enough known so that in 1763, British forces in Canada deliberately infected American Indians by distributing contaminated blankets to them.[9]

> Could it not be contrived to send the smallpox among these disaffected tribes of Indians? We must use every stratagem in our power to reduce them. {British officer Jeffery Amherst to Col. Henry Bouquet, 1763}. "I will try to inoculate the ___ with some blankets that may fall into their hands and take care not to get the disease myself." (Bouquet's reply)[10]

By the end of the seventeenth century, smallpox had become the major killer in England and throughout Europe. During the eighteenth century, it is estimated that 400,000 people died every year from smallpox in Europe. London had major epidemics at intervals as short as two years. Children were particularly vulnerable: 80 percent of children under five who contracted the disease in London died; in Berlin, 98 percent of young children who caught smallpox were killed by the disease.[11] But adults were also stricken, and epidemic waves became more and more frequent. The rich were attacked as relentlessly as the poor. Indeed, many believed that the rich actually suffered more than the poor. There were two theories as to why this might be so. The first held that the constitutions of the rich were weakened by indolence and luxury, and the second that the medical care given to the rich, the best that money could buy, actually made the disease worse and killed them. The second theory might well have had some truth to it, as physicians often prescribed torturous treatments, such as sweating the feverish sufferers by placing them near a hot fire, covering them with piles of bedclothes (often red, as an ancient tradition held that the color red had some special curative power), and not even changing the bed linens, which would become saturated with the leakage from the pustules, whose raised nodules were filled with foul-smelling pus. Some wealthier victims might have been lucky enough, however, to have a physician who subscribed to the "cold" treatment devised by the seventeenth-century English physician Thomas Sydenham. Sydenham advocated light covering, fresh air, and lots of cool beverages.[12] His method probably gave the sufferer more of a fighting chance.

In the early eighteenth century, however, Lady Mary Wortley Montagu observed a folk method of preventing smallpox while she was living in Constantinople, where her husband had been appointed ambassador. Her experience was to prove crucial to the battle against smallpox in eighteenth-century England. Having suffered a severe case of smallpox herself, which had left her with no eyelashes and a badly scarred face, she was probably

Lady Mary Wortley Montagu in Turkish dress. Stipple Engraving by W. Greatbach, 1844. © Wellcome Library, London.

more open to a folk method of smallpox prevention practiced in Turkey by old women than many Europeans might have been.

> *Apropos* of distempers, I am going to tell you a thing that will make you wish yourself here. The small-pox, so fatal, and so general amongst us, is here entirely harmless, by the invention of *ingrafting*, which is the term they give it. There is a set of old women, who make it their business to perform the operation, every autumn in the month of September, when the great heat is abated.

People send to one another to know if any of their family has a
mind to have the small-pox: they make parties for this purpose, and
when they are met (commonly fifteen or sixteen together), the old
woman comes with a nutshell full of the matter of the best sort of
small-pox, and asks what vein you please to have opened.

She immediately rips open that you offer her, with a large needle
(which gives you no more pain than a common scratch) and puts into
the vein, as much matter as can lie upon the head of her needle, and
after that binds up the little wound with a hollow bit of shell; and in
this manner opens four or five veins.[13]

Lady Montagu believed the practice to be almost entirely beneficial and
without harmful effect. She wrote that those inoculated (usually children)
would remain in perfect health until the eighth day, then have a fever for
two or three days, after which they would develop a small number of pox,
which would leave no scars. They would then be permanently immune to
smallpox. She was only partly right. Inoculation with matter taken from
actual smallpox pustules usually did result in only a minor case of smallpox,
but sometimes the inoculees had a bad case of the disease, and sometimes
they died. Even more dangerous was the fact that those inoculated could
infect others with smallpox, and those who contracted the disease in this
manner typically had as severe a form of the disease as those who caught it
from someone with the disease itself.

Unaware of these disturbing aspects of inoculation (later called variolation, or inoculation with *variola*, the medical term for smallpox), Lady
Montagu had her six-year-old son inoculated by an "old Greek woman."
Her physician, Charles Maitland, intervened after the old woman's shaky
hand (according to him) had caused the child much torture with her
attempts to incise one arm with "her blunt and rusty Needle," and he inoculated the other arm with his own instrument, which caused the child very
little pain.[14] Although the inoculation took in both arms, the boy had the
desired light case of smallpox, from which he recovered quickly.

After her return to England in 1721, Lady Montagu had Maitland inocu-
late her three-year-old daughter in April of that year in the presence of witnesses (she had delayed having the little girl inoculated in Turkey because
her nurse had not had smallpox). It was the doctor who wanted witnesses
because British doctors feared for their reputation if a patient or patients
died, even though by this time many physicians had heard about the practice and its apparent success in preventing smallpox.[15] But the smallpox epidemic in England in February and March 1721 greatly heightened Lady
Montagu's fears of the disease, and she insisted on having the child inoculated. This inoculation was successful; the little girl had an even lighter case
than her brother had had. It was now decided to experiment on six

prisoners. On August 9, 1721, three male and three female inmates of New-gate Prison were inoculated on the promise of being given their freedom (if they survived). All six survived, and one at least was proven to be immune to smallpox by exposure to two children who had the disease. Thereafter, members of the royal family began to have their children inoculated, and the practice slowly spread to the general population. Still, only about nine hundred people were inoculated in England and Scotland over the next eight years, as reports of deaths from inoculation were circulated, and also as it became more widely known that inoculees could start or worsen an epidemic.[16]

Meanwhile, in Boston clergyman Cotton Mather tried the method on a six-year-old boy and two African slaves in the same year, 1721. Mather had first heard of the method in 1716 from his slave Onesimus, who had been inoculated in Africa himself. When another epidemic threatened in 1721, Mather persuaded a physician, Zabdiel Boylston, to try the method in June. Boylston was reprimanded by the selectmen and justices of Boston because they rightly feared that inoculation might make the epidemic worse. Nevertheless, when the epidemic was over six months later, Boylston had inoculated 242 persons, and of the 855 deaths from smallpox, only six were among inoculated people.[17]

Thus inoculation, which had been practiced for centuries in Africa and Asia, became part of orthodox medical practice in Britain, the American colonies, and all over Europe during the eighteenth century. A similar practice, known as "Buying the Smallpox," had even been known in Scottish and Welsh folk medicine, apparently borrowed from Syria and North Africa, for about fifty years before its introduction in England by Lady Montagu and the royal family in 1721. A child would be sent with money or sweets to a child with smallpox, and matter from the smallpox pustules would be "bought" and rubbed or pricked into the skin of the healthy child. The practice was ignored by physicians, as it was considered merely folk medicine.[18]

As surgeons and physicians took up the practice, the method was made much more difficult and expensive by the requirement of weeks of preparation, in which the patient would be put on a special (starvation) diet, bled repeatedly, and purged. This process undoubtedly rendered patients weaker and less able to withstand the induction of smallpox, but it became common nonetheless. It gradually became recognized also that inoculees should be isolated from the rest of the population for a period of two weeks because of the danger of infecting others, a process which further increased the expense of the method for the working classes. When smallpox seemed somewhat less of a threat, therefore, the working classes tended to avoid inoculation.

The inoculation plan prepared by the inhabitants of Glynde, Sussex, however, provides an example of how working people could organize so as to make it possible for everyone to be inoculated. Faced with a threatened epidemic in 1767, villagers made plans to have half the population inoculated at one time and sent to the newly built stable block at the Glynde Estates, owned by the Bishop of Durham, who only spent six months of the year there. A doctor was paid "by the Lump," in order to make the process cheaper and include those who could not afford to pay as well as those who could. After the first set had been inoculated, they remained in the stable block for about two weeks to be "aired," that is, kept away from the rest of the population as long as they might be contagious. Meanwhile, the rest of the population carried on with the farm work and other labors.

After the airing process was completed, the second half of the population was brought in and inoculated. In all, about two hundred villagers were inoculated, along with about forty outsiders. The premises were then thoroughly cleaned and made ready for the bishop's return. The results were considered very satisfactory, as most had only a mild attack of smallpox and were chiefly bothered by the dose of "cleansing Physick" they were required to take on the fourteenth day. Only the inhabitants of the poorhouse were not included: three of them caught smallpox, and one died.[19]

In 1796, Jenner tried out the practice he called "vaccination" because it involved inserting matter from a pox taken from a cow (vacca, in Latin). This practice was to change not only the history of smallpox in Britain but the history of medicine in the world, for it eventually led to the first (and so far the only) eradication of a major epidemic disease from the entire planet. But vaccination did not replace inoculation swiftly enough to save the family of poet Samuel Taylor Coleridge from tragedy. In 1799, his nine-month-old son Berkeley died of smallpox after being inoculated, and his mother Sara also contracted smallpox, leaving her face permanently scarred and her beautiful hair "utterly spoiled." She had it all cut off and wore a wig for the rest of her life.[20]

THE VACCINATION WARS

How did it happen that an English country doctor discovered a revolutionary medical technique that was to change history? Evidence shows that Jenner did not actually discover vaccination; it had been tried by at least one other Englishman, and probably by others who are not recorded. But he was able to grasp the radical potential of vaccination and to promote its effectiveness because he had had an unusually extensive medical education for the time and had gained a prestigious place in English medical society.

Jenner had been trained by the usual method of apprenticeship to an apothecary and a surgeon, but he had then gone on to study with the well-known and influential Scottish surgeon John Hunter (see chapter 4) at St. George's Hospital in London. Hunter evidently took a liking to this particular student, who shared his interest in natural history, and helped Jenner make many important contacts. After two years' training with Hunter,

Jenner returned to his home town of Berkeley in Gloucestershire and set up general practice, which he continued for the next twenty years. Like other eighteenth-century surgeons, he performed inoculations with actual smallpox matter to protect patients, especially children, against the disease. At this time smallpox killed at least 20 percent of its victims, while inoculation claimed less than 1 percent. But that inoculation could also cause a case of smallpox almost as severe as that acquired naturally, as Jenner himself knew well, for he had had a bad case when he was inoculated at the age of eight. Accordingly, he began to collect notes from local people, milkmaids and farmers especially, who told him they knew they would never have smallpox because they had had cowpox, a mild disease of cows marked by a rash of pustules on their udders that could be contracted by humans.[21]

Jenner's interest in natural history led to his publication in 1788 of a paper on the manner in which fledgling cuckoos ejected other fledglings from the nest. This curious topic was so well received that he was subsequently elected to the Royal Society in 1789. It was probably on the basis of this success that he was able to obtain an MD from St. Andrew's University, Scotland, in 1792, for this only required a modest fee and two letters of recommendation from reputable doctors. Now qualified as a physician as well as surgeon, he turned over much of his local practice to his nephew, Henry Jenner, and began practice as a consultant, especially to well-to-do patients at the Cheltenham spa.[22]

This move gave him more leisure for his scientific researches, and he began to seriously study the question of whether infection with cowpox could confer immunity to smallpox. In May 1796, he performed the first documented case of what he later called vaccination, inoculating eight-year-old James Phipps with cowpox matter taken from a milkmaid who had an infection of this characteristically mild disease. Six weeks later he inoculated the boy in the usual manner, with smallpox matter, and recorded that the boy had no reaction, indicating that he was immune to smallpox. He then submitted a paper about the experiment to the Royal Society, but it was

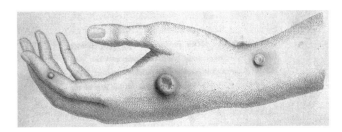

The hand of Sarah Nelmes infected with cowpox, 1798. Illustration in Edward Jenner's *An Inquiry into the Causes and Effects of the Variolae Vaccinae*, 1798. © Wellcome Library, London.

returned with the comment that "if he valued his reputation already established by his paper on the cuckoo, he had better not promulgate such ideas as the use of cowpox for the prevention of smallpox."[23]

Jenner, however, was not to be put off so easily from a new method that he was convinced could eventually result in the eradication of smallpox. In 1798 he published at his own expense a pamphlet titled *An Inquiry into the Causes and Effects of Variolae Vaccinae, a Disease, Discovered in some of the Western Counties of England, particularly Gloucestershire, and known by the Name of Cow Pox*. This pamphlet was widely read and by 1801 had been translated into six foreign languages. Although there were negative reactions of varying sorts at first (cartoons showing children growing cow horns, for example), the advantages of vaccination were recognized with astonishing rapidity: in England alone, over one hundred thousand people had been vaccinated by 1801, and the technique was also applied in the rest of Britain, Europe, and North and South America.

Jenner himself received handsome rewards for what was called the "Jennerian technique." Parliament awarded him ten thousand pounds in 1802 and twenty thousand pounds more in 1807. Napoleon, who recognized the military advantages of a vaccinated army over an unvaccinated one, had a medal made in Jenner's honor. Jenner's discovery was celebrated by governments around the globe.[24] But it also became known at the time that Jenner had not been the first to vaccinate. A farmer from Dorset named Benjamin Jesty came forward and claimed that he had vaccinated his wife and two sons with cowpox lymph in 1774. Jesty of course had neither a medical education nor the means and ability to promote the process of vaccination with cowpox, as Jenner did, but his claim to have preceded Jenner by some 22 years was taken seriously enough to be investigated by physicians at the Original Vaccine Pock Institution in London in 1805. And these physicians were sufficiently impressed to issue a statement about his extraordinary experiment in the *Edinburgh Medical and Surgical Journal* in the same year and to commission a painting of Jesty.[25]

Had it been recognized that everyone should be not only vaccinated but revaccinated at intervals, especially when epidemics threatened, smallpox might have ended in the nineteenth century. But although infant vaccination was made compulsory in Bavaria (1807), Denmark (1810), Norway (1811), Russia (1812), Sweden (1816) and Hanover (1821) in the first decades of the century, in Britain (likewise France and many other countries) vaccination remained a matter of individual choice until at least mid century. And in England resistance to vaccination became increasingly vigorous. The history of smallpox in nineteenth-century England is thus complex and contradictory. Smallpox mortality in England overall declined markedly over the century. For example, London had 755 deaths per million from smallpox in 1838–42, and only 10 per million by 1891. The provinces showed a similarly strong decline, from 547 deaths per million in 1838–42 to 13 per million in 1891–1900.[26] But there were also repeated epidemics during this time, causing spikes in the number of both cases and deaths from smallpox. It was precisely such epidemics that spurred more and more legislation to make infant vaccination compulsory. But the kinds of laws enacted in England led to protests, and eventually to a full-fledged and well-organized antivaccination movement. (In Scotland and Ireland, where infant vaccination did not become compulsory until 1863, antivaccination movements never materialized on the same scale as that in England.)

The severe European pandemic of 1837–40, for example, raised smallpox death rates in England to horrifying heights and made the urgency of population vaccination much more apparent. By 1839, thirty thousand deaths from smallpox were recorded in England. It was at this point that statistician William Farr, outraged by the death rate from what was now a preventable disease, wrote in the medical journal the *Lancet* that the outbreak was comparable to throwing children off London Bridge daily.[27] The Vaccination Act of 1840, which made vaccination free but placed it under the administration of the New Poor Law, was passed as a result of this epidemic. But this act made getting a free vaccination not only seem like receiving charity, as it had to be administered by a Poor Law doctor, but also unnecessarily difficult to obtain, as the office of the Poor Law union to which a particular family was assigned might be much farther away than that of another union office. In the following year, variolation was criminalized, but no administrative machinery was set up to enforce the act. And similarly, when the Compulsory Vaccination Act of 1853 was passed, requiring all infants to be vaccinated by the age of four months, no policy was enacted as to how parents should be notified or of what to do if they didn't bring their babies in. Some Poor Law unions put up notices about the new law, and some didn't. Also, although some were becoming aware that vaccination didn't provide lifelong protection against smallpox, many people, including John Simon, medical officer of health for London, continued to believe that it did.[28]

This was the situation at the time when Dickens's heroine Esther contracts the "contagion." There is no indication in the novel that any of the characters are aware of the need for vaccination or revaccination, only of the extreme degree of contagiousness. Typically also, the disease is represented as probably caught from a poor boy of the streets, Jo. Victorians came to believe that smallpox was a disease of the poor, though public health authorities gradually became aware that it was common among the upper classes as well. The upper classes were simply better able to conceal the disease.

Since Jo, though obviously very sick, evidently has not yet broken out in the rash of smallpox, Esther does not recognize the nature of his disease and kindly has the poor boy brought to her home, intending to care for him there. Mr. Skimpole, who was once a medical man, apparently suspects smallpox, for he says the boy has "a very bad sort of fever about him," and advises Esther and her guardian to just turn him out on the streets again.[29] This was in fact standard practice for upper-class families who, if they suspected a servant of having smallpox, often promptly sent them to a fever hospital, or even just turned them out of the house to fend for themselves, with no concern for further spread of the disease.[30] And although Esther rejects Mr. Skimpole's suggestion and instead accepts her guardian's proposal that Jo be put in a "wholesome loft-room by the stable," the boy mysteriously disappears during the night. By this time, however, Charley has caught the infection from him. In a subsequent encounter, Jo reports that he was sent to a "horspittle," where he recovers from his fever, though he later dies of what may be tuberculosis. In most cases of smallpox, the death rate ranged between 20 and 40 percent, so it is not unrealistic that although Dickens's narrative incorporates three cases of smallpox in his novel, none die of it. But they are all very seriously ill and one, Esther, is left with the disfiguring scars of the disease.

It's also realistic that in the novel, set a few years before its publication date of 1853, and thus before vaccination was made compulsory, no mention of vaccination is made. Most people were still unaware that one should be revaccinated after coming in contact with a smallpox case. Even after 1853, infant vaccination was only sporadically enforced, and only among the poor and working classes. And there was more and more opposition to the idea of infecting a healthy child with an animal disease, not only because this seemed to many a deliberate pollution of the child's purity but also because there were in fact significant risks involved. A particularly disastrous incident occurred in Italy in 1865–66 when sixty three children were vaccinated with material taken from one apparently healthy infant who turned out to be infected with syphilis. Forty-four of the vaccinated infants contracted syphilis and several died of it.[31] Opposition to vaccination in nineteenth-century England was also energized by the increasing enfranchisement of the working classes during this period and the corollary belief that the government should not have the right to invade the body of the freeborn Briton and leave its mark on his flesh.

Efforts to compel vaccination were complicated by the fact that smallpox was by no means the only epidemic disease public health authorities were trying to control. When a smallpox epidemic was expected in 1866, for example, what actually struck England was the cholera epidemic of 1866–67 (see chapter 2). The Contagious Diseases Acts, which permitted police to arrest women on suspicion of prostitution and force them to submit to gynecological examination and, if thought to have syphilis, to be detained in lock hospitals for mandatory treatment, were passed in 1864, 1866, and 1869 (see chapter 4). These acts served as examples of a new kind of public health legislation that took control of the bodies of some for the supposed good of others, thus infringing the liberties of a target population for an unproven benefit to the rest of the population. Additional acts passed in 1867 and 1871 to penalize failure to vaccinate infants and to prosecute parents were opposed by political leaders who used the same arguments for the antivaccination movement as for the movement to repeal the Contagious Diseases Acts.

When the European smallpox pandemic of 1870–72 struck England, fueled by the Franco-Prussian War (most French soldiers, despite Napoleon's support of vaccination earlier in the century, had not been vaccinated), it proved to be the worst of the century. Not only were a total of 44,500 people killed, but the mortality rate in this epidemic was unusually high. The London Smallpox Hospital records indicate that smallpox typically killed 35–47 percent of its inmates, but in this epidemic, 66–77 percent died. These figures demonstrate that smallpox incidence and mortality in England was affected not only by epidemics and pandemics elsewhere but also by changes in the virulence of the particular smallpox strain active at a particular time. It was in approximately the same era (beginning around 1860) that a different, much milder form of smallpox, *Variola minor*, is thought to have appeared in England, gradually accounting for more and more cases of smallpox (previously *Variola major*) and thus for a declining death rate from the disease. And while vaccination was the single most crucial factor in the overall decline in smallpox deaths during the century, it was gradually recognized that infant vaccination alone had no correlation with smallpox incidence, that both the supply of vaccine and the effectiveness of vaccination technique varied widely, and that vaccination did not provide lifelong protection, as Jenner had maintained.

Interestingly, efforts to enforce vaccination in British India in the late nineteenth century met with resistance for reasons very similar to those demonstrated in England. Indians had practiced variolation for centuries, accompanying it with religious rituals to the goddess of smallpox, which they believed would protect the child from the hazards of the practice. Variolation was a familiar, revered practice, while the British scientific and wholly secular method of administering vaccination was unfamiliar and even seemed sacrilegious to Indian peoples. In addition, the cow was a sacred animal for Hindus, and vaccination with matter taken from a sick cow was repugnant to them. Finally, the Indian people resisted vaccination because it left a mark on the skin which was seen as "a mark of subjection to the British Government."[32]

But while British officials could and did blame Indians as stupid and ignorant for their failure to accept vaccination, the antivaccination movement in England could not be so arrogantly dismissed. In March 1885, Jenner was hanged in effigy, and the dummy later decapitated, in the marketplace of

Leicester. The Leicester Demonstration had been carefully planned by anti-vaccination forces, who had made arrangements with railway companies for cheap excursion fares to the city, prepared banners displaying such images as a child's coffin, titled "another victim of vaccination," and successfully plotted a kind of carnival atmosphere to which a huge crowd of 80,000–100,000 was attracted. Although many of the participants probably thought of the demonstration as more entertainment than political protest, violence was just below the surface.[33]

The Leicester Demonstration marked a high point of political activism against the Compulsory Vaccination Act of 1853 and the following increasingly punitive legislation against parents who failed to comply. Calling upon parents to fight the babies' battle, antivaccinationists resorted to grotesque depictions of vaccination disasters purporting to show children who had been horribly disfigured or maimed by vaccination. Many of the leaders of the movement, such as Mary and William Hume-Rothery, were middle-class people active in a variety of Victorian political protest campaigns, not only against the Contagious Diseases Acts (see chapter 4) but also against making elementary education compulsory and the Anti-Mourning Society. But most of the protesters were drawn from the ranks of the working classes, and there was a strong linkage to dissenting religion (Methodists, Baptists, Quakers, etc.). Their insistence on the rights of the parent to decide whether to have a child vaccinated ultimately led to the New Vaccination Acts of 1898 and 1907, which permitted parents to state conscientious objection as a legitimate reason for refusing vaccination. By the end of Queen Victoria's reign in 1901, the process of vaccination that Jenner had first tested in 1796 and that had been made compulsory by midcentury was no longer required.

THE END OF SMALLPOX

The very last case of smallpox to occur on Earth happened in England in 1978. A photographer's assistant in the medical school in Birmingham, who worked a floor above a laboratory where the smallpox virus was being studied, was found to have *Variola major*. Later tests showed the infection had traveled through a service duct between the two floors.[34] The director of the laboratory, one of the world's most respected authorities on smallpox, committed suicide. The photographer's mother also contracted the disease, but recovered. The photographer, however, died. The following year, the Global Commission certified the eradication of smallpox, and in 1980, the World Health Assembly formally accepted the commission's final report on smallpox eradication.

Global eradication was achieved especially through the methods that British public health authorities had worked out during epidemics in the last years of the nineteenth century, after compulsory infant vaccination had been repealed. Faced with a smallpox epidemic in 1895 in Gloucester (a small city very near Jenner's hometown), authorities used was what called the Leicester Method: a combination of surveillance, isolation, disinfection, and vaccination of all contacts. Since vaccination is effective within three to five days, while the incubation period for smallpox is closer to twelve days, immediate isolation of all known cases of smallpox followed by vaccination or revaccination of all contacts, including people who had been in the same building or transport vehicle as a smallpox case, is quite successful at containing an epidemic if the method is pursued rigorously enough. Every known contact must be tracked down and vaccinated, and then every known contact of those contacts, a method known as ring vaccination.

For example, in December 1950 a very sick, elderly taxi driver was admitted to Bevendean Hospital in Brighton, Sussex, with a bright red rash. When he died a few days later, his disease had been diagnosed as smallpox. It was thought he had caught the disease from his daughter, who had been given a goatskin rug brought from India by her boyfriend as a gift. The daughter had had a mild illness with a rash that had not been diagnosed. The rug was burned and the taxi disinfected, but within a short time, there were more cases, all of whom were quarantined in hospital isolation as fast as diagnosed. All staff and patients in the hospital were vaccinated, and then the hospital itself was quarantined. Vaccination stations were set up, and all possible contacts, as well as anyone who asked, were vaccinated. Ultimately, about one hundred thousand people were vaccinated. But there were thirty five cases of smallpox, and ten fatalities.[35]

For some years, the story of the worldwide eradication of smallpox, though considered an amazing triumph against disease in itself, was often followed by mention of the emergence of AIDS in 1980. The end of an ancient disease was very soon succeeded, tragically, by the birth of a new, and very deadly, disease. Since 2001, another frightening possible outcome of the eradication of smallpox has arisen: that the surviving smallpox virus supplies, supposed to be held only in Atlanta, Georgia, and Koltsovo, Russia, in carefully secured laboratories, might fall into the hands of terrorists. Although supplies of smallpox vaccine sufficient to protect entire populations are held in many countries, the specter of future smallpox epidemics remains with us. Military personnel and others deemed at unusually high risk are routinely vaccinated, but because vaccination itself still carries some risk (for example, to infants with eczema or adults with compromised immune systems), most people are no longer vaccinated. It is to be hoped that they will never have to be.

6

Deafness

There are, at this time, 32 poor children, male and female, receiving education and maintenance; they are all deaf and were totally dumb: being introduced, the company (among whom were many of the Clergy) had auricular and ocular proof that they are now taught to speak, read, write, cipher, and comprehend the meaning and application of words; whereby they are raised from the low condition of mere automata to that of intellectual beings, capable of holding intercourse with their fellow rationals, and of forming suitable notions of their duty and expectations as reasonable creatures and Christians.[1]

In the year 1799, on the seventh anniversary of the London Asylum for the Deaf and Dumb, between three hundred and four hundred gentlemen who were assembled at the London Tavern at Bishopsgate Street beheld an exhibition that they regarded as little short of miraculous. Children who had been born deaf or who had been deafened before they learned to talk (now termed prelingual deafness) demonstrated their ability to read, write, do arithmetic, and even speak aloud. At a later anniversary exhibition, some of the children were reported to have actually "stood upon the tables, and pronounced a few lines, as an address to their benefactors, with a propriety and feeling that excited wonder and admiration."[2]

Until 1792 there was no school anywhere in Britain for poor children who had been born deaf or deafened by disease or accident at so early an age that language was either never learned or what had been learned was lost because the child's speech was no longer reinforced by hearing others speak. Indeed, the first school for deaf children in Britain, the Braidwood Academy founded by Thomas Braidwood, did not open until 1764, and it accepted only those students whose parents were able to pay. Before that, there was no school anywhere in Britain for the "deaf and dumb," as they were called to distinguish them from those deafened later in life who were able to retain the power of speech. (Although the term deaf and dumb has been quite rightly abandoned today, it was in common usage in the nineteenth century and I think it appropriate to use it as Victorians did. I also do not make use of the present-day distinction between "the Deaf," those who identify themselves as part of a linguistic and cultural but not disabled minority, and "the deaf," those who identify themselves as hearing impaired, as this concept had not been developed in the nineteenth century.) Such deaf and mute children were thought to be incapable of abstract thought, as they had no language to think with, and to be restricted to communication by a few simple signs and gestures. They were believed to be uneducable and to be doomed to a life of isolation and uselessness as "mere automata."

The discovery in the late eighteenth century that the deaf and dumb could be taught to read, to write, and even to speak was thus a revelation to the general public. There had actually been a few cases of education of the deaf and dumb in earlier times, but these were not generally known. The nineteenth century was the dawn of a new era for the deaf, during which their education became the norm. Large numbers of the prelingually deaf were enabled to lead reasonably normal lives for the first time in history. Yet it was also in the nineteenth century that the struggle between *manualism*, the use of sign language to enable even the most profoundly deaf to communicate, and *oralism*, the insistence on teaching the deaf to speak orally and on the complete suppression of sign language, intensified. In France, where the free education of the deaf and dumb had first been begun by Abbé de l'Epée in the 1760s, sign language was emphasized from the first. In Britain, however, a combined method was emphasized: the deaf and dumb were educated in manual language first, especially finger spelling but also signs, then in written English, and then in the attempt to produce oral speech and to read lips. This last process was infinitely more difficult than learning sign language and required intensive individual instruction to be successful. But in the late nineteenth century an international movement arose to abolish the use of sign language altogether and teach only oral speech. By 1880, when the second international conference on the deaf and dumb was held at Milan, the oralists appeared to have won, for this conference passed a resolution that oral speech had "incontestable superiority" over signs, and that oral speech and only oral speech should be taught to the deaf.[3]

This idea was not happily accepted by the prelingually deaf who had learned sign language. The first Congress of the British Deaf and Dumb Association (the name was later changed to the British Deaf Association, or BDA) was held in 1890. That congress passed a resolution of indignant protest against "the imputation of the Right Hon. Earl Granville, in his recent speech in London, that the signer and sign language was barbarous." The resolution further affirmed, "We consider such a mode of exchanging our ideas as the most natural and indispensable, and that the Combined System is absolutely necessary for the welfare of the deaf and dumb."[4]

The resolution of the 1880 Milan conference was obviously based on the belief that only the hearing were normal and that the abnormal deaf should be taught to be as like the normal hearing as possible. This attitude toward deafness as an affliction or infirmity (the terms most commonly used for physical or sensory disability in the nineteenth century) was also reflected in medical practice during the nineteenth century. Some medical practitioners now began to call themselves aurists (though there was no formal training program for this specialty) and to devise a variety of treatments and cures for the deaf, many of which were torturous and some of which actually caused or intensified deafness. Occasionally, they even killed the patient. Practitioners also began to try to understand the causes of deafness. They pinpointed many diseases, scarlet fever and syphilis in particular, as sometimes resulting in permanent deafness. No effective treatments or preventive methods were found at this time, but a number of hearing aids, such as ear trumpets, were invented for the deaf, to bring them as close to what was regarded as normal as possible.

But perhaps the most important aspect of deaf history to emerge in the nineteenth century was the representation of the deaf by themselves: Harriet Martineau and John Kitto, both well-known scholars, wrote accounts of their own experience as those labeled deaf or even deaf and dumb, though both could speak orally and neither learned sign language. In the United States, the French-born Laurent Clerc, who could read and write in both French and English but who preferred sign language and who never spoke aloud after suffering abusive attempts to teach him to speak in his youth, wrote a number of speeches that were read aloud for him, as well as an autobiographical account of his life. In addition, many of the deaf, whether British or American, wrote poetry in English. And well-known nondeaf writers such as Charles Dickens and Wilkie Collins wrote sympathetic accounts of the deaf, both nonfictional and fictional. The Victorian era culminated in what most now see as a wrong turn in education of the deaf: the increasing emphasis on oralism and on the prohibition of sign language. The profoundly disturbing rise of the eugenicist movement sought to limit the reproductive rights of the deaf. Even so, this century was also the first century when the deaf emerged as fully human: able to communicate and to become integrated members of society.

IN THE BEGINNING WAS THE SIGN

> I was about twelve years old when I arrived at the Abbé Sicard's
> school. I was endowed with considerable intelligence, but nevertheless
> I had no idea of intellectual things. I had it is true a mind, but it did
> not think; I had a heart, but it did not feel.[5]

Laurent Clerc, who was to become the first deaf teacher of the deaf in the
United States, thus described himself on his arrival at the first school established for the deaf and dumb in France. Having been deafened at the age of
one by a severe burn on his cheek incurred when he tumbled into the fire,
he had never learned to speak and had no language with which to communicate other than the few signs he and his family had invented.

It might seem that Clerc was exaggerating when he said that he did not
think and did not feel, even though he knew he had been endowed with
intelligence. But a medical writer of today, Oliver Sacks, comments that "to
be born deaf is infinitely more serious than to be born blind . . . for the prelingually deaf, unable to hear their parents, risk being severely retarded, if
not permanently defective, in their grasp of language unless early and effective measures are taken." Abbé Sicard wrote of the introduction of sign language to such deaf-mutes as Clerc as "opening up the doors of . . .
intelligence for the first time." Samuel Johnson, in describing his visit in
1773 to the Braidwood Academy, then in Edinburgh, called deafness "one of
the most desperate of human calamities" and marveled at the abilities dis-
played by the children at the school. As Sacks explains, "The languageless
deaf may indeed be *as if* imbecilic, and in a particularly cruel way, in that
intelligence, though present and perhaps abundant, is locked up so long as
the lack of language lasts."[6] It is now felt by many educators and deaf people that teaching sign language first to the prelingually deaf child is the
most effective means to teach language itself, after which reading and writing in a national language, and possibly oral speech, can be taught.

It is now known that some form of sign language was used in England as
early as 1576 when Thomas Tilsye, who was deaf, married Ursula Russel in
St. Martin's Church, Leicester, and their use of signs to exchange the marriage
vows was recorded in the parish register. Isolated instances of teaching deaf
and dumb individuals to speak and perhaps also to read and write have been
recorded across Europe since the sixteenth century. Usually this was done
because wealthy parents wished their deaf children to be able to inherit, something that was legally prohibited for the deaf and dumb in most countries. But
historical records about the use of sign language or other methods of educating
the deaf are scanty before the late eighteenth century.

A fascinating exception to the absence of such historical records is the col-
ony on Martha's Vineyard in the United States, where a deaf and dumb

man, Jonathan Lambert, settled in 1692. He brought with him knowledge of a sign language used in Kent, a county in the southeastern corner of England, very close to France.[7] A sizeable proportion of the inhabitants of Martha's Vineyard over the next two centuries had a form of inherited deafness, but the most striking thing about this community was that *all* the inhabitants, not just the deaf, used sign language. The result, as explored in Nora Ellen Groce's book *Everyone Here Spoke Sign Language: Hereditary Deafness on Martha's Vineyard* (1985), is that the deaf were regarded as no different from anyone else.

But it was Abbé de l'Epée, founder of the first public school for the deaf in France in the early 1760s, who first recognized and taught the crucial importance of sign language for the prelingually deaf. Noting that deaf-mutes almost invariably used some form of sign language, he reasoned that it would be far easier to teach the French language if the instructor first learned how to communicate by signing. Erroneously believing that the sign language used by the Parisian community of poor deaf-mutes was a universal language, the abbot learned enough of it to be able to teach it to his pupils, and then used a modified form of sign language to teach them to read and write French. Every sign language is a complete language; that is, it has grammar and syntax as well as vocabulary. But no sign language is universal, as it is always generated by a particular community of deaf people among themselves.

Abbé de l'Epée not only taught the prelingually deaf but also trained many deaf teachers of the deaf. By the time of his death in 1789, students from his school had become teachers in twenty-one schools for the deaf all over Europe, as well as elsewhere in France. The school in Paris was taken over by Abbé Sicard in 1791, and it was under his tutelage and that of one of his deaf pupils, Jean Massieu, that Clerc first learned sign language, then how to read and write French. Sicard's method of teaching the deaf, which further emphasized the value of sign language (Sicard was considered a brilliant grammarian), was introduced to England by his public exhibitions in London. On July 1, 1815, the *Times* reported that "the Abbé Sicard will deliver a lecture this day, at 12 o'clock, at the Argyll Rooms, on his system of instruction for Deaf and Dumb, exemplified by three of his pupils, Massieu, Clerc, and Dohrman."[8] Such public displays of deaf students now seem exploitative, but at the time they were seen not only as an essential means of raising funds for the education of the deaf and dumb but also as a means of educating the public about the amazing capacities of such pupils if they were appropriately taught.

The Braidwood Academy was founded in Edinburgh at about the same time as the Abbé de l'Epée's school for the poor deaf and dumb in Paris, but Braidwood used a combined method that seems to have been successful in teaching students to speak, as well as giving them a primary education in language through the use of signs of some kind. As his school was for pay-ing pupils only, Braidwood kept his method secret and taught it only to other members of the family in order to secure his profits from teaching. In 1783, Braidwood moved his school to Hackney, East London. He trained his nephew, John Braidwood, who married his daughter, in his method, and after Thomas's death, this John Braidwood ran the school until Thomas's two sons, John and Thomas, were old enough to take over. Meanwhile, another nephew, Joseph Watson, who had also been trained by his uncle, became the first princi-pal of the London Asylum for the Deaf and Dumb, founded in 1792.

After the elder Thomas Braidwood's death, Watson published two books describing the family method as based on articulation (oral speech), writing, reading, "natural gesture," and a two-handed alphabet. When Watson died, he was succeeded by his son, Thomas James Watson, who in turn was suc-ceeded by his son, the Reverend J. H. Watson, thus creating a Watson dynasty of eighty-six years. Over the course of the nineteenth century, more than twenty schools for the deaf and dumb were founded in Britain, and a variety of methods used in them.

THE RISE OF AURISM: SURGICAL SPECIALTY OR QUACKERY?

> Caddy was now the mother, and I the godmother, of such a poor little baby—such a tiny old-faced mite, with a countenance that seemed to be scarcely anything but cap-border, and a little, lean, long-fingered hand, always clenched under its chin. It would lie in this attitude all day, with its bright specks of eyes open, wondering (as I used to imag-ine) how it came to be so small and weak.[9]

Esther Summerson, the heroine of Dickens's novel *Bleak House*, describes Caddy Jellyby's baby as she first sees it. Only in the final chapter of the novel is it revealed that the little girl is deaf and dumb. Nothing is said as to the cause of her deafness. This would not have been an unusual scenario in the eighteenth and nineteenth centuries: parents often did not recognize that a child had been born deaf until it failed to learn to speak.

Once a child's deafness had been recognized, however, many different treatments were tried, and the same was true when adults became deaf, either gradually or suddenly. William Wright, who had been trained at St. Thomas's Hospital in London and styled himself a surgeon aurist though he apparently never held a medical diploma or license, proclaimed in a series of articles in the British medical journal, the *Lancet*, that the auditory organs "are so little understood by the general practitioner, that patients have had trifling cases of deafness rendered much worse, or incurable, and there are instances where the imperfect knowledge possessed by these gen-tlemen, and their self-sufficiency on the subject, have absolutely endangered the life of the patient.''[10] Over the course of the century, practitioners became more aware that most treatments for deafness did not work, and increasing emphasis was placed on hearing aids of various sorts, such as the ear trumpet.

Before that, however, an astonishing and sometimes appalling variety of treatments were attempted. One of the most common was also the simplest: pouring different liquids into the ear and letting them drain out. Clerc, for example, reported that when he was seven years old, his mother had taken him to a physician in Lyon who was said to be able to cure deafness. This physician, after examining the boy, declared that he thought he could make him hear if the boy was brought to his office twice a day for a fortnight. Clerc's mother agreed to take him, so they went regularly every day, ''and the doctor injected into my ears I do not know what liquids, but I did not derive any benefit whatever from the operation. And at the expiration of the fortnight, I returned home with my mother still as deaf as I was before.''[11]

Clerc was apparently fortunate, in that the liquids used at least seem not to have caused actual harm. But Wright reported on the case of the Duke of Wellington, who had been partially deafened by the noise of cannon and had called in a ''professional gentleman'' because of ''singing, noise and deafness'' in the ears. He was treated by the pouring into the ears of a caustic liquid which not only produced ''the most painful effects and alarming symptoms'' but ''totally destroyed the sense of hearing on one side, and seriously endangered the other.'' Trumpeting his own professional competence, Wright reported, ''When I first saw the Duke's ears they were in a state of active disease,'' but said that he had restored them to such a state of health as to enable the duke to hear with ''near perfection'' in his right ear, though his hearing remained lost in the other ear.[12]

Wright was apparently also successful in his treatment of a Miss Anna Thatcher, said to be almost deaf and mute. After a year's treatment, she could repeat words, and in 1817 she had a long conversation with Queen

Two Victorian ear trumpets. © Wellcome Library, London.

Charlotte, who subsequently appointed Wright as "surgeon-aurist-in-ordinary."[13] Wright, however, continued to promote bleeding as a treatment for certain kinds of deafness, and he also shared the common belief that hereditary deafness was the result of some fright or trauma to the mother during pregnancy. "The circumstance of a child being deaf on the same side as her mother, in consequence of the fall of the mother whilst in a state of pregnancy, is not extraordinary," he wrote.[14] Clerc described an even more appalling superstition: people believed that the mere sight of a deaf and dumb person would somehow cause those so afflicted to "multiply."[15] Such a terrifying superstition probably led to the hiding away of the deaf, especially in the vicinity of pregnant women.

Jean Marc Itard, who was appointed as resident physician of the Paris school for deaf children while it was under the leadership of Sicard and who became famous for his work with the "wild boy of Aveyron," published the first work on the diseases of the ear and of hearing in 1821. His work, which was the product of twenty years of what would today be called unethical experimentation on subjects (the children in the school) unable to give informed consent, was widely cited and extremely influential. His experiments included piercing eardrums, placing white-hot metal buttons behind the ears, threading a string through the neck with a long seton needle, and even deliberately fracturing the students' skulls by hitting them behind the ear with a hammer. His most radical and risky new technique was catheterization of the Eustachian tube—insertion of a probe through the nose and into the tube that connects the nasopharyngeal (nose and throat) area with the middle ear—and then pumping air into the middle ear through the catheter in an attempt to clear "blockage." Not until late in the century was it recognized that this technique could spread diseases, most horrifically syphilis, from one patient to another, as the need to disinfect the catheters after use was not recognized until after Lister's introduction of antiseptic techniques in the 1860s. Ultimately, Itard himself concluded: "Medicine does not work on the deaf, and as far as I am concerned the ear is dead in the deaf-mute. There is nothing for science to do about it."[16]

British practitioners were aware that many diseases could cause permanent deafness. The diseases usually contracted in childhood (measles, mumps, and scarlet fever) were especially serious, as they could cause loss of hearing before speech, and therefore language, had been acquired. Other diseases, such as smallpox, meningitis, and syphilis, could also cause deafness, and these too could strike in early childhood. Indeed, as the fetus could be infected with syphilis before or during birth by an infected mother, and thus be born deaf or become deaf shortly after birth, it was believed that syphilis could be inherited, and deafness along with it (see chapter 4). Repeated ear infections, as in Martineau's case, could cause increasing deafness. And many children and adults were deafened as the result of accidents, as in the case of Clerc and Kitto.

There was much hostility to the development of surgical or medical specialties in Britain throughout the Victorian era, including specialization in diseases of the ear. Particularly in the first half of the nineteenth century, before uniform standards for medical and surgical education began to be established, those who specialized in such fields as aurism, otology, oculism, or ophthalmology were viewed by many practitioners as mere quacks. And indeed, some of them were, as anyone could set up in business as an aurist and make a living with such easy-to-learn techniques as washing out ears. Nevertheless, some important contributions were made to knowledge of the ear and to surgical treatment of its diseases. Two men in particular, William Wilde of Dublin and Joseph Toynbee of London, both born in 1815, are credited with conferring clinical and scientific respectability to the new field of otology. Wilde, the father of writer Oscar Wilde, practiced as both otologist and oculist, that is specialist in both the ear and eye, a not uncommon combination at the time. He campaigned vigorously against quacks and patent medicines, and in 1853 he published *Practical Observations on Aural Surgery, and the Nature and Treatment of Diseases of the Ear*. Toynbee, appalled by how little was still known about the anatomy, both normal and pathological, of the ear, spent two decades on the meticulous dissection of some two thousand ears and published the results in his *Diseases of the Ear* in 1860.[17] These two works significantly furthered the new surgical specialty of otology in Britain and were recognized internationally.

Specialist hospitals for treatment of ear diseases were also founded in the nineteenth century. In 1816, John Harrison Curtis founded the Dispensary for Diseases of the Ear in London. As Curtis was a retired naval surgeon with no medical credentials whatever, licensed practitioners were not pleased, and they were even less so when the king decided to recognize the institution as the Royal Dispensary for Diseases of the Ear, and Curtis as Surgeon-Aurist to His Majesty. In 1838, surgeon James Yearsley founded the Metropolitan Institution for Diseases of the Eye and Ear, later to become the Metropolitan Ear, Nose, and Throat Hospital. This was the first hospital in the world to specialize in diseases of the ear, nose, and throat. After 1860 a number of other hospitals specializing in various combinations of the ear, nose, and throat specialties were established. Otology, laryngology, otolaryngology, and otorhinolaryngology all became recognized medical specialties during the nineteenth century.

THE TRIUMPH OF THE "PURE ORAL METHOD"

Speech is superior to signs, because it puts the deaf in the same relation to language as that enjoyed by ourselves. . . . Speech is superior to signs, because it supplies a perfect instrument of thought. . . . Speech is much superior to signs in education, because it enables the teacher to communicate directly with his pupils and to carry on his work in the language they most need to learn, as if they could hear.[18]

Until the 1860s, most British schools for the deaf used a "combined method" of some sort, combining sign language and instruction in oral speech, and they employed deaf teachers. But from the 1860s on, there was a growing movement to use only oral speech and lipreading in the instruction of the deaf and to prohibit the use of sign language entirely. Deaf teachers of the deaf were likewise increasingly excluded from education, because their deafness made it impossible for them to teach oral speech. Thomas Arnold, a hearing teacher of the deaf who became the best-known English proponent of the "pure oral method," articulated his beliefs about the superiority of speech over signs in his 1881 book, *A Method of Teaching the Deaf and Dumb Speech, Lipreading and Language*. Speech was superior to signs because it made the deaf more like "ourselves," normal hearing people. Speech was also superior to signs because it was a "perfect instrument of thought." That is, speech could communicate abstract thought, while signs were "loaded" with "indefiniteness and materialism." And speech was superior to signs because signs were "of no value for social intercourse," as only the deaf and their teachers could understand them. Signs were "a dead language," according to Arnold.[19]

Any language is, of course, a dead language to those who don't understand it, and it appears from Arnold's description of signs that he didn't understand sign language. Indeed, it's not clear today just what was meant by signs or sign language as it was referred to in Victorian Britain. Sign language was generally held to be a crude form of language until William Stokoe began his pioneering research on American Sign Language (ASL) in the 1970s. It was not until the 1980s that Mary Brennan first introduced the term British Sign Language (BSL). But these two sign languages are very different from each other, as much so as the spoken languages of English and German, for example. That's because they have quite different origins. In America, the teaching of sign language had begun with the work of Clerc, who had learned French Sign Language (LSF, or *Langes de Signes Française*), which had originated in the Parisian deaf-mute community and later been modified to conform more closely to the national French language by Abbé Sicard especially. But in the school for the deaf and dumb in Hartford, Connecticut, which Thomas Hopkins Gallaudet founded in 1817 and where Clerc was the first teacher, the students often brought with them sign languages of their own. It is thought that students from the Martha's Vineyard community, for instance, introduced their own sign language, and that the sign language used in the school was modified by that sign language.

Users of BSL and ASL cannot understand each other, while users of LSF and ASL still have some limited mutual understanding, even though the two sign languages have diverged over time.[20] BSL is also not the same as "signed English," also called "sign-supported English," in which signs have been arbitrarily assigned to English words. Although such signed English may have been used throughout the nineteenth century in the instruction of British students, most likely in conjunction with sign language, it is not in any way the same language as BSL.

In short, Arnold's comments on the inferiority of signs may not refer to BSL as it is known today. And as sign language was not written down in the nineteenth century, there is no way of learning with certainty exactly what sign language was taught in British schools for the deaf or used by deaf people among themselves. It is believed that sign language is modified by its users quite rapidly, probably more rapidly than spoken language. British students of BSL today report that they have difficulty understanding the sign language used by their grandparents and those of the older generation in general. However, in his *Memoirs of My Youth* (1865), Alexander Atkinson, a student at the Edinburgh Deaf and Dumb Institution, gives a "general view of the range and power of our sign dialect" as learned in that school. It seems clear from his description that the sign language he learned at the institution was indeed a very rich and expressive language. He writes that, in describing such subjects as the trial and execution of Charles I or the Gunpowder Plot, accounts can be given much "more truly and strikingly [in sign dialect] than they could be done by any account that could be carefully written for the then existing frame of our minds in a much longer time."[21]

But the teaching of oral speech seems to have been more successful in Britain than in France from the beginning. Jonathan Rée reports that when Sicard visited the London Asylum for the Deaf and Dumb, he was forced to admit that its oral education was "excellent," that even the voices of the deaf and dumb who had been taught to speak were "not disagreeable." The headmaster, Dr. Watson, defended his method of teaching the pupils "artificial speech" by pointing out that the deaf poor would be placed in factories where they needed to communicate orally.[22]

However, Arnold and others in Victorian Britain differed from earlier educators of the deaf in that they became part of the international campaign to prohibit sign language or manual signs of any kind from deaf education. The debate between manualism and oralism had its roots in international eighteenth-century European culture. At the time of Abbé de l'Epée's founding of the school for the deaf in Paris, based on the use of sign language, Samuel Heinecke was instituting the use of the oral method in Germany. In correspondence with the abbot, he argued strongly for the superiority of the pure oral method. Because of Heinecke's influence, children in Germany were taught by speech alone, despite the existence of several regional sign languages in the country.[23] The oral method, in fact, became known as the German method, while the use of sign language became known as the French method.

Arnold established the Oral School for the Deaf in Northampton in 1868. He had only one pupil at first, but he scored an astonishing success with this first one, Abraham Farrar. Farrar was able to pass the Cambridge University local examinations and London University matriculation. Later pupils accomplished such feats as becoming the first deaf Fellow of the Geological Society and the first deaf PhD. However, Arnold took only a few boys at a time, and he carefully selected those he thought could benefit by the oral method. But other oralists, such as Arthur A. Kinsey, Susannah E. Hull, and Mary Hare also established schools for the deaf in Britain as the international movement against sign language gained momentum.

In 1878, a small group of delegates met in Paris at the French Universal Exposition. Their aim was to promote the use of the oral method in deaf education in every European country. A second meeting was held at Lyon the following year, where it was planned to hold an international conference in Milan, Italy, the next year, 1880. It was at this Second International Congress, as it was called, that two resolutions were passed that were to dramatically and disastrously change the course of deaf education. The first resolution proclaimed "the incontestable superiority of speech over signs, for restoring deaf-mutes to social life and for giving them greater facility in language." The second resolution denounced sign language: "Considering that the simultaneous use of signs and speech has the disadvantage of injuring speech, lipreading and precision of ideas, the congress declares that the pure oral method ought to be preferred." The slogan of these hearing oralist educators was "Vive la parole!" [Long live the word!][24]

The consequences of the Milan conference were appalling, even though its resolutions represented only a consensus among hearing deaf educators of various countries. The pure oral method wiped out sign language in schools for the deaf in country after country. In Britain, hundreds of deaf teachers lost their jobs. Raymond Lee reports that over the next decade, nearly two thousand deaf teachers of the deaf in both Europe and America lost their jobs. Even nonteaching deaf personnel were fired, on suspicion that they might use sign language with the pupils.[25]

In 1886, the British Royal Commission on the Blind and the Deaf and Dumb called Edward Miner Gallaudet, son of Thomas Gallaudet and now the president of the Columbia Institution for the Instruction of the Deaf and Dumb and the Blind (renamed Gallaudet College in 1954 in honor of Thomas Gallaudet, and now Gallaudet University), and Alexander Graham Bell, best known as inventor of the telephone, to testify on the use of sign languages in deaf education. Gallaudet strongly defended the use of ASL, providing evidence in the form of superior student essays and even poetry when the students had been educated with sign language. The capacity of a born-deaf student to write actual poetry, conventionally thought to be dependent on the ability to hear rhythms and rhymes, providing irrefutable evidence that the student was capable of metaphorical language and abstract thought, was considered especially astonishing.[26]

Bell, however, argued that the signing deaf child had learned to think in "gestural language, and his most perfected English translations are only translations of his sign speech."[27] As a matter of fact, this might have been true: Clerc had explained in a letter to Frederick A. P. Barnard, written in 1835, that he was able to think more clearly, rapidly, and satisfactorily by means of signs than words because, as he wrote: "I have plenty of signs at my command to express whatever I think, whereas I want words to describe it. I can then say with propriety that I want words to express signs, as you sometimes want words to express or describe feelings of gratitude, admiration, wonder or horror."[28] It was obviously a question of one's opinion of sign language, and that depended on one's knowledge of a sign language. Thomas Gallaudet had learned LSF from Clerc at the same time he instructed Clerc in the English language. Gallaudet described the sign language used in the United States in 1847 as "a novel, highly poetical, and singular descriptive language, adapted as well to spiritual as to material objects," and said that it had a "picture-like delineation, pantomimic spirit, variety, and grace . . . the transparent beaming forth of the soul . . . that merely oral language does not possess."[29]

Unfortunately, no one came forward to defend the sign language used in Britain at the time, and the royal commission only went so far as to recommend the manualist method if a child had proved incapable of learning by the oral method after at least one year's trial.[30] Bell had other, more sinister, motives for campaigning against the use of sign language: he wanted to prevent the association of the deaf with each other insofar as possible and, in particular, to prevent the formation of deaf communities. He was an extreme eugenicist who believed that deaf individuals ought to be prevented from marrying one another, "so as to prevent as far as possible deaf babies coming into the world."[31] In 1883 he presented a lengthy paper, *Upon the Formation of a Deaf Variety of the Human Race*, to the National Academy of Sciences at New Haven, as part of his militant campaign against sign language and the reproductive rights of deaf people.

By 1900, all eighty-seven schools for the deaf in Britain were forbidden to use sign language. As Lee describes it, "British deaf children suffered a reign of terror under oralist educators and teachers, who adopted cruel methods to suppress sign language."[32] Parents were asked to stop their children from signing, in or out of school. Deaf children were largely cut off from the fund of common knowledge available to those who can chatter,

gossip, and joke while playing together. The oral method was painfully difficult for many, if not most, deaf children. Many never learned to read or
write or to speak intelligibly. As recently as 1979, a study carried out in
Britain found that most deaf school leavers had so little reading ability in
English as to be unable to read a tabloid newspaper, that their speech quality
was largely unintelligible, and that their lipreading skill was no better than
that of hearing children.[33] The victory of the pure oral method was a stag-
gering defeat for the education of deaf children.

DEAFNESS MADE VISIBLE: LITERARY REPRESENTATIONS
OF THE DEAF

> I am unwilling to quit this world, without leaving behind me some re-
> cord of a condition of which no sufferer has yet rendered an account.[34]

In *The Lost Senses*, published around 1845, Kitto begins his partially autobiographical account of deafness with this statement of his belief that his
subject is entirely new. In a similar statement in a lengthy footnote to
chapter 7 in his novel *Hide and Seek* (1854), Collins writes that he believes
no previous attempt has been made in English fiction "to draw the character
of a 'Deaf-Mute' simply and exactly after nature, or, in other words, to
exhibit the peculiar effects produced by the loss of the senses of hearing and
speaking on the disposition of the person so afflicted."[35] Martineau, in
"Letter to the Deaf" published in *Tait's Edinburgh Magazine* in April 1834,
writes that she hopes to benefit her "fellow-sufferers," for some of whom
"the discipline is newer than to myself."[36] Everywhere in Victorian literature in which the experience of deafness is described, one finds this sense of
the newness of the subject, and also of the urgency of informing the hearing
reader, as well as the deaf, about this "crushing calamity," as Kitto calls it.
The infirmity or affliction of deafness, especially of the deaf and dumb, is
represented as a new scientific discovery in the Victorian world, one that is
as sensational as tragic.

   The representation of the experience of deafness, even of being deaf and
dumb, was not in fact entirely new. Pierre Desloges, a Parisian bookbinder
and paperhanger who knew and admired Abbé de l'Epée's work, published
the first book written by a deaf-mute in France in 1779. His book is a cri-
tique of a work by Abbé Deschamps which urged the opposite method of
oralism for teaching the deaf. This short work is now available in English
translation as *A Deaf Person's Observations about An Elementary Course
of Education for the Deaf*.[37] In this little book, Desloges writes about how
he himself had become deaf and mute following a particularly bad attack of
smallpox when he was seven years old. Although by that age he had of
course already learned to speak, his illness left him not only profoundly deaf

but toothless and with damaged lip muscles, so that he could speak only with the greatest difficulty. In addition, listeners found it nearly impossible to understand his speech. When Desloges moved to Paris as a young man of twenty-seven, he did not know sign language. He writes: "I used only scattered, isolated, and unconnected signs. I did not know the art of combining them to form distinct pictures with which one can represent various ideas, transmit them to one's peers, and converse in logical discourse."[38] He learned this art from a congenitally deaf Italian who was illiterate but able to earn his living as a servant in a Parisian household.

Kitto apparently wasn't aware of Desloges's book, but he does have a chapter in *The Lost Senses* on "Massieu and Others," in which he describes the experience of Jean Massieu, "this celebrated pupil of the Abbé Sicard," as related in a little book called *La Corbeille de Fleurs* [The Basket of Flowers] (although Kitto doesn't give the author's name, it was probably Christoph von Schmid, Abbé Laurent). Kitto describes at length Massieu's childhood experience of growing up in an extended family where there were six deaf-mutes, and of how he became Sicard's pupil and later a teacher at the school in Paris, where he taught Clerc, among others. He is named in the *Times* article of July 1, 1815, quoted earlier, as one of the three pupils Sicard brought with him to London to give public exhibits of his system of instruction of the deaf and dumb.

But Desloges's book and *La Corbeille de Fleurs* were probably not known to most readers in Victorian England. To Kitto and Martineau, the infirmity or affliction of deafness, especially of the deaf and dumb (which neither Kitto nor Martineau were), seemed a new discovery in the Victorian world. In fact, until the establishment of schools for the deaf, it was widely believed that deaf-mutism was a rare condition. Many people may never have encountered a person who was unable both to hear and to speak. William Farr reported in *Vital Statistics* (1885) that there were a total of 12,533 deaf-and-dumb persons in Britain, but the proportion of such persons was only 1 in every 1,670.[39] Once schools for deaf children were established, however, the high number of applicants for places in the schools thrust the awareness of children with this affliction before the eyes of the public. Journalists and writers began to respond to this new phenomenon with articles, novels, biographies and autobiographies, poetry, and even the essays written by children in a school for the deaf.[40]

Some of this literature also was clearly part of the developing culture of invalidism with its genre of works by and about invalids (see chapter 1). Maria Frawley notes that Martineau's "Letter to the Deaf" was addressed to the same readership as her later *Life in the Sick-Room* (1844).[41] Martineau, who also wrote a novel, *Deerbrook* (1839), a series of stories titled *Illustrations of Economy*, and many other works, wrote the letter to offer advice about how to live with the kind of deafness that comes on later in life, after speech has been acquired, and in which hearing is impaired but usually not entirely lost. Martineau dwells particularly on the unnecessary "false shame" endured by one who has gradually become deaf (her hearing worsened in girlhood, apparently as the result of repeated ear infections), but also on the necessity of strategies for lessening the discomfort of those around the deaf person.

Dickens included in his *American Notes* (1842) a detailed account of Laura Bridgman, a child who had become not only deaf and dumb but also blind and deprived of the senses of smell and taste as a result of very severe illness beginning in infancy. The child's only means for learning was through her sense of touch. Dickens quotes extensively from a report written by Samuel Gridley Howe, the headmaster of the Perkins Institute for

Harriet Martineau. Lithograph by D. Maclise [A. Croquis], 1888. © Wellcome Library, London.

the Blind in Watertown, Massachusetts, calling Howe's report "a very beautiful and touching narrative."[42] Helen Keller, who was made both deaf and blind by an illness at the age of nineteen months, was later to be educated in this same school and published her autobiography, *The Story of My Life*, in 1902. Dickens also visited Hartford, Connecticut, but there he was far more interested in the inmates of the insane asylum than those of the Institution for the Deaf and Dumb, which he only mentions as "admirably conducted," like the insane asylum.

Kitto, in his *Lost Senses*, also quotes from Howe's report at length, but in keeping with his scholarly approach to the history of the deaf and those with other sensory deprivations, notes that Bridgman's case was first brought to the notice of the English public by George Combe, of Edinburgh, in his "Notes on the United States of North America" (1841), and then was "more fully illustrated by Mr. Dickens in his American Notes." Both accounts were drawn from the annual reports issued by Howe, Kitto states, and he is thus able to make some addition to them drawn from more recent reports.[43] Kitto also describes in detail the case of a British boy, James Mitchell, who was born both blind and deaf.

Kitto's descriptions of real people who had been born blind and deaf form part of the second section of his book, "Blindness." In the first part, "Deafness," he not only narrates the primal event in which his hearing was lost but follows it with an objective, carefully analyzed account of what profound deafness is like. In literary language that qualifies as a kind of psychological narrative of this moment of rebirth as a nonhearing person, he describes the terrible fall from a rooftop at the age of twelve that caused his deafness. He felt himself almost to be a deaf and dumb person at first, as he had a strong aversion to speech, even though he had retained the ability to speak. But Kitto also describes a kind of second rebirth in his later discovery of "the secret, that knowledge is power."[44] In a poignant irony, he realizes that if it had not been for his deafness he, a poor working-class boy, would doubtless never have been able to become a man of letters. Because of his deafness, however, "the pursuits which, under any circumstances, would have been chosen for my pleasures, have become my avocations and my duties."[45]

Though first sent to a workhouse and forced to work such long hours that study was impossible, kind benefactors rescued him and provided support and access to a public library. For the rest of his life, Kitto read avidly and educated himself as a biblical scholar. His *Cyclopedia of Biblical Literature* (1845), which made the higher criticism of the Bible produced by German scholars available to English readers, was so immensely popular that it was said to have become "a standard decoration for English and American parlor tables."[46] He had previously published so many works on biblical topics that he had been awarded a DD (doctor of divinity) from the German University of Giessen in 1844, an amazing achievement for a totally deaf man.[47]

Like the scholar he was, Kitto approaches the subject of deafness from multiple perspectives, carefully documenting his sources when these were not the result of his personal experience. In his chapter "Communications," he gives the history of sign language as a means of educating the deaf, quotes a number of contemporary educators of the deaf, refers to Sicard, l'Epée, and Clerc, as well as the little book on Massieu, and quotes from writings by deaf pupils. In his opinion, sign language is "undoubtedly the proper language of the deaf and dumb," but he also felt that it could only be "an imperfect vehicle for the communication of abstract ideas."[48] He himself used finger spelling, which he advocates hearing people should learn. He includes charts of both the two-handed or double alphabet and the one-handed or single alphabet to this end. He asserts that such "finger-talk" has become much more common, "especially among ladies, who, as I have been told, find it useful at school, as an inaudible means of communication, and for that purpose, teach it to one another."[49] He comments that, in the society he frequented, as many as half of the educated ladies are familiar with finger spelling, though only about one in twenty men are likely to be. In *Lost Senses*, Kitto provides an encyclopedic assemblage of what was known at the time about deafness and blindness and how to remedy some of the worst effects of early deafness through education. Together with his own searing account of his loss of hearing and his tremendous but successful struggle to overcome his "disqualifications," he thus is able to affirm the possibilities for the profoundly deaf to attain happiness.

Collins's novel *Hide and Seek* does appear to be, as Collins notes, the first attempt to realistically represent a deaf-mute in English fiction. (A novel called *Life and Adventures of Mr. Duncan Campbell,* published in 1720 and attributed to Daniel Defoe, concerns an actual person who was said to be deaf and dumb but who may have been a fraud.) Collins states in his foot-note to chapter 7 that he had found it difficult to find "reliable materials" about deaf-mutes until he discovered Kitto's book, on which much of his description of Madonna's character is based. Madonna, whose actual name is Mary Grice, loses her hearing as a child of ten when she falls from the back of a circus horse. She is represented as a beautiful and sensual, yet pure and innocent, young woman who falls in love with a man who turns out to be her half-brother. Martha Stoddard Holmes suggests that by not having Madonna's story end in marriage, Collins avoids the implications of sexuality in a disabled woman, yet "at the same time, gives readers the *frisson* of imagining, on their own time, the sensational story that doesn't take place."[50] Kate Flint, however, suggests that Madonna's story may be seen not just as an avoidance or denial of the possibility of the fulfillment of "the affective and physical desire of someone with impaired senses," but as the continuum between the able-bodied and the disabled, since they are half-brother and sister.[51]

Collins's novel encourages readers to contemplate the spectacle of a beautiful, silent (Madonna prefers to communicate only by writing on a slate or by pantomime and gesture) woman who is profoundly deaf. His plot for her does not end in marriage, the conventional Victorian plot for the conventional Victorian heroine, but in a life spent as an artist. Her story may be interpreted either as reinforcing stereotypical prejudice that the deaf should not marry and reproduce or as a radical representation of a deaf woman who is beautiful in the eye of the silent reader and is herself both confined to and enabled by the realm of the visual. The novel, like Kitto's autobiographical account and the wealth of other Victorian writings by and about the deaf and dumb, responds to cultural anxieties about the creation and the creator of the human race. Why would a benevolent God have created these afflicted yet innocent creatures? But if one explained them as the result of a godless evolutionary development, might a race of deaf human beings become a reality?

VICTORIAN CULTURE AND DEAFNESS TODAY

In an important but controversial article, Harlan Lane discusses a new surgical procedure, the cochlear implant, which was approved by the Food and Drug Administration (FDA) in the United States in 1990. While audiologists and otologists regarded the implant as a dramatic advance, offering hope that children deafened before the acquisition of language might have sufficiently restored hearing to be able to acquire language normally, the American Deaf community called the surgery a dangerous setback. For the Deaf, the implant procedure meant the prelingually deaf child would be taught to speak by a new version of the oral method, which might be no more successful than the method developed in the nineteenth century and practiced throughout most of the twentieth century, as children with cochlear implants do not regain normal hearing but are described as hearing-impaired.

Even more important, such children might never be given the opportunity to learn sign language and consequently would be denied the right to become part of the Deaf community. The National Institutes of Health Consensus Conference on Cochlear Implants called the implants a "massive intervention in the life of the child in support of the majority's rejection of minority language, culture, and values." For the better part of the nineteenth century, Lane comments regretfully, it went without saying that "you needed to know the language of the deaf community to teach deaf children, that deaf adults and deaf culture must play a prominent role in the education of this minority." But deaf people have now been medicalized, seen as candidates for surgical correction and restoration to the normal population, rather than as already normal members of a cultural and linguistic minority who happen to lack hearing but have their own language and their own cultural identity.[52]

Whether or not you agree with Lane's position, it is clear that deaf children and adults were medicalized in Victorian Britain as well, though treatments were almost always ineffectual. It is also clear that even the deaf who had become highly successful adults, such as Kitto, typically regarded themselves as having a terrible infirmity or affliction. The history of the deaf in the nineteenth century suggests that only those who were fortunate enough to live in such rare communities as that on Martha's Vineyard, where "everyone spoke sign language," did not regard themselves as different or disabled in any way.

But Victorian society nevertheless made a very important contribution to the deaf, especially those they called deaf and dumb, in that Victorians responded to their plight with tremendous interest and with attempts to generate sympathy for those who had previously been regarded as imbeciles or as freaks to be made the butt of jokes by the hearing. The promotion of sympathy was the primary aim of Victorian novelists and writers such as Dickens and Collins, though their representations of the deaf and dumb also clearly responded to cultural fascination with these children and the questions they raised. And while the success of educational methods varied, taking a turn very much for the worse after the triumph of the pure oral method, it is surely more significant that this was the era that first made it a common rule that even the child born deaf, or with multiple sensory deficits, need not grow up "senseless." The conclusion of Dickens's novel *Bleak House* undoubtedly represents the new cultural attitude towards the deaf in its best form: "I believe there never was a better mother than Caddy, who learns, in her scanty intervals of leisure, innumerable deaf and dumb arts, to soften the affliction of her child."[53] Caddy takes it as her responsibility to learn "deaf and dumb arts," so as to lessen her child's loss. Research into sign languages, including BSL, which has only been undertaken relatively recently, may be seen as a renewal of Caddy's efforts, a revitalization of an explicitly Victorian ethic.

7

Blindness

Thus with the year
Seasons return; but not to me returns
Day, or the sweet approach of eve or morn,
Or sight of vernal bloom, or summer's rose
Or flocks, or herds, or human face divine;
But cloud instead, and ever-during dark
Surround me, from the cheerful ways of men
Cut off, and for the book of knowledge fair
Presented with a universal blank
Of Nature's works, to me expunged and rased,
And wisdom at one entrance quite shut out.[1]

These lines from *Paradise Lost*, the epic poem written by the great seven-teenth-century English poet John Milton, appear in the pages of the British medical journal the *Lancet*, in October 1825, in the first lecture on "the anatomy, physiology, and diseases of the eye" written by William Lawrence of the London Ophthalmic Infirmary. "Even our great poet," the surgeon comments, always refers to his own blindness "in a tone of anguish and despondency." And although it is perhaps surprising to find that one with such a "highly-gifted mind, and the exhaustless stores of knowledge with which it was furnished," might be despondent about blindness, for others it is only to be expected.

Loss of sight is the greatest misfortune even to the rich, who can alle-viate it by purchasing the aid and services of others. How much more severely must it be felt by the poor, by the middle and lower classes of society, i.e. by 49–50ths of mankind; who, being rendered incapable of labour, and having their minds uncultivated, find their existence reduced to a dreary blank—dark, solitary and cheerless—burthensome to themselves and to those around them.[2]

Today, we are startled to find such an outburst of feeling in the midst of a medical text, let alone lines from an epic poem. One way of explaining the surgeon's manner of address to his medical audience is to see it as part of a typical Victorian "melodramatization of disability," the excess of emotion with which disabilities such as blindness are represented.[3] (Blindness is used here as the Victorians used it, to refer generally to the loss of sight, with no attempt to define differing degrees of visual impairment.) Victorians characteristically represented disabilities with what seems an over-the-top sentimentality, as in Charles Dickens's portrayal of Tiny Tim, the little crippled boy in the ever-popular *A Christmas Carol*. The surgeon's impassioned literary style here certainly demonstrates how the meanings of blindness have been shaped for him by the early nineteenth-century culture in which he lived, practiced, and taught others about diseases affecting the eye, commonly referred to in medical literature as the organ of the noblest sense. But the surgeon's opening also can tell us a great deal about the contradictory constructions of blindness common to this period in Britain.

On the one hand, for example, the surgeon invokes the romantic image of the blind poet whose loss of human sight signals his gain of insight, or visionary power. References to the figure of the blind poet as a metaphor for visionary power are common in Victorian literature and culture. The figure is so familiar it can be parodied, as in George Eliot's novel *Middlemarch*, where the literally shortsighted Dorothea Brook deludes herself that her husband Casaubon, a dry and dull scholar, is a latter-day version of the visionary Milton. Blind men are also typically represented in Victorian literature as highly romanticized heroes, such as the blinded Rochester in Charlotte Brontë's *Jane Eyre* (1847), who loses (only partially, it turns out) his sight as the result of his heroic effort to save his insane wife from the mansion she has set afire. Romney Leigh, the hero in Elizabeth Barrett Browning's immensely popular novel-poem *Aurora Leigh* (1857), loses his sight after a strikingly similar fire, when the poor to whom he has turned over his family mansion decide to burn it down. Amyas Leigh, the naval hero in Charles Kingsley's popular novel *Westward Ho!* (1856), is blinded in an apocalyptic lightning strike after fighting courageously in a great sea battle. He is subsequently rewarded with the doglike devotion of the woman who becomes his wife and wants to be his slave forever. Blindness has a heroic position in Victorian literature that is strikingly different from that of deafness, which appears infrequently and almost always as an attribute of a minor character such as Wemmick's father, the Aged Parent in Charles

Dickens's novel *Great Expectations*. Wemmick cheers his father by setting off a small cannon every night, as it's the only thing the "intensely deaf" old man can hear.[4] (Perhaps this is even an intended irony on Dickens's part, as the Duke of Wellington had lost his hearing at the Battle of Waterloo as a result of just such deafening cannon noise.)

On the other hand, the surgeon speaks of the blind as reduced to a dreary blank of existence because of their inability to work or to be educated. Blindness was so great a misfortune as to make many think their existence would be better terminated than to live without this "precious sense," he grimly proposes. Similarly, Henry Mayhew, in his interviews with street people first published in the *Morning Chronicle* in 1850–51 (later published as *London Labour and the London Poor*), dwells on the blind street sellers and musicians who are reduced to the lowest kind of labor, and to those reduced even lower, to begging in the streets, by the loss of sight. As in the surgeon's candid comment, social class made all the difference in how the blind were seen by others. The poor blind, who often were visibly, sometimes grotesquely, disfigured by diseases such as smallpox and syphilis that had caused their blindness, were at best to be pitied, at worst despised. Above all, they were to be put to work. The blind beggar was shadowed by the image of the fraudulent blind beggar, one who pretended to be blind in order to be supported by the charity of others. Victorians were particularly affronted by impostor blind beggars, perhaps in part because of the romanticized status of blindness; such not-blind blind beggars were not only cheating the honest donor but insulting blind heroes by their deceptive performance as well.

Contradictory values are also to be found in the history of Victorian attempts to educate and assist the blind. Residential schools or asylums for the blind, first founded in the last decade of the eighteenth century but proliferating in the nineteenth, were divided as to whether teaching the blind to read and write was as important as teaching them a trade and thus providing them with a means to support themselves. Institutions for the blind also differed as to whether they emphasized providing not only a trade but actual employment in institutional workshops, or teaching a trade that could make the blind independent of the institution, such as piano tuning. Although it was recognized by the 1820s that the blind could be taught to read through the use of embossed or raised type, reading was probably not part of the curriculum at most schools for the blind in Britain until midcentury. And educators could agree on no single form of such type until late in the century, a situation referred to as the "Battle of the Types." Even the literate blind were thus limited to reading books published in the particular form of embossed type in which they had been educated. By the end of the century, however, Braille had finally become the almost universally accepted type. And in 1893, when the state mandated education for blind as well as deaf children, instruction in reading and writing through the use of Braille became the norm rather than the exception.

The surgeon's opinion is even more revelatory of the contradictions in the history of British medicine in the area of eye diseases, still almost exclusively practiced at this point in the century by those qualified as surgeons, not physicians. In his later publication *A Treatise on the Diseases of the Eye* (1833), Lawrence states, "In the fifteenth, sixteenth, seventeenth, and first half of the eighteenth century, the management of the diseases of the eye was left to quacks, mountebanks, and itinerant practitioners."[5] There were no accepted fields of specialization of any kind in surgery or medicine at this time: such restriction of practice to a single part of the body was generally disdained as the work of men with no more education than that of a barber. But restriction of practice to the eye was held in particular contempt. The most commonly practiced form of treatment for cataract (a clouding or growing opacity of the lens of the eye) was called "couching" and referred to pushing the cataract down and out of the line of vision in the eye with a needle. This operation was considered so far beneath the level of expertise of most qualified surgeons that it was usually left to "oculists," "itinerant practitioners" who often had little surgical and no medical training.

But new interest in the field of eye diseases had been spurred by an epidemic of infectious eye disease called the Egyptian ophthalmia brought back by soldiers fighting against Napoleonic forces in Egypt at the turn of the century, and also by a new surgical technique for the extraction or total removal of cataracts, and resulting cure of blindness, developed in mid-eighteenth-century France by Jacques Daviel. Qualified surgeons such as Lawrence became increasingly interested in these new diseases of the eye and new surgical treatments for blindness and began to devote a larger part of their practice to them. The surgeon's quotation from *Paradise Lost* and his lofty lament about the dreary "blank" of existence for the blind is doubtless thus also part of a calculated strategy both to represent himself as a gentleman, educated in the humanities as well as the sciences, and to distance the entire new field about which he was lecturing, which only later was to be dignified by the name ophthalmology, as far as possible from quackery.

The surgeon's poetic opening may also be read, however, as part of his radical medical politics, viewing both the new, postrevolutionary Parisian medicine and its concern for care of the poor with admiration. His favorable attitude toward French developments in physiology provoked attack from his more conservative British colleagues but it was the French and the Austrians who were making strides in treatment of eye diseases at this time.[6] This new field was in fact to become one of the few success stories in nineteenth-century medicine. Not only in Britain, but all over Europe, the proportion of blind persons to the general population fell steadily during the second half of the century. In Britain, it dropped from 1,110 blind persons per million in 1851 to 830 in 1901, due to improvements in surgery, vaccination against smallpox (a major cause of blindness), and advances in the prevention of infectious eye diseases, particularly in the newborn.[7] The Victorian era in Britain, therefore, can be seen as a time of real, though limited, progress against blindness itself and toward improvement in the lives of the blind.

EDUCATION OF THE BLIND IN VICTORIAN BRITAIN

Many of the blind men are under the protection of a Society, which furnishes them with books printed in raised type which they decipher by the touch. Others provide their own books, and are allowed to sit on door steps or in the recesses of the bridges without molestation from the police. It has been found in inquiry that these afflicted persons are really what they appear to be—poor, helpless, blind creatures, who are totally incapacitated from earning a living, and whom it would be heartless cruelty to drive in the workhouse, where no provision is made for their peculiar wants.[8]

The midcentury scene in the London streets described here in a contribution to Mayhew's *London Labour and the London Poor* demonstrates not only the amazing advance made possible in education of the blind by the new print technology which the blind were able to "decipher by the touch" but also the failure of that achievement thus far to bring about a similar advance in the general condition of the blind in Victorian society. The blind men were not reading books for their own amusement or improvement but to support themselves. They elicited contributions from passers-by who were entertained by this new spectacle of the blind reading aloud from books, books of a newfangled kind that were read not by the eyes but the fingers. The police refrained from "molestation" of such blind readers, that is, they did not arrest them for begging in the streets, which would have resulted in their being sent to the workhouse, because they judged them to be genuinely blind. Most blind adults were regarded as helpless because they were generally unable to find employment of any kind. Almost the only benefit of learning to read embossed or raised type, aside from the religious edification they received (most books printed in such type during the first half of the century were of a religious nature), was that, while it remained a novelty, people would pay to hear the blind read aloud. And at midcentury, it was still a novelty.

The first school for the blind to be established in Britain was the Liverpool School for the Indigent Blind, founded in 1791 by Edward Rushton.

Rushton was motivated in part by his experience of an epidemic of ophthalmia (infectious eye disease) on a slave ship. (He later became partially blind himself.) The Liverpool School, like all subsequent institutions for the blind founded in nineteenth-century Britain, was a charitable enterprise. The state did not take responsibility for education of the blind until passage of the 1893 Elementary Education Act (Blind and Deaf Children). But by midcentury, the idea of residential schools or asylums for the blind had caught on to such an extent that such institutions had been founded all over Britain. In time, as historian John Oliphant notes, "an institution for the blind came to be regarded as one of the hallmarks of a self-respecting Victorian city, along with the railway station and, later, the Town Hall."[9]

But such schools did not necessarily teach the blind to read. As institutions supported by charity, every school or asylum decided on its own curriculum. The overwhelming emphasis in most institutions was, first, religious instruction and, second, the teaching of trades designed to make the blind self-supporting. The Liverpool School, for example, did not begin to teach reading until 1862. The blind were, in effect, simply confined in these institutions, rather than given an education as the term is understood today: taught to read and taught various kinds of knowledge through the study of books. The blind inmates were also compelled to work, and though some institutions paid them for their labor, others did not. Some institutions attempted to teach the blind trades that they could pursue independently, such as piano tuning, but others employed the blind in their own workshops, maintaining that most would not otherwise be able to find employment, and thus effectively warehousing them for life.

Such institutions did serve to protect the blind from the casual cruelty of a society that still enjoyed such spectacles as bear baiting, dog fighting, and public hangings. People still toured madhouses for amusement: Charles Dickens records such a visit to an American insane asylum in his *American Notes*.[10] It was, in fact, just such a cruel spectacle of blindness that is reported to have made a Frenchman, Valentine Haüy, vow to find a way to teach the blind to read. In 1771, while walking in the streets of Paris, he saw a group of blind men tricked out in grotesque robes and dunces' caps, wearing huge pasteboard spectacles which exaggerated the emptiness of their sightless eyes, pretending to play stringed instruments and read music by lighted candles. The crowd watching them was highly amused by this self-mockery of the state of blindness, but for Haüy it was an epiphany. He later wrote:

Why was it that a scene so dishonorable to humanity did not perish the instant of its conception? Why was it that poetry and picture should lend their divine ministration to the publication of this atrocity? Ah! It was without doubt, that the scene reproduced before my eyes, and conveying to my heart profound sorrow, might inspire and arouse my soul. "Yes," I said to myself, seized by an exalted enthusiasm, "I will substitute the truth for this mockery, I will make the blind read."[11]

Haüy, who had also been inspired by the work of Abbé de l'Epée in the education of deaf-mutes (see chapter 6), went on to experiment with various kinds of raised type. He worked with a blind beggar boy, François Lesueur, and taught him to read with raised type in six months. He then went on to found a school in 1784, L'Institution National des Jeunes Aveugles (the National Institution for Blind Young People), which later included deaf-mute children. The students at this school presented demonstrations and concerts to gain public support, as did the early schools for the deaf and dumb in Britain.

But the students at the School for the Indigent Blind in Liverpool would have been unable to give a public demonstration of reading, at least not until some time after 1862. What they were taught in the schools and asylums were such trades as basket-weaving, turning (making wheels), brush-making, and mattress-making—trades it was thought could be pursued profitably by a sightless worker. Whether this assumption was correct, however, was doubted by one of the blind street people interviewed in Mayhew's *London Labour and the London Poor:*

"There's many a blind basket-weaver playing music in the streets 'cause he can't get work. At the trade I know one blind basket-maker can make 15s. a-week at his trade, but then he has a good connection and works for his-self; the work all comes home. He couldn't make half that working for a shop. At turning wheels there's nothing to be done; there's so many seeing men out of employment that's glad to do the work at the same price as the blind, so that unless the blind will go into the workhouse, they must fly to the streets."[12]

Students were also taught music in the first half of the nineteenth century, as it was thought the blind had a special sensitivity to sound and therefore aptitude for music. They learned not only to sing (especially hymns and other church music) and to play instruments but also the trade of piano tuning. Later in the century, some schools began to include massage, or "medical rubbing," and eventually typewriting. But from the beginning, the emphasis was on instilling a work ethic. In the first years at the Liverpool School, for example, the students were to acquire "habits of industry." The women were set to spinning yarn and picking oakum, the men to making baskets and whips.[13] The schools soon became, in effect, small factories producing objects that could be sold. It was common for the inmates to be paid wages for the many hours they spent in this productive labor, although institutions probably didn't pay them what they could have made had they been able to work independently. Institutions doubtless also saw to it that wages didn't add too much to the cost of maintaining these blind workers. At the Edinburgh Asylum, for instance, records indicate that wage cuts were imposed for idleness, that the workers had to maintain savings accounts, and that they had to contribute to a system of sick pay. For some institutions, profits from the sale of what the inmates made were a very important source of institutional income.[14]

What was life like inside these institutions for the blind? It appears that there was plenty of food, and it may even have been quite good. The Liverpool School "scouse" (stew) was made with meat, potatoes or rice, and a variety of vegetables. Until midcentury, when temperance movements became more powerful, a ration of beer was included at both lunch and dinner. Clothing was also provided. But days were long, often beginning with religious worship at 6:00 A.M., followed by workdays of seven or eight hours and additional prayers and religious instruction later in the day. And discipline was strict. Students might be punished for such infractions as lateness, improper language, "indecency," or immorality by solitary confinement, a bread and water diet, longer hours at work, or even beatings and floggings.[15] Not surprisingly, a visitor to the Liverpool School reported, "There was no whispering or pushing or punching, but a general apathetic listlessness, both of manner and expression, as if the poor little fellows had no interest in life and didn't want to have any."[16]

But Victorian schools for the blind were becoming interested in the new idea of teaching the blind to read by using raised type. In 1832, the Edinburgh Society for the Encouragement of the Useful Arts in Scotland offered a prize for the best type for the blind. The medal was awarded in 1837 to Dr. Edmund Fry of London for a system of plain Roman capitals. Only a short while later, Louis Braille, a student at the Paris school for the blind, published a pamphlet describing his system of raised dots. However, his system did not become official even in the school where it had been developed until 1854, two years after Braille's death.[17] In the intervening years, what Thomas Rhodes Armitage called a "Babel of systems" appeared in Britain. Another tactile system of the Roman alphabet was invented by John Alston of Glasgow in the 1830s. James Gall devised a system in which curves were removed from the Roman alphabet. William Moon came up with a script that simplified the shapes of the Roman alphabet, with the intention of making it more easily readable by the toughened fingers of laborers. Thomas Lucas and James Frere developed even more "arbitrary" systems, meaning those in which the raised type had even less relation to the Roman alphabet used by sighted readers of English.

The difficulty with all of these systems of script designed for the blind was that, as they became easier to read with the fingers, they became harder or impossible to read with the eyes. Promoters of the various kinds of types became increasingly passionate, producing the public debate known as the "Battle of the Types." W. H. Illingworth, for example, documented in his 1910 *History of the Education of the Blind:*

> So lately as 1884, a superintendent of one of the best schools for the blind in the kingdom, when pressed to introduce the Braille system, exclaimed: "What! That barbarous and heathen system of reading? Never! It had not the smallest resemblance to ordinary print! How are we teachers to learn it?"[18]

In *Blind People: Their Works and Ways* (1867), the Reverend B. G. Johns pointed out that a letter pricked out with stamps that used the Roman alphabet by a blind student in an institution could be read by his parents, whereas one written in an arbitrary script would be meaningless to them. In other words, the controversy over which form of raised type was best was based not only on resistance to a type that would have to be learned by sighted readers such as the teachers of the blind but also on the desire to incorporate the blind as fully as possible into sighted culture.[19] And as with sign language for the deaf, the medium of communication most useful to those deprived of a sense might not be useful in helping them to communicate with those not so deprived.

Matters were eventually resolved by Armitage, a physician who had lost his sight gradually in midlife. He was one of the founders of the British and Foreign Blind Society, so named because of his consciousness that the blind from other countries were coming together in a common movement to improve their lot. In his book *The Education and Employment of the Blind: What It has been, Is, and Ought to Be* (1871), Armitage surveyed the existing systems of raised type, including Braille, and urged not only that a single system be adopted but that the choice of system should be made *only* by those who were blind. Braille, he noted, was now the only system in use in France, and it was fast becoming the system most used all over Europe and in North and South America.[20] Armitage further emphasized the crucial importance of education to all the blind, stating that literacy was important even in the learning of trades. He later came to espouse eugenicism, arguing that the blind should not intermarry, so as not to produce more blind children, and an elitist position on education for the blind, urging that only the most talented of the blind poor should receive higher education. Still, his influence is generally felt to have vastly benefited the blind in Britain.

Worcester College, the first "college" (high school) for the blind in Britain, was founded in 1866. It accepted only the blind sons of gentlemen, or "persons of the male sex afflicted with total or partial blindness, and belonging by birth or kinship to the upper, the professional or the middle classes of society."[21] As Oliphant comments, "Its foundation emphasized the depth of the Victorian conviction that class differences were to be preserved in and through education."[22] It also was committed to preserving the Victorian understanding of gender differences. Not until 1921 was a similar institution, Chorleywood College, opened for girls. However, the founding of Worcester College did attest to the emerging belief that the blind could achieve higher education: many of the students went on to attain university degrees.

Armitage had been involved in the founding of Worcester College, and he later was instrumental in the founding of the Royal Normal College and Academy of Music for the blind. He persuaded Francis J. Campbell, a blind teacher of music at the Perkins Institute in Watertown, Massachusetts, to open the school and, as Campbell was unable to find suitably trained teachers in Britain, he applied to the Perkins Institute, still under the management of Howe, to help him find teachers. The result was that the Royal Normal College was dominated by the American approach to education of the blind, including the employment of blind teachers. Campbell traveled throughout England and found jobs for organists and piano tuners trained in his school. Later, the school also taught typing and shorthand. Campbell's work was so admired that he was knighted in 1909.[23]

The schools benefited chiefly older children and young adults, although ages ranged as high as eighty in those that maintained workshops for the inmates. By the 1880s, students were mostly aged eleven to thirty-five. Since it was calculated at that time that nine-tenths of the blind in Britain were over twenty-one, that the average age at which people became blind was thirty-one, and that the average age of the existing blind population was forty-nine, it is clear that the lives of most of the blind were not affected by the founding of schools, asylums, and colleges for them.[24] The blind were, if we listen to Mayhew's informants, "disabled" by Victorian society. They could not do most kinds of work profitably even if they had been trained to do such work in a school for the blind. Most had been trained in an occupation or profession before they became blind and were then unable to continue in that work after sight was lost. Perhaps because Victorian society had no recourse for the adult blind except charity, blind people abound in Mayhew's accounts of street vendors, performers, and beggars (no deaf or deaf-mutes are mentioned). In the surgeon Lawrence's view, for the poor and the middle and lower classes of society, loss of sight meant loss of the capacity for work, and reduction of existence to that of "a dreary blank." This attitude was probably shared by virtually all sighted Victorians, and perhaps by many of the blind themselves.

THE EMERGENCE OF OPHTHALMOLOGY

I was confined on my back—a month in a dark room, with bandages over my eyes for the greater part of the time—and had a careful nurse, to attend me both night, & day—I was bled with 8 leeches, at one time, & 6, on another, (these caused but little pain) in order to prevent, inflammation—.[25]

Patrick Brontë, a clergyman of the Church of England, age sixty-nine, thus described his recovery from cataract surgery in August 1846. His daughters Charlotte and Emily, later to become famous authors, had visited Manchester in order to find a surgeon sufficiently skilled to perform the operation of cataract extraction. They were referred to William James Wilson, founder of the specialist eye hospital in Manchester, former president of the Manchester Medical Society and recently elected Honorary Fellow of the Royal College of Surgeons, thus able to append the letters "FRCS" to his name. He agreed to examine Charlotte and Emily's father and set a date for three weeks later. On seeing the old man, whose blindness had become so advanced that he was reduced to sitting in a dark room doing nothing most of the time, the surgeon set a date for the operation just a few days later. He explained that he would operate on only one eye, in case infection set in and all sight was lost in the operated eye.

On the day of the surgery, Monday, August 24, Wilson and two assisting surgeons performed the operation, which involved cutting into the left eye and extracting the entire lens, the small, and normally transparent, structure in the eye that focuses light rays onto the retina (the nerve layer that lines the back of the eyes). There was no anesthetic, as the use of ether would only be introduced later that year in Britain, following its demonstration at an operation at Massachusetts General Hospital on October 16. Patrick probably sat in a chair facing the surgeon, who would have been seated on another chair, while an assistant standing behind the patient held and steadied his head. This was the traditional position for cataract surgery.[26]

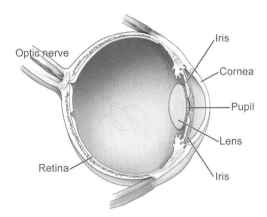

Diagram of eye anatomy. National Eye Institute.

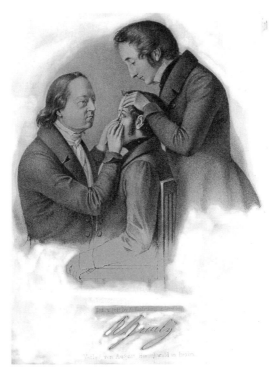

Traditional seated position for cataract surgery, 1843. © Wellcome Library, London.

The operation lasted a quarter of an hour and was endured by the patient with "extraordinary patience and firmness," as Charlotte wrote to her friend Ellen. Patrick himself later made notes in the margins of his copy of Graham's *Modern Domestic Medicine*: "Belladonna a virulent poison—was first applied, twice, in order to expand the pupil—this occasioned very acute pains for only about five seconds—The feeling, under the operation—which lasted fifteen minutes, was of a burning nature—but not intolerable—as I have read is generally the case, in surgical operation. *My lens* was *extracted* so that cataract can . . . never return in that eye."[27]

After the operation, Patrick and Charlotte (Emily had not come to Manchester this time) remained in lodgings for nearly five weeks. Charlotte had hired a nurse who took care of Patrick during this time. She herself, though suffering from a raging toothache, made use of the time to begin writing what would become her revolutionary novel about a woman's life, *Jane Eyre* (which ends, as previously noted, with the partial blinding of the hero). After the recovery period, Patrick found his sight so completely restored as to be able to read and write as well as to find his way about without a guide. Almost a year later, he wrote to the local paper, the *Leeds Mercury*, to defend the new anesthetic agent, ether. Although many had fears about the consequences of using ether, Patrick declared, "It appears to me to be evident, that as it regards the inhalation of the vapour of ether, a great, a useful, and important discovery has been made, and one that ought to be patronized by every friend to humanity."[28]

Surgery for the extraction of cataracts, such as was undergone by Patrick Brontë without benefit of ether, was one of the major improvements in the treatment of eye disease and prevention or cure of blindness achieved in the nineteenth century. Until 1753, when the French surgeon Jacques Daviel first reported on his procedure for the extraction of a cataract, the only operation performed anywhere in Europe was known as couching, a term taken from the French *coucher*, to lie down. This operation, which had been performed since ancient times by Indian and Arab surgeons (the Greeks had no knowledge of it), involved the insertion of a needle into the eye and thence into the cataract. The cataract would be pushed downward in the eye, dislocating it from the line of vision, or couching it. If the cataract stayed where it had been moved, all well and good; if it rose again, the surgeon might try puncturing it with the needle, so that the contents would spill out and eventually be absorbed in the fluid within the eye.[29] But if the cataract had grown sufficiently hard, this tactic might not work. And cataracts that had been couched might remain dislocated for an indeterminate period of time, only to rise again, blocking the line of vision, anytime from a few weeks to many years later. This is why Patrick's surgeon explained that, because the clouded lens had been actually removed from the eye, it could never return to block his regained vision.

But although Daviel had proved that a cataract could be successfully removed from the eye, it was another hundred years before most surgeons adopted this procedure rather than couching. For one thing, although couching was considered so easy that it was generally left to barber-surgeons or itinerant oculists, cataract extraction was difficult enough to require a skill and precision that was beyond the abilities even of many of the better-trained surgeons during the first half of the nineteenth century. English surgeons especially attacked the new French surgery, with the famed English surgeon Percival Pott dismissing it as just a "kind of fashion." Georg Joseph Beer, an Austrian qualified in both medicine and surgery who risked the disdain of his peers by limiting his practice to diseases of the eye, suggested four reasons for British antipathy to cataract extraction: "Some of the English ophthalmologists rejected the extraction method in order to please Mr Pott, others in order to stand out among the crowd. A third group did it out of national pride and out of hate of all French. And a fourth group did it because they had bad results due to prejudice or clumsiness."[30]

Consequently, both couching and cataract extraction continued to be practiced well into the nineteenth century in Britain. The esteemed surgeon George Critchett lectured in 1855 about the three operative procedures by which a cataract might be removed from the field of vision: "solution," or puncturing the lens capsule with a needle and allowing a soft cataract to flow out and dissolve in the aqueous humor, the watery fluid in front of the eye; "extraction," or removal of the lens from the eye; and "couching," also now known as "depression" or "reclination." Critchett, who did not limit his surgical practice to eye surgery, also suggested that the patient could be placed either in a sitting or a recumbent position, although he preferred the latter. Among the arguments in favor of "solution" are, he notes, its painless character and the slight amount of confinement and inconvenience suffered by the patient. However, as the cataract might not dissolve as fully as desired, the operation might have to be repeated several times. The same was true for couching, of course. Another reason in favor of this procedure, he candidly admitted, was the relative rapidity with which the necessary amount of dexterity could be acquired for this operation.[31]

Critchett appears not to have considered anesthesia of any type necessary, at least for such operations as solution or couching. Indeed, as late as 1886, surgeon C. Bell Taylor commented that "for years past I have operated without any anesthetic" because both ether and chloroform had been found to cause dangerous vomiting. However, fortunately for patients, "the splendid discovery of cocaine" as a local anesthetic had been made in 1884, and a few drops could be used to numb the eye without the risks of general anesthesia.[32]

During the latter half of the century as new techniques of surgery were developed, and also as the need for antiseptic technique was recognized, the extraction of the cataract was increasingly the surgery of choice. Cataract extraction was particularly crucial to those blind from infancy with congenital cataracts for, if sight was not restored early, the child would not have learned how to see, that is, how to interpret the sensory information received through the eye. In the late seventeenth century, William Molyneux had proposed that a person blind from birth, on having sight restored, might not be able to recognize through seeing what he had learned to know by touch. For example, such a person might not be able to differentiate a round from a square shape by sight even though he could by touching.[33] John Locke's *Essay Concerning Human Understanding* (1690) took up the debate in response to Molyneux's hypothesis, exploring the philosophical issue as to whether innate ideas existed in the mind of the newborn or all knowledge had to be gained through sensory experience. When William Cheselden, an English surgeon, operated on a boy and published his "Account of some Observations made by a young Gentleman, who was born blind, or lost his sight so early, that he had no Remembrance of ever having seen, and was couch'd between 13 and 14 years of Age" in the journal

Philosophical Transactions in 1728, the boy provided evidence that Molyneux had been right.[34] Not only was he unable to tell a round from a square
by sight but, to his continual embarrassment, he was unable to distinguish
between his dog and his cat unless he touched them. Interest in this historic
surgery clearly continued in the nineteenth century, for Wilkie Collins
makes unmistakable reference to it in his 1872 novel *Poor Miss Finch*.[35]
Critchett, who was Collins's eye surgeon, had himself published *A Case of
Blindness from Birth: In Which Sight was Restored in a Female by an
Operation at the Age of Twenty-Two* in 1855. Critchett reported that, as in
the case of Cheselden's patient, the young woman he treated was unable to
recognize objects or even faces despite the ability to see them.

The increasingly successful surgical treatment of cataracts was only one
of the important advances made in the newly emerging field termed ophthalmology. But British practitioners were still so hostile to any kind of specialization that as late as the 1860s a campaign was organized by the British
Medical Association and the *British Medical Journal* against this growing
professional trend. By that time, however, knowledge of the eye and its diseases, and international circulation of this knowledge in the swelling numbers of medical journals, had produced a professional organization of men
who were increasingly willing to allow themselves to be recognized as specialists in the treatment of diseases of the eye.

The epidemic of Egyptian ophthalmia, contracted by British soldiers sent
to Egypt to oppose Napoleon's campaign to seize the country and disrupt
British trade, first sparked interest in the field. By 1801 both French and
British soldiers were suffering horribly from some form of infectious con-
junctivitis which often left them blind within a matter of weeks, sometimes
from actual rupture of the eyeball. This disease, described as "unexpected,
widespread, incomprehensible and horrid," catapulted the treatment of eye
disease from a small and relatively insignificant part of a surgeon's practice
to a large and economically important aspect of the nation's health.[36] Major
proportions of entire regiments might be admitted to hospitals, such that
the army's capacity to fight was seriously impaired. If soldiers and sailors
lost their sight permanently, they became dependent on public support for
the rest of their lives. Most disturbing of all to those practitioners who studied the disease, it became more and more apparent that at least some of this
"purulent ophthalmia" was actually the venereal disease gonorrhea, which
had been "displaced" upward to the eyes. It was the same disease that
caused "sore eyes," or ophthalmia neonatorum, often leading to blindness
in newborns, and it was morally, as well as physically, repulsive.[37] Another
infectious disease of the eye, trachoma, also flourished in this epidemic. Trachoma has now been identified as a sexually transmitted disease (STD)
caused by the bacterium *Chlamydia trachomatis*, but in the nineteenth century the disease was generally thought to be caused simply by unhygienic

conditions, especially the sharing of towels and drinking cups by soldiers. Trachoma can in fact be spread by nonsexual transmission, and both types of ophthalmia can be passed to a newborn as it passes through the birth canal of an infected mother. The epidemic of ophthalmia, of whatever kind, was brought home to England by returning military men and spread throughout the country, where it became endemic. By 1879, it was found that 25 percent of all blind children had lost their sight from ophthalmia neonatorum.[38] Lawrence's first book demonstrates equally the connection of his specialty to the Egyptian opthalmia epidemic: published three years before his *Treatise on the Diseases of the Eye*, it is titled *Venereal Diseases of the Eye* (1830) and describes gonorrheal as well as syphilitic diseases as they affected the eye. Both diseases can cause blindness.

The size of the Egyptian ophthalmia epidemic spurred the founding of eye hospitals. No fewer than three were founded in London alone in the decade or so following the Egyptian campaign, one of which later became the famed Moorfields or Royal London Ophthalmic Infirmary. They soon cropped up all over Britain, with as many as fifty-two eye, or eye and ear, hospitals established between 1808 and 1889. Ophthalmology became the fastest growing subspecialty of surgery, and later of combined medicine and surgery, not only in Britain but throughout Europe.

But it was not until 1850, when Hermann von Helmholtz invented the ophthalmoscope, that specialization in diseases of the eye became respectable. This instrument made it possible to look directly into the living eye and actually see such anatomical features as blood vessels and the optic nerve. In Helmholtz's original discovery, his instrument used mirrors to reflect light into the eye and obtain an optical image of the retina and other structures in the interior of the eye, making possible new leaps in the knowledge of the anatomy and pathology of the eye.[39] The very first atlas of the pathology of the eye, James Wardrop's *Morbid Anatomy of the Human Eye*, had only been published in 1808. It was based entirely on observations made by dissection of the nonliving eye. Although it was followed and improved upon by several European works on eye pathology, the invention of the ophthalmoscope was followed by works based on observations on the living eye made with this revolutionary instrument. From about 1885 onward, a handheld electric ophthalmoscope was developed, and the ophthalmoscope in use today is basically an improved version of that one.

Of course, the ophthalmoscope did not receive immediate acclamation and acceptance. Some surgeons feared that reflecting "naked light" into the eye might damage it.[40] Others, however, recognized its epoch-making character. In 1886, Frans Cornelius Donders commented:

[Helmholtz] never thought, or at least he never said, that the new instrument implied the dawning of a new era for ophthalmology. Von

Graefe felt it immediately. When he for the first time saw the background of the eye, with its nerve entrance and its blood-vessels, his cheeks reddened, and he called out excitedly, "Helmholtz has unfolded to us a new world!"[41]

The First International Ophthalmological Exhibition was held in London in 1851, and it was here that ophthalmologists from all over Europe learned of Helmholtz's invention for the first time. The next two decades were thought by some to be the "Golden Age of Ophthalmology," and new articles continually appeared in medical journals announcing exciting discoveries about the living eye and how it functioned in health and disease.[42] It was the ophthalmoscope that made possible Albert von Graefe's discovery of a surgical cure for one type of glaucoma, another cause of blindness that became preventable in the nineteenth century. With the ophthalmoscope, the surgeon (or physician, for in the latter half of the nineteenth century, British practitioners were increasingly qualified in both medicine and surgery) could detect indications of illness elsewhere in the body, such as hypertension (high blood pressure), diabetes, heart disease, and brain tumors.

With sufficient training, the ophthalmologist could also use this instrument to obtain precise measurement of the refractive (focusing ability) errors of the eye and thus prescribe spectacles that could substantially improve vision even for those with very poor vision. At about the same time the ophthalmoscope was invented, the use of a box of trial lenses (lenses graded according to type and strength) began to become more common. Prior to that time, most spectacles were sold by peddlers who recommended them based largely on the customer's age. But in the latter half of the century, ophthalmologists increasingly considered refractive examination using both the ophthalmoscope and a box of trial lenses something that should be part of every examination, and eyeglasses became something that could help even some of those previously considered "as good as blind" to have useful vision.[43]

Nevertheless, one ophthalmologist commented in 1871 that "the number of physicians who are working with the ophthalmoscope in England may, I believe, be counted on the fingers of one hand."[44] And although the German obstetrician Karl Siegmund Franz Credé announced in 1881 that a single drop of a 2 percent solution of silver nitrate placed into the eyes of a newborn would prevent almost all cases of ophthalmia neonatorum, children continued to be partially or completely blinded by other diseases, such as syphilis, smallpox, scarlet fever, measles, and meningitis, contracted in infancy or early childhood. However, the emergence of ophthalmology in the nineteenth century did make significant advances in the prevention and treatment of blindness, whether total or partial.

BLINDNESS AND GENDER IN VICTORIAN LITERATURE AND LIFE

> Woman without the aid of man is naturally weak, and how incompa-
> rably so must they be who are not only debarred from having man's
> aid, but are also deprived of the inestimable blessing of sight![45]

Such is the opinion of William Hanks Levy, published in his book *Blindness
and the Blind; or, A Treatise on the Science of Typhology* (1872). Levy was
himself a blind man, and a married man. But blind women, he asserts, are
rarely able to have "man's aid," as in marriage. Although "men without
sight . . . enter into the bonds of matrimony quite as frequently, in proportion to their numbers, as their sighted neighbors, . . . with blind women, it
is far otherwise," he comments soberly.[46] Levy is not alone in this opinion.
In most Victorian literature, blind women do not marry. In Charles Dickens's *Cricket on the Hearth*, for example, blind Bertha provides the music
for the culminating dance, but does not join in it herself, a metaphor for her
exclusion from the dance of marital partnership. Commenting on this story,
Elisabeth G. Gitter states that "blind women in the nineteenth century were
not generally thought to be marriageable" and adds that in fiction, "through
the often melodramatic contrivance of medical recovery, lovers could be
cured of blindness and made fit for marriage."[47] Dickens's heroine in *Bleak
House*, for example, recovers her sight after losing it temporarily during her
illness with what is most probably smallpox, and thereafter marries (see
chapter 5). In real life, such an unmarried young woman, if permanently
blinded by smallpox, as many smallpox victims were, would probably not
have been able to marry. Elizabeth Gilbert, to whom Levy dedicated his
book and who had been blinded by scarlet fever in early childhood, had to
renounce her ideal of marriage, according to her friend and biographer Frances Martin, when she realized the impossibility of achieving a home and
family of her own.[48] Though the daughter of a bishop and independently
wealthy at the age of twenty-one through the inheritance of a godmother's
estate, she found herself literally excluded from the balls to which her sisters were invited. Fortunately for the blind poor, she decided to devote her
life to helping them support themselves through providing workshops in
which they could keep the full profits from their labor. Gilbert and Levy
worked together in this endeavor.

The case is strikingly different with the representation of blind men in
Victorian fiction. Not only are they marriageable, but the heroines who
marry them are delighted, according to the conventional Victorian marriage
plot, to have a greater opportunity than most wives to devote themselves to
lifelong service to their husbands. Jane Eyre, after marrying the blind and
crippled (one hand has been amputated) Rochester, exclaims to the reader
that she became "his vision" and that "never did I weary of gazing for his

behalf . . . never did I weary of reading to him; never did I weary of conducting him where he wished to go: of doing for him what he wished to be done."[49] Ayaconara, the heroine of Charles Kingsley's novel *Westward Ho!* (1855), throws herself on her knees at the feet of her blinded hero, sobbing that she cannot bear to see him weep and begging him, "Only let me fetch and carry for you, tend you, feed you, lead you, like your slave, your dog! Say that I may be your slave!"[50] And even the feminist heroine Aurora Leigh, in Elizabeth Barrett Browning's novel-poem, ends the narrative by "seeing" for the blinded hero a vision of "perfect noon," an apocalyptic future that they will inhabit together.[51]

Such perfect unions of blind man and sighted wife, however, allow for more than one interpretation. They certainly represent the most conventional myth of marriage in Victorian times, that women were born to love and serve men and were happiest in doing so. But as numerous feminist literary critics have pointed out, the relationship between a blind man and sighted wife in Victorian literature may also be seen as more equal in some ways, for the wife is empowered even as she becomes more of a slave to her husband's happiness. It is now the man who becomes dependent on the woman.

This reversal, or at least equalization, of position may actually have been the case in the marriage of at least one blind man married to a sighted woman in the Victorian era. When Henry Fawcett, who became the best-known blind man in British public life, married Millicent Garrett, a woman fourteen years younger than he, in 1867, the marriage was as radical as the political principles shared by both.[52] Henry, a professor of political economy at Cambridge University and also a member of Parliament, had always been interested in women's rights, and Millicent later described herself as a "woman suffragist . . . from my cradle." Though Millicent was prepared to be the "eyes and hands" of her husband, who had lost his sight in a tragic hunting accident, she was also his intellectual companion, his secretary, and his co-campaigner for women's rights, and she became a much-published and successful author in her own right. After she led her husband to the door of the House of Commons each day, the young wife (she was only nineteen at the time of marriage), proceeded up the stairway to "the Ladies' Cage," where she could listen to the debates on political and social issues in which she was deeply interested.[53] By the 1870s, she had become well known as a public speaker, at a time when it was still highly unusual for women to speak in public.[54] It was a union in which both partners stood to gain, and the woman unusually so, in this era when women did not have the vote and were by no means equal partners under the laws and customs of Victorian marriage.

Wilkie Collins's second novel, in which he states that he hopes to exhibit a major disability, in this case blindness, "as it really is," was published nearly twenty years after *Hide and Seek* (1854), which features a deaf and dumb heroine (see chapter 6). In *Poor Miss Finch* (1872), the heroine is a twenty-two-year-old woman who has been blind since about the age of one year, when her blindness came on unexpectedly, with no apparent cause. The plot of this novel is radical in the sense that the blind woman does marry in the end, although it appears she becomes the most conventional of Victorian wives, completely occupied with her children, her husband, and domestic life. The plot is anything but radical in its representation of the operation performed on Lucilla by a German oculist, whose name, Herr Grosse, suggests not only his corpulence and fondness for rich foods but his gross manners in general. The surgery performed by Herr Grosse, which is not explicitly described, does restore Lucilla's sight, but not her vision. As with Cheselden's surgery in the eighteenth century on the boy blind from birth, while Lucilla's ability to see is restored, she is unable to recognize by sight what she can recognize by touch. And her blindness soon returns, an event which strongly implies that the German oculist has merely couched congenital cataracts, the likely cause of her becoming blind in early infancy without an evident cause such as illness. After Lucilla's blindness returns, in a plot that is, as Catherine Peters notes, "a spider's web of improbabilities,"[55] she is able to once again correctly recognize which of two twins it is whom she truly loves, by touch. When her sight was restored, she was able to see that this twin's skin complexion was of a hideous, dark blue color, attributed to the drug, silver nitrate, with which he was being treated for his epilepsy, and her sight thus led her to the false conclusion that this could not be the twin she loved. Once she is again blind, she knows her true love by touch, and happily marries him.

Lucilla's story, in fact, is another twist on the literary tradition of the visionary power possessed by the blind poet-prophet—only in this case, her visionary power is that of touch. But she makes it clear that she is better off blind, as she sees better without sight:

> "Do you think I wish to see him disfigured as he is now? No! I wish to see him—and I *do* see him!—as my fancy drew his picture in the first days of our love. My blindness is my blessing. It has given me back my old delightful sensation when I touch him; it keeps my own beloved image of him—the one image I care for—unchanged and unchangeable."[56]

Blindness is represented here, as in most Victorian literature, as a metaphor for insight rather than as actual sensory loss. As Naomi Schor acknowledges in her autobiographical essay "Blindness as Metaphor," there is no way the metaphor of blindness as insight, and its corollary of sightedness as blindness, can simply be outlawed, because these metaphorical uses of blindness have become ubiquitous in our language and culture. But she repeats, with emphasis, Susan Sontag's fear about the consequences of speaking of illnesses such as cancer in metaphors:" [It] inhibit[s] people from seeking treatment early enough, or from making a greater effort to get competent treatment. *The metaphors and myths, I was convinced, kill.*"[57] Collins's novel is an unfortunate instance of just such killing—in this instance, blinding—actually encouraged by his improbable reworking of the old saw that true love is blind. In *Poor Miss Finch*, Collins has the English surgeon, tellingly named Sebright (obviously superior to the German oculist, Herr Grosse), state that the operation should never have been performed on Lucilla because her chances of regaining vision are very slim.[58] The surgeon never explains, as Collins's own surgeon Critchett did in his *A Case of Blindness from Birth*, that surgeons almost never saw such cases after the 1850s because congenital cataracts were usually removed in the first year of life, thus making it possible for the growing child to develop vision, which does not depend simply on sight but on the capacity to interpret sensory information from the eyes. This was one form of blindness that the new knowledge of ophthalmology had learned how to prevent, if surgery was performed soon enough. But Collins, like many other Victorian writers, prefers to play with metaphors rather than represent "as it really is" what the surgeon Lawrence had called "the greatest misfortune even to the rich." "Blindness," Lucilla chirps, "is my greatest blessing." Collins's novel is an extreme form of the melodramatization of blindness.

8

Victorian Women
as Patients and Practitioners

There is, however, in almost all public discussions upon the social
position of women, an odd peculiarity which betrays itself here with
great distinctness: it is, that writers on the subject invariably treat
this half of humankind as a distinct creation rather than as a portion of a general race—not as human creatures primarily, and
women in the second place, but as women, and nothing but
women—a distinct sphere of being, a separate globe of existence, to
which different rules, different motives, an altogether distinct economy, belong.[1]

That the well-known Scottish writer Margaret Oliphant could so clearly
state in 1858 the "peculiarity" that women were not commonly thought
of as part of the same human race as men indicates how accepted the
notion had become even by midcentury (as well as what an astute feminist
thinker she was). Ornella Moscucci, whose 1990 study on the rise of gynecology (the science of woman) in the nineteenth century has become a
classic in medical history, states Oliphant's insight even more succinctly:
because of her role in reproduction, woman was regarded as a "special case,
a deviation from the norm represented by the male."[2] By the end of the
century, beliefs that women were a "distinct" kind of being ruled by a
"distinct economy" had reached ridiculous and dangerous extremes in the
medical realm. In 1891 surgeon Thomas Spencer Wells attacked what he
then realized had become a sort of epidemic of ovariotomies (removal of
the ovaries) with a scathing portrait of what would happen if andrology

(the science of man) should become as common a part of surgical practice as gynecology:

> Fancy the reflected picture of a coterie of the Marthas of the profession in conclave, promulgating the doctrine that most of the unmanageable maladies of men were to be traced to some morbid change in their genitals, founding societies for the discussion of them and hospitals for the cure of them, one of them sitting in her consultation chair, with her little stove by her side and her irons all hot, searing every man as he passed before her; another gravely proposing to bring on the millennium by snuffing out the reproductive powers of all fools, lunatics, and criminals . . . if too, we saw, in this magic mirror, ignorant boys being castrated almost impromptu, hundreds of emasculated beings moping about and bemoaning their doltish credulity.[3]

The rise of gynecology in the nineteenth century identified women as a special group of patients, while at the same time it supported the ideology that women, because they were specialized for reproduction, were unfit to become medical practitioners or, for that matter, to undertake any kind of rigorous intellectual study that might undermine the health of their reproductive organs. At the same time, it supported the theory that women (and only women) should become nurses, for, as Florence Nightingale famously said, "Every woman is a nurse."[4] An 1878 editorial in the *Lancet* declared that "in the economy of nature . . . the ministry of woman is one of help and sympathy." "Complete surrender" of judgment and "implicit obedience in spirit, as well as letter, which are the first essentials of a good nurse" were natural to women, but not to men. For women to aspire to become doctors, *leaders* in the medical realm, was a "revolt against the reign of natural law."[5]

But the very vehemence of this increasing medical dogmatism on the "natural" difference between women and men spurred the feminist response against it. Part of this response was to strengthen some women in their determination to become doctors, regardless of the medical profession's resistance to them. In the closing decades of the nineteenth century, a small group of women managed to become medical practitioners in Britain. Ironically, the very notion that women were a special group of patients, distinct from men, also created an opportunity for women who wished to enter the field of medicine, for it was logical that such patients might desire a practitioner of their own sex. And because in medicine women were classed with children (it was traditional for lectures to be given in medical schools on the "diseases of women and children"), there was more tolerance in the medical field for women physicians who wanted to specialize in the new field of children's diseases, or pediatrics. Although the medical/surgical specialties of gynecology and obstetrics had been in the process of development from the eighteenth century on, it was not until these new specialties had medicalized women (made the female body the object of specialized medical scrutiny and treatment) that the medical profession had to acknowledge that women physicians might be the natural choice for women patients. By the end of Queen Victoria's reign, the "science of woman" had transformed women into a special class of patients, but it had also facilitated the entry of women into the medical profession.

VICTORIAN WOMEN BECOME PATIENTS: THE RISE OF GYNECOLOGY

Thurs 7 March, 1850

Administered Chloroform to Mrs. Dickens, 29 Tibberton Square, whilst Mr. Baker Brown removed a large multilocular [multiple fluid-filled sacs] ovarian cyst from which 24 pints of liquid were first evacuated. . . . An incision of about 8 inches in length was first made exposing the tumour. Two of the cysts were opened and the contents were evacuated. The incision was then extended . . . [to] 12 or 14 inches in length. Mr. Brown then introduced his hand and removed the tumour. . . . The patient, after the tumour was drawn out, appeared to breathe entirely by the ribs and care was taken not to push the narcotism [anesthesia] too far. . . . Some brandy being given, the pulse improved. There was a little sickness 2 or 3 hours afterwards which was relieved by swallowing bits of ice. Died of peritonitis early on the 4th day.[6]

John Snow, whose education as a doctor is described in chapter 1 and researches on the transmission of cholera in chapter 2, began to keep "case books," or brief notes on cases he attended, in July 1848. At this time he had become deeply interested in the use of ether and chloroform, anesthetic gases first introduced into surgery in late 1846. He had already published *On the Inhalation of the Vapour of Ether in Surgical Operations* in 1847. The operation he describes in somewhat more detail than usual here, removal of an ovary, had been only rarely performed before the introduction of anesthesia, even though ovarian cysts could become so enlarged as to confine a woman to bed, sometimes causing severe pain as well. But the pain of abdominal surgery made both surgeons and patients reluctant to risk surgery. And there was an even greater risk: any penetration of the abdominal cavity most commonly led to infection, as it did here. The patient died of peritonitis, infection of the peritoneum (lining of the abdominal cavity), four days after the operation. Hence, Baker Brown's operation on Mrs. Dickens on March 7, 1850, was something of a radical innovation in nineteenth-century surgery.

The first ovariotomy known to medical history was performed in 1809 by an American surgeon, Ephraim McDowell, who had studied medicine and surgery at the University of Edinburgh in 1793–94 and then returned to Danville, Kentucky. He was sent for by doctors who had seen a forty-seven-year-old woman, Jane Todd Crawford, who was believed to be pregnant but whose pains did not seem to be labor pains. Her doctors sent for McDowell, who had to travel sixty miles to reach her. McDowell examined Crawford and found that she was not pregnant. He concluded that she had an enormously enlarged ovary and that there was no way she could be helped except by trying to remove it. He feared the tumor might kill her if it was not removed, but he also feared that abdominal surgery might kill her. He left the decision up to her, but told her he would operate only in his own house where, among other things, he would have the assistance of his nephew, James McDowell, an MD.

Crawford had to make the lengthy trip to Danville on horseback, as there were no roads, but she managed the trip, supporting her tumor on the saddle horn. There in McDowell's home she had the operation, which lasted twenty-five minutes. Some eight years later, McDowell wrote that the tumor was so large he could not take it out in one piece. He extracted fifteen pounds of a "dirty gelatinous substance," and then the sack, which weighed seven pounds. Crawford is reported to have recited psalms throughout the operation. McDowell probably gave her what he called "cherry bounce," or a mixture of opium and alcohol. Miraculously, the patient recovered. On the fifth day after the operation, McDowell found her not only out of her bed but making it up. Nearly a month later, she rode home and lived for thirty years more.[7]

McDowell later wrote that he had done thirteen other ovariotomies, or what he called "Extirpation of the Ovaries." Only one of his patients died, an almost unbelievable record for this operation at that time. Surgeons who read his reports of his operations were skeptical, but nevertheless, ovariotomies began to be attempted in Britain. John Lizars, surgeon and lecturer in anatomy at Edinburgh University, operated on a young woman in 1824, but discovered that she had no ovarian tumor but was simply obese. She at least survived the operation, however, whereas the next three attempts by Lizars resulted in the death of the patient. But in 1838, a general practitioner named William Jeaffreson reported a successful ovariotomy, and thereafter more of the operations were attempted.

Such surgeries of course became more common, like all surgery, after the introduction of anesthesia. But some surgeons now began to claim that the "disease" of ovarian cysts regularly progressed toward enlargement, local irritation, constitutional exhaustion, and death. It was even claimed that patients developed a peculiar facial appearance that Spencer Wells, who was at this time on the side of surgical intervention, called *facies ovariana*. The mere "tapping" of an ovarian cyst, or drawing off fluid without removing the ovary, was called only palliative, simply delaying the patient's death by a few years.[8] Ovariotomies, accordingly, were performed more and more frequently, despite awareness of an appalling death rate. Baker Brown's first three ovariotomies all ended in death, yet he had such faith in the "ultimate efficacy of ovariotomy" that he next operated on his own sister, who fortunately recovered.[9] Between 1854 and 1856, Baker Brown performed nine ovariotomies, and only two patients survived.

But there was also a strong backlash against ovariotomy in midcentury. In November 1850, Robert Lee, MD, analyzed 162 operations for ovarian tumors and found that a third of the cases had been found to be inoperable or to have no tumor. (One of the problems with ovariotomies at this time was that surgeons still sometimes could not distinguish between a large ovarian cyst and simple obesity, or even pregnancy.) Of the 102 completed operations, 42 had ended in the patient's death. Charles West gathered statistics in 1855 showing that, of 200 ovariotomies, 44.5 percent ended in the death of the patient. These statistics, plus strong opposition from a group of conservative surgeons, made ovariotomy less popular for a time.

But in 1857, Spencer Wells began to perform the operation, and over the next twenty-one years, his mortality for the surgery declined from 50 to 11 percent.[10] This was achieved partly through improvement of surgical technique and partly through his introduction of Listerian antisepsis in the 1870s. Paralleling this reduction in mortality for the operation was a ballooning of the myth that removal of the ovaries could cure women of many kinds of mental instability caused by the functioning of their reproductive systems. In 1873, Robert Barnes delivered the Lumleian lectures to the Royal College of Physicians on the subject of "The Convulsive Diseases of Women." By this he meant such conditions as "menstrual epilepsy," hysteria, and other types of female "fits."[11] Belief in such kinds of mental instability peculiar to females and associated with menstruation (or its absence) was not new. As early as 1828, George Man Burrows, a respected general practitioner who became an alienist, or specialist in mental disorders, wrote in his *Commentaries on the Causes, Forms, Symptoms and Treatment, Moral and Medical, of Insanity*: "Everybody of the least experience must be sensible of the influence of menstruation on the operations of the mind. In truth, it is the moral and physical barometer of the female constitution. . . . The functions of the brain are so intimately connected with the uterine system, that the interruption of any one process which the latter has to perform in the human economy may implicate the former."[12] By 1883, Thomas Clouston, physician-superintendent of the Royal Edinburgh Asylum, wrote: "Disturbed menstruation is a constant danger to the mental stability of some women; nay the occurrence of normal menstruation is attended by some risk in unstable brains. The actual outbreak of mental disease, or its worst paroxysms, is coincident with the menstrual period in a very large number of women indeed."[13]

Ovariotomies, now dignified by the name oöphorectomy or salpingo-oöphorectomy (removal of Fallopian tubes as well as ovaries), began to be done in the 1870s and 1880s for such disorders as ovaries that were said to be prolapsed though otherwise healthy, dysmenorrhoea (painful menstruation), menstrual epilepsy, and even more ambiguous disorders such as "ovarian cyrrhosis."[14] The basic process of ovulation, or release of the ovum from the ovary, had only been discovered in 1831, and very little was actually known about menstruation, which was commonly referred to as the time when a woman was "unwell." But men rushed to fill in the gaps in knowledge with theory. In 1873, Edward Clarke of Harvard College published *Sex in Education*, in which he argued that menstruation was disabling and that higher education was already destroying the reproductive functions of American women by overworking their minds. Henry Maudsley, a British psychiatrist, in turn rushed to publish *Sex in Mind and Education* in 1874, utilizing Clarke's theories to argue that menstruation was an absolute bar to higher education for women. And in 1877, surgeon Lawson Tait wrote in *Diseases of Women* that girls and women should be treated as invalids. If a girl had "curse pains," she should be removed from school for six months and should have no instruction of any kind, especially not music, which he felt was responsible for "menstrual mischief."[15]

As Elaine Showalter comments, women themselves contributed to the problem: their willingness to accept drastic surgical remedies for a wide range of symptoms made it possible for surgeons such as Spencer Wells and Tait to perform hundreds of ovariotomies and other operations on women's sexual and reproductive organs. One doctor commented in 1894 that "pelvic operations on women has [sic] become a fad."[16] But it's also likely that the increasing number of abdominal and pelvic surgeries performed on women in the later decades of the nineteenth century had something to do with the increasing number of doctors. In England and Wales, the number of doctors increased between 1861 and 1891 by 53 percent, rising from 17,300 to 26,000. As the American physician Mary Putnam Jacobi wrote in 1895, "I think, finally, it is in the increased attention paid to women, and especially in their new function as lucrative patients, scarcely imagined a hundred years ago, that we find explanation for much of the ill-health among women, freshly discovered today."[17] Removal of healthy ovaries for a variety of supposed though unproven health benefits remained popular among both gynecologists and their patients not only in the late Victorian period but throughout much of the twentieth century.

Snow's case report on the unfortunate Mrs. Dickens is also interesting because the surgeon who performed this operation later became famous—and then infamous—for another type of gynecological surgery that he began practicing in the late 1850s, after Snow's death. Baker Brown, who was at this time a respected member of the Obstetrical Society of London, believed that masturbation, which he termed "peripheral excitement," caused madness, and that removal of the clitoris would prevent or cure it. He set up a private clinic in London in 1859, and from then until 1866 he performed numerous clitoridectomies there and elsewhere. He increased the range of conditions for which clitoridectomy was a supposed cure to include girls' disobedience to their mothers and wives' unhappiness with their husbands. Then in 1866 he published a book on his work, *On the Curability of Certain Forms of Insanity, Epilepsy, Catalepsy, and Hysteria in Females*. This led to outrage from many fellow surgeons, who believed that clitoridectomy would be seen as a slur on a respectable woman's character and that women would cease to consult gynecologists at all for fear of this operation. Reports that Baker Brown had operated on women who didn't understand the nature of the surgery he was performing on them also began to appear. The death knell for his career came when it was discovered that he had performed clitoridectomies on institutionalized women without their consent or that of their families. On April 3, 1867, the Obstetrical Society of London held a hearing on Baker Brown and his practice of clitoridectomy. The outcome was that he was expelled from the society. His health failed, and he died a few years later, in February 1873.[18] However, clitoridectomies continued to be performed for wholly unproven benefits, especially in the United States, well into the twentieth century.

Yet another aspect of Baker Brown's career ties him to a development in gynecological surgery which has been more problematic to assess in terms of ethics than that of clitoridectomy. During the American Civil War, an American gynecologist named J. Marion Sims spent time in London, and while he was there, he demonstrated his operation for the repair of vesico-vaginal fistula to Baker Brown. Vesico-vaginal fistula is an injury usually sustained during an obstructed labor, when the baby is too big or in the wrong position to pass through the birth canal. Obstructed labor is particularly likely to occur in malnourished women, whose pelvises are too small for the baby to pass through. The prolonged pressure of the baby's head against the pelvis can cause tissues in the vagina, uterus, and bladder, also sometimes the rectum, to die, resulting in the formation of a permanent opening or connection between two organs, or between one organ and the outside of the body. The resulting injury leaves the woman completely incontinent of urine, and sometimes of stool. Such a fistula does not kill the woman, but leaves her in so terrible a condition that many nineteenth-century victims wished they were dead. Fleetwood Churchill, a well-known gynecologist, described the problem as follows:

The escape of faeces or urine is attended with so marked and irrepressible an odour, that the patient is placed *hors de société* [excluded from society]. Obliged to confine herself to her own room, she finds herself an object of disgust to her dearest friends and even to her attendants. She lives the life of a recluse, without the comforts of it, or even the consolation of it being voluntary.[19]

The horrors of the condition had been known since ancient times, and they continue today in undeveloped countries. A *New York Times* article published February 24, 2009, described women in Tanzania with such fistulas and noted that they frequently become outcasts because of the odor, their families forcing them to leave home or building them a separate hut. Surgical cure is still not easy: one of the women interviewed had already endured two painful operations but was hoping a third would be successful.[20]

Until Sims's work in mid-nineteenth-century America, there were no successful surgical techniques for repair of these terrible birth injuries. Sims performed many operations between 1845 and 1857 in attempts to learn how to repair the fistulas, and he finally developed effective procedures. He was celebrated for this accomplishment during his lifetime and after his death: he was even called "the father of gynecology." But in the 1970s, scholars began to question the ethics of Sims's surgery, for it was realized that he had experimented with the various techniques on the bodies of slave women, some of whom he had purchased for this very purpose. He operated repeatedly on some slaves without anesthesia, though he apparently did give them opium to relieve their pain.[21] Historians continue to have mixed opinions about the ethics of Sims's surgical experimentation, some pointing out that it's likely the slaves who had the condition were grateful when he succeeded in curing them, even if it took repeated, torturous operations, and others maintaining that it is unquestionably unethical to perform such surgeries on women who were unable to give their consent, even if those women might have done so had they been free.

Regardless of one's assessment of Sims's development of treatment for vesico-vaginal fistula, no one is likely to approve of his later career, for Sims went on to practice clitoridectomy, as well as ovariotomy, once he was back in the United States. It seems likely that Baker Brown demonstrated his operation for clitoridectomy to Sims, as Sims demonstrated his for fistula repair, during the time when Sims was in London. But whereas clitoridectomy was no longer respectable in Britain after Baker Brown's trial and expulsion from the Obstetrical Society of London, its popularity continued in the United States for many years and Sims was one of its chief promoters.[22]

The rise of gynecology did have some beneficial effects for Victorian women. By the end of the century, gynecological surgery was able to safely and effectively cure many women of real ailments of the reproductive system, such as ovarian cysts, uterine tumors, some cancers of the reproductive organs, and birth injuries. But the science of woman had also developed an ideology of the female body as inherently "unwell," whether menstruating or ceasing to menstruate, and this ideology continued to have unhealthful consequences for girls and women throughout the twentieth century. Referring to the development of gynecological endocrinology (the study of female hormones) in the early twentieth century, and to Blair Bell's argument that "it is because of all the internal secretions that woman is what she is," Moscucci comments: "For the scientist, the march of progress had pushed the boundaries of gynaecology forward. The historian will be more inclined to view this development as the expression of an enduring ideology."[23] The prescription of hormone replacement therapy (HRT) to millions of menopausal women during the second half of the twentieth century in the belief that female hormones would prolong women's youthfulness and benefit their health—in the absence of any large-scale, double-blind, gold-standard study to prove or disprove this belief—is a striking demonstration of the power of this "enduring ideology." Not until 2002, when the National Institutes of Health halted its carefully designed study of the overall risks and benefits of taking the hormones estrogen and progestin, was it known that these hormones actually increased the risks of breast cancer, heart disease, stroke, blood clots, and urinary incontinence.[24] The Victorian science of woman should continue to be studied in order to expose its ongoing influence on modern medicine.

VICTORIAN WOMEN AS OBSTETRIC PATIENTS

Thursday 7 April [1853] At a twenty minutes past twelve by a clock in the Queen's apartment I commenced to give a little chloroform with each pain, by pouring about 15 minims by measure on a folded handkerchief. The first stage of labour was nearly over when the chloroform was commenced. Her majesty expressed great relief from the application, the pains being very trifling during the uterine contractions, and whilst between the periods of contraction there was complete ease. The effect of the chloroform was not at any time carried to the extent of quite removing consciousness. Dr. Locock thought that the chloroform prolonged the intervals between the pains, and retarded the labour somewhat. The infant was born at 13 minutes past one by the clock in the room (which was 3 minutes before the right time); consequently the chloroform was inhaled for 53 minutes. The placenta was expelled in a very few minutes, and the Queen appeared very cheerful and well, expressing herself much gratified with the effect of the chloroform.[25]

Queen Victoria was indeed much gratified with the effect of chloroform during this, her eighth labor. She chose to have it again with her ninth and last delivery, although this time, according to Snow's report, the chloroform was less gratifying. Her physician, dissatisfied with the progress of the labor, had administered some powdered ergot, a drug known since the eighteenth century (at least) to increase uterine contractions. After the second dose, the queen "kept asking for more chloroform, and complaining that it did not remove the pain."[26] At the final stage of the labor, when Locock wanted the queen to bear down, she complained that she could not make the effort. Snow left off giving the chloroform for three or four pains, after which the royal patient found she was able to make the effort, and the baby was born.

The queen's experience of childbirth represents both the unusual and the usual in Victorian obstetrics. The administration of chloroform during labor was definitely unusual at this time. Irvine Loudon comments that it was only when Queen Victoria had chloroform for her eighth delivery that opposition to anesthesia in childbirth began to collapse. After that, it was known as "chloroform à la reine" [like the queen], and those who could afford to pay for it began to inhale the pain-killing gas during their labor.[27] Snow found himself giving anesthesia to many women because of his experience with the queen. One woman refused to inhale any more chloroform until told what the queen had said when she was breathing it. Snow is said to have replied: "Her Majesty asked no questions until she had breathed very much longer than you have; and if you will only go on in loyal imitation, I will tell you everything." But when the woman later regained consciousness, Snow had already left the hospital.[28]

Snow's reports on the queen's last two childbirths indicate both the benefits and the risks of anesthesia during labor: mothers could be spared at least some pain, but it was obvious from early on in its use that anesthesia could also prolong labor. In addition there were protests from those who felt that the pain of labor was divinely ordained, quoting the text from the King James translation of the Book of Genesis that "in sorrow thou shalt bring forth children" (Genesis 4:16). Even more scandalous, some practitioners maintained that they had seen women exhibit signs of sexual excitement when they were anesthetized: that one woman actually "went unconsciously through the movements attendant on the sexual orgasm, in the presence of numerous bystanders."[29] James Simpson Young, professor of midwifery at Edinburgh University, who had first used chloroform for a woman in labor in November 1847, tried to counter such arguments. But the debate raged on in medical journals and pamphlets until Queen Victoria requested anesthesia for her eighth delivery. Even after that, doubts and objections continued with sufficient vigor that the Royal Medical and Chirurgical Society of London appointed a committee in 1863 to study the physiological effects of chloroform. As Mary Poovey notes, "It had become apparent by that time that no one actually understood how anesthesia worked."[30] By that time also it had been reported that 123 patients had died, apparently from the use of chloroform rather than from the operation for which it was administered.

The queen's choice of a physician rather than a midwife to attend the birth, unlike her decision to have anesthesia, was by that time very usual and customary. Locock had begun his education as an accoucheur (midwife or obstetrician) as a private pupil of Benjamin Brodie, a surgeon at St. George's Hospital, and then attended lectures at the medical school on Great Windmill Street (the same one Snow was to attend later). Locock had then graduated with his MD from the University of Edinburgh in 1821. On Brodie's recommendation, he decided to devote himself to the practice of midwifery. He became very successful as an accoucheur, for many years having the largest practice in London, and in 1840 he was appointed "first physician accoucheur" to the queen. He attended the births of all nine of her children and was created a baronet in 1857.[31]

Although Locock was unusual in that he had had more medical education than most men who practiced midwifery at this time, it was not at all unusual for a woman to have a medical man rather than a female midwife attend the birth in the Victorian era. Until the early eighteenth century, most births had been attended by a female midwife and/or a group of female friends, often called "gossips," who might or might not have had experience with childbirth. The midwife also might or might not have had any apprenticeship or training in midwifery. Loudon points out that England was very backward in this respect: in most European countries, midwives had been trained and licensed for centuries. In Germany, for example, midwives were supervised and licensed from the mid-fifteenth century. In the Netherlands by the mid-seventeenth century, midwives had to be able to read and write, to have served a long apprenticeship, and to be women of good reputation in order to obtain a license. In mid-eighteenth-century France, the midwife Madame Du Coudray, "a woman of impressive charisma, talent, and literacy with a profound knowledge of the management of childbirth," was charged by King Louis XV with touring the entire country and training hundreds of students in each region.[32]

In England, by contrast, there was no formal system for licensing midwives until the Midwives' Act of 1902. And although it is now known that eighteenth-century midwives were better trained than had been formerly supposed, midwifery in Europe not only was much better regulated but had much more control over what would now be called obstetric practice. In England, however, employment of a man-midwife became much more common from the second half of the eighteenth century, and by the 1790s, between one-third and one-half of all births were attended by men-midwives. The exact reasons for this shift are not known. Some historians have attributed it to the influence of the Chamberlen family and their carefully guarded secret of the use of forceps, which they claimed to have discovered around 1645. By the early eighteenth century, this secret (similar but somewhat different instruments had been used since ancient times to extract the infant in an obstructed labor) had leaked out, and men-midwives may have monopolized the use of such instruments.

Loudon argues that the increase in men-midwives was due to an increase in surgeon-apothecaries, or men who had some education in both surgery and medicine (see chapter 1), and to a new "spirit of inquiry." By the end of the eighteenth century in England, there had been an "explosion of knowledge" on new forms of maternal care.[33] A small group of London accoucheurs, including William Smellie, William Hunter, Thomas Denman, and William Osborn, not only practiced but also published textbooks that became classics. William Hunter's lavishly produced *Anatomy of the Gravid* [pregnant] *Uterus* (1794) was illustrated by a superior draftsman, Jan van Rymsdyk. Although some of the illustrations have been interpreted by feminist critics as implicitly violent because of their graphic representation of the dissected female body, they conveyed new knowledge of the pregnant womb and the fetus within it.[34]

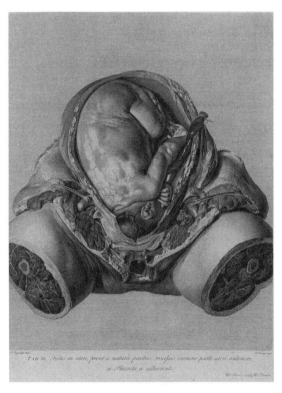

William Hunter, *The Anatomy of the Human Gravid Uterus exhibited in Figures*, Plate VI, 1774. Normal full-term infant. © Wellcome Library, London.

From "To a Little Invisible Being Who is Expected Soon to Become Visible" (1825)

For thee the nurse prepares her lulling song,
The eager matrons count the lingering day;
But by far the most thy anxious parent longs
On thy soft cheek a mother's kiss to lay.

She only asks to lay her burden down,
That her glad arms that burden may resume;
And nature's sharpest pangs her wishes crown,
That free thee from thy living tomb.

She longs to fold to her maternal breast
Part of herself, yet to herself unknown;
To see and to salute the stranger guest,
Fed with her life through many a tedious moon.

Come, reap thy rich inheritance of love!
Bask in the fondness of a Mother's eye!
Nor wit nor eloquence her heart shall move
Like the first accents of thy feeble cry.

Haste, little captive, burst thy prison doors!
Launch on the living world, and spring to light!
Nature for thee displays her various stores,
Opens her thousand inlets of delight.

—Anna Laetitia Barbauld

William Smellie's treatise on midwifery showed how to use forceps and how to measure the size of the pelvis in order to predict difficult deliveries. Thomas Denman's *An Essay on Natural Labours* (1786) describes the three stages of labor so clearly that, in Loudon's opinion, "with a few minor alterations, it could serve as a text for students today."[35]

Another form of new obstetric knowledge was developed on the Continent early in the nineteenth century, when Jean Lejumeau de Kergaradec learned how to use Laënnec's stethoscope to detect the fetal heartbeat. Until this discovery, there had been no way to be assured of a woman's pregnancy until quickening (first perceived motions of the fetus in the womb), and even that was not certain. Anna Laetitia Barbauld's poem "To a Little Invisible Being Who is Expected Soon to Become Visible" expresses both the joy

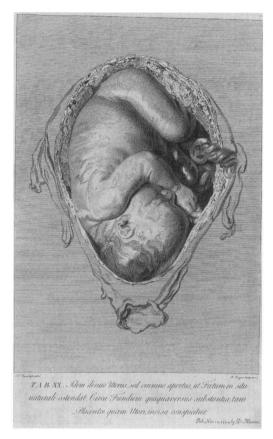

William Hunter, *The Anatomy of the Human Gravid Uterus exhibited in Figures*, Plate XX, 1774. Placenta praevia. © Wellcome Library, London.[36]

of anticipated birth and the fear and anxiety of having no certainty that this "little captive" will burst its prison doors, or even that it is alive in its "living tomb."

Clare Hanson recounts the story of Judith Milbanke, who in October 1791 wrote her aunt about her suspicion (and anxiety) that she might be pregnant after fifteen years of childless marriage and two miscarriages. She and her aunt corresponded throughout the next several months, with her aunt recommending that she consult the fashionable accoucheur Dr. Denman. Eventually, the aunt actually had a consultation with Dr. Denman herself and was reassured by him that he didn't think "there was any necessity for your having more pains or worse time on account of your Age."[37] In May 1792,

Milbanke gave birth to a daughter, Annabella, who married Lord Byron in 1815. The fact that Milbanke did not herself consult a midwife or medical practitioner of any kind before the birth was typical for this time, and for most of the nineteenth century as well. The American physician Thomas Bull, whose *Hints to Mothers* (1837) became a very popular guide to women on both sides of the Atlantic throughout the nineteenth century, describes four symptoms that may help a woman determine whether she is pregnant: ceasing to be "unwell," morning sickness, changes in the breasts, and quickening. He does not suggest she consult a physician or that a stethoscope could be applied to the abdomen to detect the fetal heartbeat.

Pelvic examinations were only rarely performed in Britain before the 1830s, and then only because disease of some sort was suspected, not to ascertain pregnancy. Until the speculum was brought back from Paris by students who had learned to use it there, the practitioner was unable to visualize the cervix (neck or mouth of the womb). The examination was usually performed with the woman standing, the practitioner kneeling on the floor and placing one hand beneath the woman's skirts. In order not to offend delicacy or produce indelicate sensations, the practitioner customarily looked away during the examination. Anne Lister, a lesbian who feared she had picked up syphilis or some venereal disease, described having such an examination in August 1823.[38] Even when the speculum was in use in Britain, there was great outcry against its being used on "innocent" women, whom medical men suspected of becoming addicted to its use and begging to be examined.[39] It was probably just as well that the instrument was not used to routinely diagnose pregnancy, as until antiseptic technique was introduced, its use would doubtless have spread infectious disease.

The queen's nine deliveries all took place in the royal home, and in this they were very typical. Throughout the nineteenth century, 90 percent of all deliveries in Britain were home deliveries, despite the existence of a number of different types of lying-in hospitals and maternity wards in general hospitals, as well as workhouse hospitals. The fact that the queen and her infants survived all nine deliveries was, however, less typical. Whether delivered in a hospital or at home, maternal and infant mortality rates were extremely high. In the second half of the century, between four and five mothers died for every thousand births. Pat Jalland comments that this statistic almost certainly does not represent the real toll of maternity, as statistics did not include deaths from miscarriage (which could be as dangerous as childbirth).[40] Also, the cause of death after childbirth was sometimes described so vaguely as to be useless for purposes of classification, and in order to reduce their mortality statistics, some hospitals, midwives, and doctors failed to identify deaths from hemorrhage or infection as connected to childbirth, especially if the death occurred some weeks after delivery. Multiple childbirths also increased the risk of maternal death. Robert Barnes warned in 1859 that the risk of death rose sharply after the fifth labor, and this was true for middle- and upper-class women as well as working women. The infant death rate, meaning infants who died before the age of one year, was still more shocking: it remained constant at around 153 per thousand throughout the nineteenth century. (Today, by comparison, it's about 5 per thousand.) And this figure is also almost certainly too low, as stillbirths were usually not recorded.

The two principal causes of death in childbirth were puerperal or "childbed" fever, an infection Pasteur discovered in 1880 to be caused by a bacterium later named *Streptococcus pyogenes*, and a second, more general category called "accidents in childbirth."[41] This could include death from bleeding, eclampsia (convulsions), mismanaged delivery of obstructed labor, or unskilled use of instruments such as forceps. This category also accounted for many stillbirths. The risk of both causes of maternal death was almost certainly increased by the ignorance of both practitioners and midwives. Loudon writes that "the teaching of midwifery in the nineteenth and twentieth centuries was often disgraceful" in Britain.[42] Elizabeth Garrett Anderson, the first woman to qualify as a physician in England, wrote in 1896 that "puerperal mortality all over England is higher than it ought to be" and that the responsibility lay largely in the poor quality of education in midwifery.[43] Medical students typically had only a few weeks of midwifery training, often consisting of delivering poor women with little instruction or supervision. While certain groups of midwives might be trained carefully, most were not.

The major cause of death in childbirth throughout the nineteenth century and until the late 1930s, when sulphonamides were introduced, was puerperal fever. Although the queen's physician knew nothing of antisepsis or bacteria, whose existence had not been established as yet, he presumably did know of the benefits of strict hygiene, especially hand-washing, since the queen never had puerperal fever. Snow's publications on cholera make it clear that he, and presumably all well-educated medical practitioners, was aware that infections could be passed by unclean hands. There had been no fewer than three studies of puerperal fever by the mid-nineteenth century that offered convincing evidence that the disease was passed from birth attendants to women. In the late eighteenth century, Alexander Gordon studied an epidemic of puerperal fever in the Scottish town of Aberdeen that lasted from 1789 to 1792 and published a paper showing that the disease was passed from one lying-in woman to another by the birth attendant. In 1843, Oliver Wendell Holmes had published a paper on the contagiousness of puerperal fever. And in 1847, Ignaz Phillip Semmelweis, observing that a maternity clinic staffed by student midwives had a much lower mortality rate than another staffed by medical students, concluded that the medical students carried something on their hands from the corpses they were dissecting to the bodies of the women they were delivering. He insisted that the medical students wash their hands in a chlorine solution before examining a woman in labor, and the mortality rate in their clinic instantly dropped to the same level as that of the student midwives' clinic.[44] Although Semmelweis did not publish his observations until a decade later, his recommendations were spread by word of mouth. The tragedy is that, until Lister introduced his system of antisepsis in the 1860s (and indeed, until a couple of decades later), most medical practitioners simply ignored the glaring evidence that attention to the cleanliness of the birth attendants could make the difference between whether a woman lived or died as a result of childbirth. But the queen's physician, one can be sure, washed his hands, as her anesthesiologist doubtless also did.

Deaths from puerperal fever in lying-in hospitals continued to rise even as understanding of its cause and strategies for its prevention also increased, not only in Britain but also in Europe and the United States. One method of prevention was simply to close a hospital for a period of time, allowing it to air out. The Chelsea Hospital for Women, for example, was reported to have kept infection at bay by closing the hospital for one month every year.[45] But by the 1870s, hospital epidemics of puerperal fever had become so devastating that mass closure of lying-in hospitals was being considered. The institution of Listerian antiseptics in the late 1870s, however, had a dramatic effect: puerperal fever was almost completely abolished in hospitals. Most births in Britain, however, continued to take place in the home, and puerperal fever continued unabated there, even after the Midwives' Act of 1902 began to produce trained and supervised midwives. In fact, the maternal mortality rate actually rose between 1900 and 1930. The risk of a mother dying in childbirth was as high in 1934 in England and Wales as it had been in the 1860s. Investigations found that general practitioners making home deliveries were not only careless about antiseptic procedures but too eager to apply forceps in normal labors after putting the mother under anesthesia. Some used forceps and anesthesia in as many as 50 percent of their normal midwifery cases. By contrast, in European countries where a high proportion of home deliveries were supervised by trained midwives, the mortality rate was low. Loudon concludes, "In retrospect one can see that before the Second World War wherever there was a country or a region in which there was a high proportion of home deliveries by trained midwives and a low amount of interference by doctors in normal labours, there was a high standard of maternal care characterized by a low rate of mortality."[46]

VICTORIAN WOMEN AS NURSES AND MIDWIVES

In nearly every country but our own there is a Government School for Midwives. I trust our School may lead the way toward supplying a long felt want in England.[47]

Unfortunately, the plan for a school for midwives that Florence Nightingale described in an 1861 letter to her friend Harriet Martineau led only to a program that lasted for five years (1862–67) at King's College Hospital and that probably trained no more than forty midwives, if that. But Nightingale's recognition of the need for midwives trained in a government-regulated school, such as existed in many European countries, demonstrates her awareness that carefully trained midwives could make a vast difference in the maternal mortality rate. In her *Introductory Notes on Lying-in Hospitals*, published in 1871, she stated, "With all their defects, midwifery statistics point to one truth; namely that there is a large amount of preventable mortality in midwifery practice, and that, as a general rule, the mortality is far, far greater in lying-in hospitals than among lying-in at home."[48]

Nightingale herself never believed in germ theory, that is, that invisible microorganisms caused disease. "There are no specific diseases," she argued, even after Robert Koch had demonstrated that specific bacteria caused tuberculosis and cholera.[49] But she believed in hygiene: a rigorous regime of scrupulously clean, well-ventilated hospital wards. And she invented the idea of the scrupulously clean, trained, and disciplined professional nurse. Nursing was a sanitary mission, in Nightingale's view. It was also strictly a feminine profession: "You cannot be a good nurse without being a good woman," she was fond of saying, and throughout her phenomenally successful promotion of what came to be called "the Nightingale nurse," she reinforced the most traditional Victorian notions of proper gender roles. Nurses, who were to be female, were to be subordinate to doctors, who were, and ought to remain, male. Nightingale was not a feminist.

Born into a wealthy family, and spending most of her youth on country estates, interspersed with visits to London, Nightingale was nevertheless an unhappy young woman whose adolescence was marked by bouts of depression. At the age of sixteen, she felt she had been called to God's service, and she became deeply interested in the writings of Christian mystics. In 1850, while traveling in Europe with friends, she managed to visit the Institute of Protestant Deaconesses at Kaiserwerth in Germany, a Protestant nursing sisterhood, and she later visited the Sisters of Charity in Paris, a Roman Catholic nursing sisterhood. When she returned to England, she took an unpaid position as administrator at the Establishment for Gentlewomen during Illness on Harley Street in London. Here she first demonstrated her talent for administration, as well as her fervor for hygiene, for she literally cleaned up the institution, instituting rigorous standards of cleanliness and order. While she was working at Harley Street, the cholera epidemic of 1854 hit London, and Nightingale went to help out at the Middlesex Hospital, where she again demonstrated "a remarkable flair for imposing her will on institutions."[50]

In October 1854, she was called upon by the government to help out in the desperate need to reform nursing care for soldiers in the hospitals set up in the Crimean War theater. She took with her a mixed group of ladies from nursing sisterhoods (among whom was an aunt of Christina Rossetti) and working-class nurses and, on arrival, set about cleaning up the hospitals in the Crimea. Among the most serious problems there was the epidemic of cholera (see chapter 2), which her emphasis on keeping water, as well as air, unpolluted by the miasma from chamber pots probably helped to restrain. In May 1855, she herself collapsed with what was called "Crimean fever" or typhus fever, but what was probably brucellosis, an infection that affects animals such as sheep and goats but that can be acquired by humans.[51] She slowly recovered and continued to work at Scutari, where she continued to exercise her gift for administration, as well as actually nursing the sick herself, according to later accounts by soldiers. Her work was heavily publicized in the *Times* and other media, and by the time she returned to England in 1856, she had become a national heroine, the revered "Lady with the Lamp." The Nightingale Fund was set up to enable her to establish a "permanent institution for the training, sustenance and protection of nurses."[52] She accordingly established the Nightingale School for Nurses at St. Thomas's Hospital in London and went on to promote various kinds of nursing and hospital programs, such as the unfortunately short-lived one in midwifery at King's College Hospital. But her chief preoccupation after her return to England in July 1856 was to reform the Army Medical Services. This became her main goal.

While at the Statistical Congress held in 1860, where she worked frenetically to promote a scheme for collecting uniform hospital statistics, Nightingale suddenly became severely ill with what was probably sequelae of the Crimean fever. Thereafter she lived the life of an invalid, but she turned out mountains of papers from the seclusion of her sickroom. Scholars have recently produced much new research based on the voluminous archives of writings left by this formidable woman. As of 2008, there are eleven published volumes of her writings, each volume consisting of but a small proportion of her writings on a specific topic. In the process, Nightingale's image as a selfless and heroic woman who singlehandedly reformed nursing has undergone revision. Details of what she was and was not able to accomplish have emerged. Historians now cite as her major accomplishment in nursing that of making nursing a respectable occupation for middle-class women and eventually transforming it by her vision of a secular but dedicated professional ideal. She is also credited with the development of a recognized body of nursing skills and behaviors, such that by the end of the nineteenth century, the Nightingale model had metamorphosed into the modern professional nurse.[53] But the extent of Nightingale's investment in class and gender hierarchy has now also been exposed, and much more is now known about the somewhat less than well-planned way in which the training of Nightingale nurses began.

Before Nightingale, women who wished to become nurses simply learned by doing. The heroine of Elizabeth Gaskell's *Ruth* (1853) exemplifies this practice. The revelation that Ruth is a "fallen woman" (the fact that her child was born out of wedlock has come to light) leads to the loss of her position as governess and inability to obtain any other kind of "respectable" work. When Wynne (the parish doctor) asks her if she would go out as a "sick nurse" because he thinks he could find her employment, she readily agrees. But when her friend Jemima exclaims that she doesn't think the gentle Ruth is "fitted" for it, Ruth says she thinks she is fitted, simply because she likes being about sick and helpless people, she feels sorry for them, and she thinks she has "the gift of a very delicate touch" and would try to be "very watchful and patient." Jemima thinks Ruth is too good for this job because she's well educated, but Ruth says that her knowledge of Latin, for instance, would come in handy because she'll be able to read the prescriptions. Jemima replies that of course the doctors would rather she did not read the prescriptions, meaning that doctors wouldn't want a nurse who knew as much as they did.[54]

The novelist's account demonstrates both the low esteem in which nurses were held at the time Nightingale began her career and the absence of any formal training programs for nurses. Even the Anglican sisterhoods which began in the 1840s and Elizabeth Fry's Institute of Nursing in London founded in 1840 were based on the assumption that the chief qualifications for nursing were having a good "character," that is, reputation, especially sobriety (nurses and midwives, like Charles Dickens's Sairey Gamp, were stereotyped as being fond of the bottle), being a moral, even overtly religious woman, and being willing to work hard and obey the doctor's orders.

Nightingale intended to reform this traditional training in which nurse trainees picked up skills on the ward or in the sickroom and to institute instead a structured program of nursing education. But diaries of student nurses suggest that their instruction was catch-as-catch-can, like that of medical students in the early decades of the century. Rebecca Strong, a student at the Nightingale school in 1867 recalled:

> Very little was expected from us, as progress was slow in regard to organized teaching. Kindness, watchfulness, cleanliness, and guarding against bedsores were well ingrained. A few stray lectures were given, one I remember especially, I think it was on the Chemistry of Life, or some such title. . . . There was a dummy on which to practice bandaging, and some lessons were given, also a skeleton, and some ancient medical books, one, fortunately, on Anatomy for those who attempted self-education.[55]

Nightingale actually disapproved of student nurses receiving medical education: their job was to control the hospital (or sickroom) environment and to assist doctors, not to substitute for them. She feared that if nurses were to be taught the new scientific knowledge, such as ideas about bacteria, they might simply be distracted from their primary mission, which was that of providing a sanitary environment.

Nevertheless, some medical teaching was integrated into the training at St. Thomas's: some lectures were given by doctors, some by matrons (head nurses), and in time the curriculum was better planned. Throughout her career, however, Nightingale wanted women, whether nurses or midwives, to remain distinct from the medical profession. The problem became especially acute in relation to training in midwifery, when she wrote, "Would we could induce the women doctors to take up midwifery and nursing while they are moving heaven and earth to go in for ordinary men's examinations."[56] What was meant by "ordinary men's examinations" here was examinations for qualification as medical practitioners, which at this time (1865) were still separately taken for licensing as apothecary, surgeon, or physician, although more and more were qualifying as both apothecary and surgeon, and/or were graduating with an MB or MD. But the 1858 Medical Registration Act still did not require training in midwifery in order to register as a medical practitioner of any kind. (Qualification in midwifery was not required until the 1886 Medical Act Amendment Act.) Nightingale's comment indicates she had a separate vision for men and women in medicine: men were to practice medicine, to take the lead in medical treatment, while women were to serve in the traditionally feminine roles of nurse and midwife, caring, nurturing, nursing, and especially caring for women in the exclusively female function of childbirth.

Nightingale wished not only to exclude women from medicine but also to exclude men from nursing. This is especially ironic in that her initial rise to fame in nursing occurred in the military context of the Crimean War, where until the arrival of Nightingale and her faction of women nurses, the only nursing care available to the sick and wounded men was that of men nurses and orderlies. These men nurses continued to work alongside the women nurses, but Nightingale's writings always assumed that nurses were female. Yet an 1874 article in *Fraser's Magazine* noted, "In hospitals the first peculiarity to be noticed is, that women are employed to nurse both sexes; whereas in private families men nurses are frequently, if not generally, in attendance on men." Arlene Young comments that "the ultimate casualty of the new system of nursing was the male nurse," a group that lacked "class status or cultural cachet."[57]

St. Thomas's nursing school was also structured by class, and from the beginning this made for uneasy relationships among women in the school. Middle- or upper-class women entered as "lady probationers" and were expected to go on to become matrons. Working-class women were simply probationers and were not expected to go on to leadership positions. The upper-class women who became matrons sometimes appeared threatening even to the medical practitioners, many of whom, especially surgeons, came from lower-class backgrounds. Practitioners also saw matrons as a threat to their authority. The issue of just who should be in charge of controlling nursing schedules and rotations, the matron or the medical men, caused a hot conflict at Guy's Hospital that went on through 1879 and 1880.[58]

By the end of the Victorian era, however, Nightingale-style nurses had become an accepted segment of hospital staffing. Nurse education had gradually encompassed more medical and scientific knowledge, as well as more highly skilled nursing practices, and at the same time medical staffs began to recognize how crucial nurses were to the functioning of the hospital. Nevertheless, it took another war to finally bring nurses official recognition as a profession. The British Nurses Association had been founded in 1888 with the specific goal of achieving legal status for the profession, but it was not until after World War I that the Nurses Registration Act was passed. Historians debate whether this was due to the more glamorous image of the nurse in military service and a sense of national gratitude, as happened with Florence Nightingale and the raising of the Nightingale Fund after the Crimean War, or was merely the eventual outcome of the prolonged campaign for nurse registration. Hospitals resisted the passage of this act, fearing that it would lead to longer, more expensive nurses' training, and that this in turn would further intensify an already existing nursing shortage. And some general practitioners also continued to see nurses as competitors, and the registered nurse as a possibly even stronger competitor in the medical marketplace.

The Nurses Registration Act passed in 1919 set up a General Nursing Council (GNC) to supervise the registration process and establish standards for nursing. However, historians argue that the act was itself "a piece of political compromise" that served the needs of hospitals and doctors by leaving issues of pay, conditions, and the content of nurse training in their hands.[59] Nurses only had to have one year of formal training, or three years of practice, and be willing to pay a guinea, in order to be registered. The GNC could set up a model training syllabus, but nursing schools did not have to comply with it. The Ministry of Health could overturn the GNC rulings. Anne Witz states:

> The passage of the Nurses Registration Act in 1919 did not represent a victory for pro-registrationist nurses. The nursing profession had not come to power. Instead nurses were henceforth to be tightly constrained within a state-profession relation within which they were the weaker partner, as well as within the employment relation between hospitals and nurses and the inter-professional relation between doctors and nurses.[60]

VICTORIAN WOMEN AS GENERAL PRACTITIONERS

> Again, "the woman question" in relation to the practice of physic and
> surgery, is forced upon us by the wise decision of the British Medical
> Association to exclude female practitioners; and, by a curious coinci-
> dence, we are, at the same moment, invited by an able article in the
> last number of the *Spectator*, to consider the peculiar physical state
> and mental susceptibilities of "Invalids." The two topics, thrown to-
> gether, not inopportunely, suggest the comparison, or contrast, as it
> will be found, of woman as doctor and woman as nurse. In the one
> character she is as awkward, unfit, and untrustworthy, as she is at
> home, capable, and thoroughly worthy of confidence in the other.[61]

This 1878 editorial in the *Lancet* is comparatively gentlemanly in its
handling of "lady doctors." In 1871, the "boys of Philadelphia," medical
students at the Pennsylvania Hospital in the United States, had greeted the
first women allowed into its clinics with "insolent and offensive language . . .
missiles of paper, tin foil, tobacco-quids, etc. . . . while some of these men
defiled the dresses of the ladies near them with tobacco juice."[62] When Sophia
Jex-Blake and her fellow female students tried to enter classes at the University of Edinburgh, the gates of the medical school were slammed in their faces
by "rowdies," young men who were smoking, passing about bottles of
whisky, and abusing the women in "the foulest possible language."[63] After a
sympathetic medical student wrenched open the gate and the women had
gained entrance to the anatomical classroom, a sheep was pushed into the
classroom by the rioters outside. On the way out of the classroom, mud was
hurled at them.

Thomas Neville Bonner comments that "the path to a medical degree
for a woman, strewn with obstacles as it was in 1871, was incomparably
smoother than it had been twenty years before."[64] Yet at the time of
the 1878 editorial in the *Lancet*, women not only were excluded from
the British Medical Association but were not admitted to any British
hospitals except their own, and they were kept out of all medical schools
except those established exclusively for women. In 1881, they were not
allowed to participate in the International Medical Congress held in London, and by 1882, only twenty six women, almost all with degrees
acquired outside of Britain, had been able to gain recognition as registered practitioners.

The first woman to be accepted onto the medical register in Britain was
Elizabeth Blackwell, who had gained her degree in 1849 from a little back-
woods medical school in Geneva, New York. She graduated first in a class of
150 students, receiving her MD in an event that was publicized all over Britain as well as the United States Realizing that she needed clinical experience, she travelled to Paris and enrolled at La Maternité, then the leading

school for midwives in Paris (no medical school in Paris would admit her). While syringing the eye of an infant with purulent ophthalmia (see chapter 7), a drop of discharge got into her own eye. She contracted the disease herself and wound up becoming blind in one eye and with impaired vision in the other. Surgery was, of course, now barred to her. She returned to New York and opened a dispensary for poor women and children in 1853.

But in 1858 she visited London again and here was able to register as an MD because of a loophole in the Medical Registration Act that hadn't been foreseen. The act, which registered all qualified practitioners annually, but without specifying whether they were qualified as physicians, surgeons, or apothecaries, contained a clause allowing doctors with foreign degrees practicing in England before 1858 to register. Blackwell was the only woman to register. She then returned to New York (though born in Bristol, England, she had emigrated to the United States with her family at the age of eleven), where she continued to develop the New York Infirmary for Women, a hospital run by medical women for women. She did not come back to England until 1869.[65]

Opposition to women entering the medical profession was intense, fueled everywhere by Victorian gender ideology. Ladies were simply not supposed to have anything to do with bodies, in particular. When Elizabeth Garrett, older sister of Millicent Garrett Fawcett (who was to marry the blind Henry Fawcett in two years and become a feminist campaigner [see chapter 7]), told her father that she intended to become a physician, his response was that "the whole idea was so disgusting." Elizabeth asked him why it was all right for ladies to be nurses in the Crimea but not for them to train to be doctors. In time he came around to the position that he would prefer to have a woman doctor treat his wife and daughters if he could be absolutely sure that she was fully qualified.[66] Garrett attempted to enroll as a student at several London teaching hospitals and also to matriculate at the universities of Edinburgh, St. Andrews, and London, but was rejected everywhere. However, she eventually managed to gain qualification by threatening legal action against the Society of Apothecaries if they refused to allow her to sit the examination even after she had studied privately with teachers from recognized medical schools and served an apprenticeship under a licensed apothecary. The society didn't have an actual rule against it, so they had to allow her to take the exam, and when she passed, they had to award her the License of the Society of Apothecaries, or LSA. The Society of Apothecaries accordingly made a new rule that only those who had studied in a recognized medical school could be a candidate for the examination. But Garrett was now entered on the medical register, the first woman qualified in Britain to do so. She then proceeded to the University of Paris, where she obtained an MD in 1870. In 1873 she was admitted to the British Medical Association, but later the BMA voted against the admission of further women. Garrett is undoubtedly the unnamed subject of the 1878 *Lancet* editorial, cited above, which applauds the BMA for voting to exclude female practitioners from its ranks. However, Garrett stubbornly remained the only woman member for the next nineteen years. (Her friend and assistant physician at the New Hospital for Women, Frances Hoggan, was ejected from the BMA on the grounds that she had not been registered when elected, as she had a foreign degree from Zurich University.) She had set up a practice in London, and in 1866 had established the St. Mary's Dispensary for Women and Children in the Marylebone district of London. In 1871 she had opened ten beds above the dispensary as the New Hospital for Women. This was the first hospital in Britain to have only women appointed to its medical staff. In the same year she married James George Skelton Anderson, who had chaired her successful election campaign to the London School Board.

Meanwhile, Sophia Jex-Blake had begun her campaign to become a physician. Jex-Blake had originally planned a career in teaching, although she knew she had no need to support herself, as she came from a well-off, upper-class family. She studied at Queen's College in Harley Street, London, where she demonstrated such unusual proficiency in mathematics that she became a college tutor in the subject. She worked with Elizabeth Garrett in 1862, helping her prepare her application to the University of Edinburgh. Following that, she travelled to Europe and to the United States. In Boston she stayed at the New England Hospital for Women while working there as clerk and nursing assistant. This experience led to her decision to become a physician rather than a teacher. She also now heard that Garrett had passed the Society of Apothecaries examination and become the second woman to be registered on the British medical register. But the society had now come up with a new rule to prevent this happening again: in the future, a woman would be unable to attend lecture courses that were made compulsory for examination candidates.[67]

In 1869, Jex-Blake began her campaign to be admitted to the University of Edinburgh medical school. The university went through all sorts of shameful shenanigans to avoid the threatening prospect of a female medical student. At first they told her she couldn't attend the men's classes, and it would be impracticable for the university to hold classes for just one woman. Jex-Blake accordingly rounded up four other women, and they all took the matriculation examination and passed. The lecturers charged them high fees because of the small size of their classes, but Jex-Blake was able to offer financial help to the other women. At the end of the first term, all of them passed their examinations, four with distinction, but opposition merely increased. Their numbers also increased, as two more women joined the group, now dubbed the "Edinburgh Seven."

But when the women applied to begin their clinical training at the Edinburgh Royal Infirmary in 1871, their application was simply refused for that year. Joseph Lister, who had only taken the chair in clinical surgery in 1869, was one of their chief opponents. Although some professors opposed the notion of female students because they feared the traditional bawdy medical jokes in the lecture hall would embarrass them, Lister was so devout and serious a Quaker that rude jokes were not an issue in his classroom. However, he declared that he "could not bear the indecency of discussing with women the secrets of the 'fleshly tabernacle.'"[68] In 1878, he was one of those who pressed the BMA to expel its two female members at the time, Elizabeth Garrett Anderson and Frances Hoggan. Although it managed to find a reason for expelling Hoggan, the organization was unable to come up with a rationale to get rid of Anderson.

Although Lister apparently had no objection to allowing women patients to listen to his lectures (see chapter 1), he would not allow women medical students to attend his lectures in clinical surgery, and they were not permitted to view major operations in the infirmary. In 1872, the university court decided that degrees could not be granted to women medical students. Jex-Blake appealed the decision, but ultimately a panel of twelve judges decided in 1873 that the university had never been empowered to accept women students. Even then, Jex-Blake and her group did not quite give up. Despite the fact that they were, in effect, expelled, they stayed in Edinburgh for another year, gaining experience in the infirmary wards. Jex-Blake then moved to London, where she raised funds for the London School of Medicine for Women (LSMW). She pressed Elizabeth Garrett Anderson to join forces with the LSMW, even though the two were not particularly good friends, having very different personalities. In 1876, Russell Gurney's Enabling Bill made it possible for any of the nineteen different licensing bodies to accept women candidates for examination, but did not require them to do so. Gurney correctly predicted that some of the licensing bodies would accept women if they were not compelled to do so. Jex-Blake, among others, sat the examination held by the King and Queen's College of Physicians in Ireland and was qualified by them. (She had by then obtained the MD at Bern, Switzerland.) During the same year of 1877, she successfully completed negotiations with the London Free Hospital allowing students from the LSMW to gain clinical experience there. British women at last had access to both comprehensive medical training and to registration.

None of the women who managed to become physicians in Britain in the latter half of the nineteenth century were "great women" who succeeded in their ambition by individual heroic effort alone. Their campaign was part of a wider struggle for women's higher education and for the vote. They were supported by such prominent feminists as Emily Davies and Frances Power Cobbe. Cobbe in particular became a close friend of Elizabeth Garrett Anderson, and Frances Hoggan was her personal physician. The thirty-nine women who had studied medicine at Edinburgh between 1869 and 1873 formed a lifelong network for professional support. Just as to have been one of "Lister's men" became a proud boast, women associated themselves with Jex-Blake.[69]

Of course, there were divisions. Garrett Anderson had always felt that women who wanted to be physicians should be discreet and womanly in their approach. "It is a great thing for anyone in my position to be alive to the necessity for exercising tact and showing womanliness of manner and externals," she wrote in a letter to her father.[70] Arthur Munby commented in December 1870 that he had seen Garrett looking "youthful and charming—one of the belles of the room: 'tis amusing, to see this learned and distinguished M.D. moving about in rose-coloured silk and pointlace, with flowers in her hair, and receiving due homage, in both capacities, from the men."[71] Jex-Blake, on the other hand, was known for her "naturally hasty temper and imperious disposition."[72] When, in 1877, members of the council for the London School of Medicine for Women failed to appoint her as honorary secretary of the school because they thought her "forthright, militant approach" was no longer appropriate, she was so hurt that she returned to Edinburgh and set up her practice there.[73] Frances Hoggan resigned from her position as assistant physician at the New Hospital for Women in 1878 because she disagreed with Garrett Anderson's willingness to undertake the high-risk surgery of ovariotomy. She and her husband, who was also a physician and who had an Edinburgh MB, had both been very critical of Jex-Blake's confrontational tactics at Edinburgh.

But the campaign by British women to gain entry to the medical profession, which, by the end of the nineteenth century, had become the elite profession of modern medicine, was predicated both on the needs and the strengths of other women. Because all Victorian women had been made into a special class of patients, identified as having weaknesses peculiar to their sex and modesty peculiar to their gender, a few Victorian women were able to make it into the highest class of medicine, the doctor. Not until what has been called second-wave feminism arose in the late twentieth century, however, did women begin to be able to enter the profession in numbers something like those proportionate to men.

GLOSSARY

Accoucheur: midwife or obstetrician. Term used especially for men who specialized in midwifery.

Alienist: specialist in mental disorders.

Animal magnetism: power to attract or fascinate others in a sensual or hypnotic way.

Antiseptic technique: disease-killing technique, such as the use of carbolic acid and other antiseptic agents believed to kill bacteria, instituted by Joseph Lister.

Apothecary: In early decades of nineteenth century, an apothecary was legally prohibited from dispensing medical advice, and was restricted to compounding drugs prescribed by physicians. However, most apothecaries did dispense medical advice, prescribed as well as compounded drugs, and generally acted as medical practitioners.

Aseptic technique: prevention of introduction of disease-causing bacteria by techniques such as sterilization of instruments.

ASL: American Sign Language.

Aurist: specialist in diseases of the ear.

Blister: poultice or piece of gauze to which a substance capable of raising a blister on the skin has been applied.

BSL: British Sign Language.

Chancroid: a localized genital infection.

Clap: common slang term for gonorrhea.

Couching: Earliest surgical procedure for treatment of cataracts: a needle or knife inserted in the eye to push the clouded lens down and out of the line of vision in the eye.

Egyptian ophthalmia: infectious disease of the eye that could cause blindness and was contracted by military troops during the Napoleonic wars in Egypt.

Endemic: infectious disease (or other property) that is always present in a particular region, though sometimes reaching a higher rate of infection than at other times.

Epidemic: outbreak of infectious disease within a certain area, such as a nation, region, or city.

Facies ovariana: term invented for a peculiar facial appearance thought to accompany the presence of an ovarian cyst.

Fomite: an inanimate object, such as clothing, bed linens, or dust, that may carry contagion from dried pustules, as in the transmission of smallpox.

Forensic medicine: investigative and legal medicine.

Foul: common slang term for syphilis.

Friendly societies: early nineteenth-century form of medical insurance, in which groups of workers joined together to pay common fees for provision of medical care.

GMC: General Medical Council. Created by the Medical Act of 1858 to register all qualified practitioners annually.

Gonorrhea: sexually transmitted disease characterized by discharge from urethra or vagina. Could also be transmitted to newborns, causing opthalmia neonatorum and blindness.

GP: General practitioner. Used by medical practitioners from the late eighteenth century on to refer to men who were educated in both medicine and surgery, but with no required national standards or qualifications.

GPI: general motor paralysis of the insane. A combination of partial but generalized paralysis and insanity that may appear as part of the last, or tertiary, stage of syphilis.

GRO: General Register Office, instituted in 1837. Among other things, it required registration of cause of death.

Guaiacum: type of wood believed to cure syphilis.

Homeopathy: medicine based on cure of illnesses by treatment with like medicine, or tiny doses of drugs believed to cause symptoms like those of the disease being treated.

Hospital fever: infectious disease acquired in a hospital.

Hospital gangrene: infectious disease of wounds acquired in a hospital.

Hutchinson's triad: three symptoms that indicate presence of congenital syphilis: interstitial keratitis (inflammation of the cornea), notched incisor teeth, and deafness.

Hydropathy: various forms of water cures involving drinking and bathing in water believed to have special therapeutic powers.

Indoor position: employment for an apprentice or assistant that provided room and board.

Inoculation: introduction of infectious matter, such as that from smallpox pustules, into the body with intent to produce a mild case of the disease and confer immunity to it thereafter.

Laudanum: mixture of opium and alcohol that was one of the most commonly used medicines of the Victorian era.

Lock hospital: hospital for treatment of venereal diseases.

LSA: license of the Society of Apothecaries.

LSF: *Langes de Signes Française,* or French Sign Language.

Lymph, cowpox: matter from cowpox pustules taken from cows or calves and used to vaccinate against smallpox.

Magdalene home: penitentiary for fallen women, or prostitutes.

MB: bachelor of medicine.

MD: doctor of medicine.

Mercury: most commonly used drug for treatment of syphilis until the twentieth century.

Mesmerism: hypnotism as practiced by F. A. Mesmer (1734–1815) in connection with his theory of animal magnetism.

Midwifery: art and science of assisting childbirth.

MRCS: Member of the Royal College of Surgeons.

Multilocular: multiple fluid-filled sacs; most often used in describing ovarian cysts.

Narcotism: term used for anesthesia in the nineteenth century.

Oöphorectomy: medical term for removal of ovaries.

Opthalmia neonatorum: term for infection of the eye in the newborn, most often caused by gonorrhea but also by trachoma and syphilis.

Opthalmology: specialty in diseases of the eye.

Opthalmoscope: instrument used to see the interior of the eye.

Otology: specialty in diseases of the ear.

Ovarian cyst: tumor of the ovaries that could be benign or malignant.

Ovariotomy: removal of one or both ovaries.

Pandemic: outbreak of infectious disease that spreads across many countries or even around the world.

Physician: in the early decades of the 19th century, most often the holder of an MD, in Britain usually a graduate of Oxford or Cambridge who was educated in classical Greek medical theory. In later decades, holders of an MB, or bachelor of medicine, might claim status as physician, and by the late nineteenth century, this was the most usual qualification for a doctor.

Pox: common slang term for syphilis.

Puerperal fever: infectious disease acquired during or after childbirth or miscarriage.

RCP: Royal College of Physicians.

RCS: Royal College of Surgeons.

Salpingo-oöphorectomy: medical term for removal of Fallopian tubes and ovaries.

Speculum: instrument used for examination of the vagina and cervix.

Sphygmomanometer: instrument used to measure blood pressure. Invented in 1896 by Scipione Riva-Rocci.

Stethoscope: instrument used to listen to sounds within the body. Invented by Réné Laënnec in 1819.

Surgeon: During early decades of the nineteenth century, this term could refer to anyone who had had an apprenticeship with a surgeon and therefore learned techniques of basic surgery such as tooth-pulling, setting fractures, and dealing with external injuries. In later decades, surgeon increasingly referred to a man (women were excluded from this practice) who had passed qualifying exams set by the Royal College of Surgeons; he could append the letters FRCS, Fellow of the Royal College of Surgeons, to his name. From the 1830s onward, surgeon commonly referred to a medical man who had some qualifications in medicine as well as surgery and who was actually a general practitioner, or GP.

Surgeon-apothecary: medical practitioner with dual qualifications in medicine and surgery; a general practitioner, or GP.

Tapping: drawing off fluid from ovarian cyst, as opposed to removing the cyst.

Tertiary syphilis: third stage of syphilis that often appears many years after earlier stages.

Tracheotomy: surgical opening in the trachea or windpipe.

Trachoma: venereal disease caused by *Chlamydia trachomatis* that can be spread by sexual or nonsexual transmission and that can cause ophthalmia neonatorum, or infection of the eye in newborns.

Treponema pallidum: bacterium that causes syphilis.

Unwell: euphemism for menstruation.

Vaccination: introduction of lymph from a cow infected with cowpox, in order to confer immunity to smallpox.

Variola major: usual form of smallpox, which is very severe.

Variola minor: much milder form of smallpox.

Variolation: inoculation with infection matter from smallpox (variola).

Venereologist: practitioner who treats venereal (sexually transmitted) diseases.

Vibrio cholerae: bacterium that causes cholera.

Wassermann blood test: blood test to detect syphilis.

WHO: World Health Organization.

Workhouses: facilities for the working poor, instituted under the Poor Law of Elizabethan times, but made into more disciplinary institutions that were more like prisons under the New Poor Law of 1834 in order to discourage pauperism.

NOTES

INTRODUCTION

1. Duffin, *History of Medicine*, 241.
2. Ibid., 351–52.
3. Jordanova, "Social Construction of Medical Knowledge," 361, 368.
4. Ibid., 363–66.

CHAPTER 1: PRACTITIONERS AND PATIENTS IN VICTORIAN ENGLAND

1. Eliot, *Middlemarch*, 136.
2. Ibid.
3. Ibid., 116.
4. Ibid., 415.
5. Hardy, *Health and Medicine in Britain since 1860*, 5–6.
6. Ellis, *Case Books of Dr. John Snow*, 3.
7. Loudon, *Medical Care and the General Practitioner*, 154.
8. Vinten-Johansen et al., *Cholera, Chloroform, and the Science of Medicine*, 21–22.
9. Ibid., 43.
10. Ibid., 61.
11. Ibid., 64.
12. "John Snow Archive and Research Companion," http://johnsnow.matrix.msu.edu/.
13. Peterson, *The Medical Profession in Mid-Victorian London*, 15.
14. Dawson and Royal, eds., *An Oxfordshire Market Gardener*, 60.
15. Hardy, *Health and Medicine in Britain since 1860*, 7.

16. Haley, *Healthy Body and Victorian Culture*, 12–13.

17. Martineau, *Life in the Sick-Room*, 14.

18. Martineau, *Letters on Mesmerism*, 243–45.

19. Hardy, *Health and Medicine in Britain since 1860*, 2–3.

20. Wohl, *Endangered Lives*, 11.

21. Jewson, "The Disappearance of the Sick-Man from Medical Cosmology, 1770–1870," 225–44.

22. Ackerknecht, *A Short History of Medicine*, 187.

23. Digby, *Making a Medical Living*, 77–78.

24. Cathell, *The Physician Himself*, Preface.

25. Digby, *Making a Medical Living*, 244.

26. Ibid.

27. Ibid.

28. Ibid., 130.

29. Cobbe, "The Medical Profession and Its Morality," 297.

30. Mitchell, *Frances Power Cobbe*, 280.

31. Hardy, *Health and Medicine in Britain since 1860*, 80.

32. Goldman, *Lister Ward*, 80.

33. Ibid., 50.

34. Ibid., 58–59.

35. Ibid., 59, 84.

36. Jewson, "The Disappearance of the Sick-Man from Medical Cosmology, 1770–1870," 235.

37. Brunton, ed., *Health, Disease and Society in Europe, 1800–1930*, 28–30.

38. Ibid., 30–31.

39. Ibid., 25.

40. Ibid., 32–33.

41. Ibid., 26.

42. Goldman, *Lister Ward*, 55.

43. Brunton, ed., *Health, Disease and Society in Europe, 1800–1930*, 25.

44. Ibid., 39.

CHAPTER 2: CHOLERA

1. Kingsley, *Two Years Ago*, 85.

2. As quoted in Morris, *Cholera 1832*, 14.

3. Wohl, *Endangered Lives*, 372n5.

4. Gairdner, as quoted in Haley, *Healthy Body*, 6.

5. Trevelyan, *Life and Letters of Lord Macaulay*, 162.

6. Briggs, "Cholera and Society in the Nineteenth Century," *Collected Essays*, 153.

7. Snow, *On the Mode of Communication of Cholera*, 2nd ed., 1855.

8. As quoted in Arnold, *Colonizing the Body*, 160–61.

9. Durey, *Return of the Plague*, 7.

10. Evans, "Cholera in Nineteenth-Century Europe," 160.

11. Arnold, *Colonizing the Body*, 168.

12. Ibid., 169.

13. Hays, *Epidemics and Pandemics*, 270.

14. Morris, *Cholera 1832*, 23.

15. Ibid., 39–40.

16. Bourdelais, *Epidemics Laid Low*, 58.

17. Morris, *Cholera 1832*, 45.

18. Durey, *Return of the Plague*, 171, 176–78.

19. Morris, *Cholera 1832*, 15.

20. Durey, *Return of the Plague*, 27–29.

21. Briggs, *Collected Essays*, 154.

22. Wohl, *Endangered Lives*, 118.

23. Mort, *Dangerous Sexualities*, 13–61.

24. Lewis, ed., *Letters of Elizabeth Barrett Browning to Her Sister Arabella*, August 31 [1849], 1:276; August 17 [1849], 1:271.

25. Wohl, *Endangered Lives*, 118.

26. Bynum, *Science and the Practice of Medicine*, 78, 83.

27. *Times*, "Asiatic Cholera in the Pool of London," October 16, 1848, 7.

28. *Times*, July 23, 1849, 7; June 26, 1849, 8; July 14, 1849, 8; July 17, 1849, 8.

29. Vinten-Johansen et al., *Cholera, Chloroform, and the Science of Medicine*, 187.

30. Ibid.

31. Snow's publications on chloroform are available on "The John Snow Archive and Research Companion," http://johnsnow.matrix.msu.edu/.

32. Vinten-Johansen et al., *Cholera, Chloroform, and the Science of Medicine*, 242.

33. Bynum, *Science and the Practice of Medicine*, 79.

34. *Times*, September 26, 1849, 4.

35. Snow, *On the Mode of Communication of Cholera*, 38–55.

36. Vinten-Johansen et al., *Cholera, Chloroform, and the Science of Medicine*, 288.

37. Snow, *On the Mode of Communication of Cholera*, 38–55.

38. Ibid.

39. Whitehead, "The Broad Street Pump," 116.

40. Ibid.

41. Ibid.

42. Ibid., 113.

43. Hempel, *The Strange Case of the Broad Street Pump*, 177.

44. Whitehead, "Broad Street Pump," 113.

45. Ibid., 115.

46. Ibid., 114.

47. Ibid., 120.

48. Ibid., 121.

49. Ibid., 121–22.

50. Snow, *On the Mode of Communication of Cholera*, 1–38.

51. Ibid.

52. Ibid.

53. Ibid.

54. Vinten-Johansen et al., *Cholera, Chloroform, and the Science of Medicine*, 39.

55. Snow, *On the Mode of Communication of Cholera*, 55–98.

56. Bynum, *Science and the Practice of Medicine*, 80–81.

57. Vinten-Johansen et al., *Cholera, Chloroform, and the Science of Medicine*, 303; 316n66.

58. Nightingale, *Notes on Nursing*, 18.

59. Ibid., 13.

60. Hays, *Epidemics and Pandemics*, 267.

61. Ibid., 270.

62. Briggs, *Collected Essays*, 165–66.

63. World Health Organization Media Centre. "Cholera." http://www.who.int/mediacentre/factsheets/fs107/en/.

CHAPTER 3: TUBERCULOSIS

1. Letter to William Smith Williams, December 20, 1848, in Barker, *The Brontës*, 577.

2. Ibid., 137, 139.

3. Jones, "Captain of All These Men of Death," 26n65.

4. McKeown, *Modern Rise of Population*, 128–42.

5. Szreter, "The Importance of Social Intervention in Britain's Mortality Decline c. 1850–1914"; Hardy, *The Epidemic Streets*, 211–12; Jones, "Captain of All These Men of Death," 3–7.

6. Jones, "Captain of All These Men of Death," 1–7.

7. Dubos and Dubos, *The White Plague*, 5.

8. Wootton, *Bad Medicine*, 30–31.

9. Kiple, "The History of Disease," 37.

10. Dubos and Dubos, *The White Plague*, 9.

11. In 1956 it was recognized that although 95 percent of adult scrofulous infections are caused by the tuberculosis bacillus, most scrofulous infections in children are caused by a nontuberculous bacterium. See McClay, "Scrofula," section 2.

12. Porter, "Consumption: Disease of the Consumer Society?" 67.

13. Smith, *Retreat of Tuberculosis*, 41.

14. Dubos and Dubos, *The White Plague*, 35.

15. Smith, *Retreat of Tuberculosis*, 4.

16. Porter, "Consumption," 65–68.

17. Dubos and Dubos, *The White Plague*, 73, 75.

18. As quoted in Dubos and Dubos, *The White Plague*, 94.

19. Jones, "Captain of All These Men of Death," 1–3.

20. Dubos and Dubos, *The White Plague*, 8–9.

21. Hays, *Epidemics and Pandemics*, 201.

22. Duffin, *To See with a Clearer Eye*, 155–56.

23. Smith, *Retreat of Tuberculosis*, 3.

24. Barker, *The Brontës*, 168–69.

25. Ibid., 700, 731, 820.

26. Dubos and Dubos state that Patrick Brontë's death was most likely due to tuberculosis and that he may have been the original source of infection that destroyed his entire family (*The White Plague*, 35, 38–39).

27. Ibid., 84.

28. Duffin, *To See with a Clearer Eye*, 155.

29. Bynum, *Science and the Practice of Medicine*, 35–37.

30. Dubos and Dubos, *The White Plague*, 79–80.

31. Barnes, *Making of a Social Disease*, 29.

32. Dowling, *Holmes in Paris*, xiv.

33. Duffin, *History of Medicine*, 77.

34. *Lancet* 90, issue 2302 (October 12, 1867), 452.

35. Ackerknecht, *Short History of Medicine*, 177.

36. Duffin, *History of Medicine*, 81.

37. Smith, *Retreat of Tuberculosis*, 48.

38. Warboys, *Spreading Germs*, 206.

39. Ibid., 209.

40. Sontag, *Illness as Metaphor*, 3, 12–16.

41. Gates, "When Life Writing Becomes Death Writing," 72.

42. Dubos and Dubos, *The White Plague*, 59, 247n3.

43. Ibid., 11–17.

44. Frawley, *Invalidism and Identity*, 49–50.

45. Gates, ed., *Journal of Emily Shore*, 165–66.

46. Ibid., 264.

47. Yonge, *The Heir of Redclyffe*, 12.

48. Unsal, Erbil, et al., "Limping Child," *Pediatric Rheumatology Online Journal*.

49. Ashton, *G. H. Lewes*, 248.

50. Ibid., 248–50.

51. Vinten-Johansen et al., *Cholera, Chloroform, and the Science of Medicine*, 389.

52. Jones, "Captain of All These Men of Death," 2, 5. In Ireland, however, mortality did not begin to decline until 1904.

53. As quoted in Hardy, *Epidemic Streets*, 255.

54. Ibid., 257.

55. As quoted in Rosenkrantz, "Introductory Essay," xxii.

56. Ibid., xxvi.

57. Hays, *Epidemics and Pandemics*, 465–71.

CHAPTER 4: SYPHILIS

1. Warren, *Passages from the Diary of a Late Physician*, 98.

2. Ibid., 87.

3. Walkowitz, *Prostitution*, 49–50.

4. Ibid., 270n9.

5. Rossetti, "Jenny," lines 163–66.

6. See "Disease Watch: Syphilis."

7. Spongberg, *Feminizing Venereal Disease*, 1.

8. As quoted in Quétel, *History of Syphilis*, 10.

9. Ackerknecht, *Short History of Medicine*, 100.

10. Hays, *Epidemics and Pandemics*, 75–76; McAllister, "Stories of the Origin of Syphilis in Eighteenth-Century England," 24.

11. Hays, *Epidemics and Pandemics*, 70.

12. Siena, "The 'Foul Disease' and Privacy," 217.

13. Ibid., 220.

14. Ibid., 222.

15. Siena, *Venereal Disease, Hospitals, and the Urban Poor*, 62–77.

16. Merians, "The London Lock Hospital and the Lock Asylum for Women," 132–35.

17. Duffin, *History of Medicine*, 317.

18. Merians, "The London Lock Hospital and Lock Asylum for Women," 137–43.

19. Rossetti, "Jenny," lines 253–66.

20. McAllister, "Stories of the Origin of Syphilis in Eighteenth-Century England," 37.

21. Ibid., 37.

22. Acton, *Functions and Disorders of the Reproductive Organs*, 209.

23. Quétel, *History of Syphilis*, 111.

24. Ibid., 82–83; Dracobly, "Theoretical Change and Therapeutic Innovation," 538–39.

25. Quétel, *History of Syphilis*, 111.

26. As quoted in Dowling, *Oliver Wendell Holmes in Paris*, 65.

27. Walkowitz, *Prostitution*, 51; Duffin, *History of Medicine*, 100.

28. De Méric, "Hereditary Syphilis," *Lancet* (October 23, 1858), 435; Bayfield, "Hereditary Syphilis," *Lancet* (October 30, 1853), 453.

29. Ricord, as quoted in Ernst Finger, *Gonorrhea: Being a Translation of the Sexual Organs and Its Complications* (New York, 1924), 11, as cited in Walkowitz, *Prostitution*, 272n37.

30. Walkowitz, *Prostitution*, 53.

31. Dracobly, "Theoretical Change and Therapeutic Innovation," 548.

32. Walkowitz, *Prostitution*, 56–57.

33. Ibid., 59.

34. Mahood, *The Magdalenes*, 35.

35. Spongberg, *Feminizing Venereal Disease*, 47.

36. Acton, *Prostitution*, 3.

37. Ibid., 58; also see all of chapter 6, pp. 52–73.

38. Ibid., 55.

39. Spongberg, *Feminizing Venereal Disease*, 59.

40. Ibid., 63.

41. Ibid., 66–71.

42. Walkowitz, *Prostitution*, 94.

43. Ibid., 93–94.

44. Mitchell, *Frances Power Cobbe*, 194.

45. Webster, "A Castaway," 192–93.

46. Doyle, "The Third Generation," 34.

47. Silverstein and Ruggere, "Dr. Arthur Conan Doyle," 210.

48. Quétel, *History of Syphilis*, 134–35, 160–70.

49. Ibid., 167.

50. Spongberg, *Feminizing Venereal Disease*, 143–59; Smith, *Victorian Demons*, 98–99; Showalter, *Sexual Anarchy*, 197–200.

51. Stutfield, "Tommyrotics," 836.

52. See Liggins, "Writing against the 'Husband-Fiend,' and Kennedy, 'Syphilis and the Hysterical Female.'"

53. As quoted in Liggins, "Writing against the 'Husband-Fiend,'" 178.

54. Brown, *Advice to Single Women*, 143–44.

55. Davidson and Hall, *Sex, Sin, and Suffering*, 6.

56. Quétel, *History of Syphilis*, 219–33; Brandt, *No Magic Bullet*.

57. U.S. Public Health Service Syphilis Study at Tuskegee.

58. Brandt, *No Magic Bullet*, 5.

CHAPTER 5: SMALLPOX

1. Dickens, *Bleak House*, 504.

2. Ibid., 572.

3. As quoted in Hopkins, *The Greatest Killer*, 38.

4. Ibid.

5. Ibid., 76.

6. Ibid., 4.

7. Hardy, *Epidemic Streets*, 112–13.

8. Hopkins, *The Greatest Killer*, 98.

9. Barquet and Comingo, "Smallpox: The Triumph over the Most Terrible Ministers of Death," 2; Duffin, *History of Medicine*, 153.

10. Quoted in Duffin, *History of Medicine*, 153.

11. Barquet and Comingo, "Smallpox," 3.

12. Miller, *Adoption of Inoculation*, 34–36.

13. Letter from Lady Mary Wortley Montagu to Sarah Chiswell, dated April 1, 1717, as quoted in Hopkins, *The Greatest Killer*, 47–48.

14. Glynn, *Life and Death of Smallpox*, 46.

15. Miller, *Adoption of Inoculation*, 65–68.

16. Hopkins, *The Greatest Killer*, 49.

17. Miller, *Adoption of Inoculation*, 93.

18. Crook, *Defying the Demon*, 21–22.

19. Ibid., 56–66.

20. Shuttleton, *Smallpox and the Literary Imagination, 1660–1820*, xiii.

21. Baxby, "Jenner, Edward (1749–1833)."

22. Ibid.

23. Hopkins, *The Greatest Killer*, 79.

24. Sherman, *The Power of Plagues*, 204.

25. Pead, "Benjamin Jesty: The First Vaccinator Revealed."

26. Hardy, *The Epidemic Streets*, 111.

27. Hopkins, *The Greatest Killer*, 87.

28. Hardy, *The Epidemic Streets*, 116–17.

29. Dickens, *Bleak House*, 493.

30. Hardy, *The Epidemic Streets*, 131–33.

31. Hopkins, *The Greatest Killer*, 85.

32. Arnold, *Colonizing the Body*, 136, 143.

33. Durbach, *Bodily Matters: The Anti-Vaccination Movement in England, 1853–1907*, 50–51.

34. Glynn, *Life and Death of Smallpox*, 227.

35. Crook, *Defying the Demon*, 108–14.

CHAPTER 6: DEAFNESS

1. *Times*, May 10, 1799.

2. *Times*, May 4, 1808.

3. Grant, *Deaf Advance*, 8.

4. Lee, *Beginner's Introduction to Deaf History*, 52.

5. Krentz, ed., *A Mighty Change*, 10.

6. Sacks, *Seeing Voices*, 8, 19, 1.

7. Lee, *Beginner's Introduction to Deaf History*, 235.

8. Advertisement, *Times*, July 1, 1815.

9. Dickens, *Bleak House*, 768.

10. Wright, "Causes and Treatment of Deafness," 413.

11. Krentz, ed., *A Mighty Change*, 23.

12. Wright, "Causes and Treatment of Deafness, No. IV," 566.

13. Power, "Wright, William (1773–1860)."

14. Wright, "Causes and Treatment of Deafness, No. II," 464.

15. Clerc, *Address*, 12.

16. Lane, "Cochlear Implants," 282–83.

17. Hawkins, "Wilde and Toynbee," 129–34.

18. Arnold, *Method of Teaching*, 9.

19. Ibid., 7.

20. Baynton, *Forbidden Signs*, 13.

21. Atkinson, *Memoirs of My Youth*, 92–93.

22. Rée, *I See a Voice*, 196–97.

23. Ibid., 12; Lee, *Beginner's Introduction*, 37.

24. Lee, *Beginner's Introduction*, 41–42.

25. Ibid., 42.

26. Esmail, "Power of Deaf Poetry," 349.

27. As quoted in Esmail, "Power of Deaf Poetry," 353.

28. Krentz, *A Mighty Change*, 21.

29. As quoted in Baynton, "A Silent Exile on This Earth," 132.

30. Grant, *Deaf Advance*, 10.

31. Lee, *Beginner's Introduction*, 42.

32. Ibid.

33. "History of British Sign Language," deafsign.com.

34. Kitto, *Lost Senses: Deafness*, 5.

35. Collins, *Hide and Seek*, 165.

36. Martineau, "Letter to the Deaf," 231.

37. Lane, ed., *Deaf Experience*, 28–48.

38. Ibid., 32.

39. Farr, *Vital Statistics*, 56.

40. *Essays by the Pupils at the College for the Deaf and Dumb, Rugby, Warwickshire.*

41. Frawley, ed., *Life in the Sick-Room*, 13–14.

42. Dickens, *American Notes*, 43.

43. Kitto, *Lost Senses: Blindness*, 41.

44. Kitto, *Lost Senses: Deafness*, 81.

45. Ibid., 96.

46. Pardes, "Remapping Jonah's Voyage," 271.

47. Hamilton, "Kitto, John (1804–1854)."

48. Kitto, *Lost Senses: Deafness*, 124, 122.

49. Ibid., 99.

50. Holmes, *Fictions of Affliction*, 83.

51. Flint, "Disability and Difference," 159.

52. Lane, "Cochlear Implants," 273–81.

53. Dickens, *Bleak House*, 987.

CHAPTER 7: BLINDNESS

1. As quoted in Lawrence, "Lectures," 145.

2. Ibid.

3. Holmes, *Fictions of Affliction*, 26.

4. Dickens, *Great Expectations*, 238–39.

5. Lawrence, *Treatise on the Diseases of the Eye*, 8.

6. Jacyna, "Medicine in Transformation, 1800–1849," 51.

7. Oliphant, *Early Education of the Blind in Britain*, 51.

8. Mayhew, *London Labour and the London Poor*, 4:431.

9. Oliphant, *Early Education of the Blind in Britain*, 10.

10. Dickens, *American Notes*, 97–101.

11. As quoted in Farrell, *Story of Blindness*, 19.

12. Mayhew, *London Labour and the London Poor*, 1:397.

13. Oliphant, *Early Education of the Blind in Britain*, 139.

14. Ibid., 141.

15. Ibid., 133, 157–58.

16. Ibid., 133.

17. Farrell, *Story of Blindness*, 99.

18. As quoted in Warne, "So That the Sense of Touch May Supply the Want of Sight."

19. Ibid.

20. Armitage, *Education and Employment of the Blind*, 5.

21. Oliphant, *Early Education of the Blind in Britain*, 86.

22. Ibid.

23. Farrell, *Story of Blindness*, 35.

24. Oliphant, *Early Education of the Blind in Britain*, 37, 132.

25. Barker, *The Brontës*, 507.

26. Jeffries, *Lectures on the Diseases of the Eye*, 192.

27. Barker, *The Brontës*, 507.

28. Ibid., 519.

29. Blodi, "Cataract Surgery," 166.

30. Ibid., 169.

31. Critchett, "Diseases of the Eye, Lecture XIII," 381–83.

32. Taylor, "Clinical Lectures on Diseases of the Eye, II," 866.

33. Farrell, *Story of Blindness*, 13.

34. Davidson, "Identities Ascertained," 329n131.

35. Peters, "Introduction," viii–ix.

36. Davidson, "Identities Ascertained," 315.

37. Ibid., 314–16.

38. Farrell, *Story of Blindness*, 227.

39. Albert, "The Ophthalmoscope and Retinovitreous Surgery," 188.

40. Ibid.

41. Ibid., 189.

42. Ibid., 191–92.

43. Albert, "Ocular Refraction and the Development of Spectacles," 109, 115–16.

44. Albert, "The Ophthalmoscope and Retinovitreous Surgery," 192.

45. Levy, *Blindness and the Blind*, 373.

46. Ibid.

47. Gitter, "The Blind Daughter," 675–76.

48. Martin, *Elizabeth Gilbert*, 73–74.

49. Brontë, *Jane Eyre*, 451.

50. Kingsley, *Westward Ho!*, 634.

51. Browning, *Aurora Leigh*, IX:961.

52. Goldman, "Henry Fawcett, 1833–1884." *ODNB Online*.

53. Rubinstein, "Victorian Feminists: Henry and Millicent Garrett Fawcett," 73–74.

54. Howarth, "Fawcett, Dame Millicent Garrett (1827–1928)."

55. Peters, "Introduction," xvi.

56. Collins, *Poor Miss Finch*, 417–18.

57. Schor, "Blindness as Metaphor," 77.

58. Collins, *Poor Miss Finch*, 199–200.

CHAPTER 8: VICTORIAN WOMEN AS PATIENTS AND PRACTITIONERS

1. Oliphant, "Condition of Women," 216.

2. Moscucci, *Science of Woman*, 2.

3. As quoted in Moscucci, *Science of Woman*, 1.

4. Nightingale, *Notes on Nursing*, 3.

5. Editorial, *Lancet*, August 17, 1878, 226–27.

6. Ellis, ed., *Case Books of Dr. John Snow*, 113–14.

7. Dally, *Women under the Knife*, 8–19.

8. Moscucci, *Science of Woman*, 138.

9. Roy, "Brown, Isaac Baker, (1811–1873)."

10. Moscucci, *Science of Woman*, 152.

11. Dally, *Women under the Knife*, 88.

12. Burrows, *Commentaries*, 146.

13. As quoted in Dally, *Women under the Knife*, 87.

14. Moscucci, *Science of Woman*, 156–57.

15. As quoted in Moscucci, *Science of Woman*, 93–94.

16. Showalter, *Sexual Anarchy*, 131.

17. Dally, *Women under the Knife*, 95.

18. Roy, "Brown, Isaac Baker, (1811–1873)."

19. Churchill, *Diseases of Women*, 567.

20. Grady, "After a Devastating Birth Injury, Hope."

21. Duffin, *History of Medicine*, 260–61; Dally, *Women under the Knife*, 20–34.

22. Barker-Benfield, *Horrors of the Half-Known Life*, 120.

23. Moscucci, *Science of Woman*, 206.

24. National Cancer Institute, "Menopausal Hormone Replacement Therapy Use and Cancer."

25. Ellis, ed., *Case Books of Dr. John Snow*, 271.

26. Ibid., 471.

27. Loudon, "Childbirth," 213.

28. Miller, "'Temple and Sewer': Childbirth, Prudery, and Victoria Regina," 25.

29. As quoted in Poovey, *Uneven Developments*, 31.

30. Poovey, *Uneven Developments*, 25.

31. Bettany, "Locock, Sir Charles, First Baronet (1799–1875)." *ODNB Online*.

32. Loudon, "Childbirth," 208–9.

33. Ibid., 210.

34. Jordanova, *Sexual Visions*, 60–62.

35. Loudon, "Childbirth," 209.

36. *Placenta Praevia* is a condition in which the placenta lies across the mouth of the uterus, preventing birth of the baby and usually causing profuse bleeding. In this case hemorrhage caused the death of the mother.

37. Hanson, *Cultural History of Pregnancy*, 1–2.

38. Whitbread, ed., *I Know My Own Heart*, 288.

39. Moscucci, *Science of Woman*, 116.

40. Jalland, *Women, Marriage, and Politics, 1860–1914*, 171.

41. Wohl, *Endangered Lives*, 13.

42. Loudon, "Childbirth," 212.

43. As quoted in Loudon, "Childbirth," 213.

44. Loudon, "Childbirth," 214.

45. "Centenary: Chelsea Hospital for Women," *Lancet*, October 16, 1971.

46. Loudon, "Childbirth," 218.

47. Baly, *Florence Nightingale*, 67.

48. As quoted in Baly, *Florence Nightingale*, 65.

49. Baly, *Florence Nightingale*, 23.

50. Baly and Matthew, "Nightingale, Florence (1820–1910)." *ODNB Online*.

51. Ibid.

52. Baly, *Florence Nightingale*, 9.

53. Bynum, "Rise of Science in Medicine, 1850–1913," 161–62; Rhodes, "Women in Medicine," 165.

54. Gaskell, *Ruth*, 388–89.

55. As quoted in Summers, *Angels and Citizens*, 93.

56. As quoted in Baly, *Florence Nightingale*, 75.

57. Young, "'Entirely a Woman's Question?'" 20, 21.

58. Rhodes, "Women in Medicine," 169.

59. Ibid., 176.

60. As quoted in Rhodes, "Women in Medicine," 176.

61. Editorial, *Lancet*, August 17, 1878.

62. Bonner, *To the Ends of the Earth*, 4.

63. Blake, *Charge of the Parasols*, 125–26.

64. Bonner, *To the Ends of the Earth*, 6, 61.

65. Elston, "Blackwell, Elizabeth (1821–1910)." *ODNB Online*.

66. Blake, *Charge of the Parasols*, 57–58.

67. Roberts, "Blake, Sophia Louisa Jex- (1840–1912)."

68. Crowther and Dupree, *Medical Lives*, 152.

69. Ibid., 154.

70. Blake, *Charge of the Parasols*, 63.

71. Mitchell, *Frances Power Cobbe*, 205.

72. Roberts, "Blake, Sophia Louisa Jex- (1840–1912)." *ODNB Online*.

73. Ibid.

BIBLIOGRAPHY

Ackerknecht, Erwin H. *A Short History of Medicine*. Baltimore: Johns Hopkins University Press, 1955, 1968, 1982.

Acton, William. *Functions and Disorders of the Reproductive Organs*. 8th ed. Philadelphia, 1894. *Google Book Search (full view)*.

———. *Prostitution, Considered in its Moral, Social and Sanitary Aspects, in London and other large Cities; with Proposals for the Mitigation and Prevention of Its Attendant Evils*. London, 1857. *Google Book Search (full view)*.

Advertisement. *Times* (London), July 1, 1815. *Gale Times Digital Archive*.

Albert, Daniel M. "Ocular Refraction and the Development of Spectacles." In Albert and Edwards, eds., *The History of Ophthalmology*, 107–23.

———. "The Ophthalmoscope and Retinovitreous Surgery." In Albert and Edwards, eds., *The History of Ophthalmology*, 177–202.

Albert, Daniel M., and Diane D. Edwards, eds. *The History of Ophthalmology*. Cambridge, MA: Blackwell Science, 1996.

Arnold, David. *Colonizing the Body: State Medicine and Epidemic Disease in Nineteenth-Century India*. Berkeley: University of California Press, 1993.

Arnold, Thomas. *A Method of Teaching the Deaf and Dumb Speech, Lipreading and Language*. London, 1881. Web. *Google Book Search (full view)*.

Ashton, Rosemary. *George Henry Lewes: A Life*. Oxford: Clarendon Press, 1991.

"Asiatic Cholera in the Pool of London." *Times* (London), October 16, 1848. *Gale Times Digital Archive*.

"Asylum for the Deaf and Dumb." *Times* (London), May 10, 1799. *Gale Times Digital Archive*.

"Asylum for the Deaf and Dumb." *Times* (London), May 4, 1808. *Gale Times Digital Archive*.

Atkinson, Alexander. *Memoirs of My Youth*. Feltham, England: British Deaf History Society, 2001. Orig. pub. 1865.

Baly, Monica. *Florence Nightingale and the Nursing Legacy*. London: Routledge, 1986.

Baly, Monica E., and H. C. G. Matthew, "Nightingale, Florence (1820–1910)." *Oxford Dictionary of National Biography Online*. OUP, 2004–9.

Barker, Juliet. *The Brontës*. New York: St. Martin's Griffin, 1994.

Barker-Benfield, G. J. *The Horrors of the Half-Known Life: Male Attitudes toward Woman and Sexuality in Nineteenth-Century America*. New York: Harper Colophon, 2000.

Barnes, David S. *The Making of a Social Disease: Tuberculosis in Nineteenth-Century France*. Berkeley: University of California Press, 1995.

Barquet, Nicolau, and Pere Domingo. "Smallpox: The Triumph over the Most Terrible of the Ministers of Death." *Annals of Internal Medicine* 127, no. 8 (October 15, 1997): 635–42.

Baxby, Derrick. "Jenner, Edward (1745–1823)." *Oxford Dictionary of National Biography Online*. OUP, 2004–8.

———. *Forbidden Signs: American Culture and the Campaign against Sign Language*. Chicago: University of Chicago Press, 1996.

Baynton, Douglas. "'A Silent Exile on This Earth': The Metaphorical Construction of Deafness in the Nineteenth Century." In Davis, ed., *The Disabilities Studies Reader*, 129–50.

Bettany, G. T. "Locock, Sir Charles, First Baronet (1799–1875)." Rev. Anne Digby. *Oxford Dictionary of National Biography Online*. OUP 2004–8.

Blake, Carolina. *The Charge of the Parasols: Women's Entry to the Medical Profession*. London: Women's Press, 1990.

Blodi, Frederick C. "Cataract Surgery." In Albert and Edwards, eds., *The History of Ophthalmology*, 165–76.

Bonner, Thomas N. *Becoming a Physician: Medical Education in Britain, France, Germany and the United States, 1750–1945*. Oxford University Press, 1995.

———. *To the Ends of the Earth: Women's Search for Education in Medicine*. Cambridge, MA: Harvard University Press, 1992.

Bourdelais, Patrice. *Epidemics Laid Low: A History of What Happened in Rich Countries*. Trans. Bart K. Holland. Baltimore: Johns Hopkins University Presss, 2006. Orig. pub. as *Les épidémies terrassé: Une histoire pays riches*. Paris, Éditions de La Martinière: c. 2003.

Brandt, Allan M. *No Magic Bullet: A Social History of Venereal Diseases in the United States since 1880*. Oxford University Press, 1985.

Briggs, Asa. *The Collected Essays of Asa Briggs*. Vol. 2: *Images, Problems, Standpoints, Forecasts*. Brighton, England: Harvester Press, 1985.

Brown, Haydn. *Advice to Single Women*. London: Sisley's, c. 1899.

Browning, Elizabeth Barrett. *Aurora Leigh*. Norton Critical Edition, ed. Margaret Reynolds. New York: W. W. Norton, 1996.

Brunton, Deborah, ed. *Health, Disease and Society in Europe, 1800–1930: A Source Book*. Manchester, England: Manchester University Press with the Open University, 2004.

———. ed., *Medicine Transformed: Health, Disease and Society in Europe, 1800–1930*. Manchester, England: Manchester University Press, 2004.

Burrows, George Man. *Commentaries on the Causes, Forms, Symptoms and Treatment, Moral and Medical, of Insanity*. London, 1828. Web. *Google Book Search (full view)*.

Bynum, W. F. "The Rise of Science in Medicine, 1850–1913." In Bynum et al., *Western Medical Tradition, 1800–2000,* 111–239.

———. *Science and the Practice of Medicine in the Nineteenth Century.* Cambridge University Press, 1994.

Bynum, W. F., Anne Hardy, Stephen Jacyna, Christopher Lawrence, and E. M. (Tilli) Tansey. *The Western Medical Tradition, 1800–2000.* Cambridge University Press, 2006.

Cathell, Daniel Webster. *The Physician Himself.* New York: Arno Press and *New York Times,* 1972. Orig. pub. 1882.

Churchill, Fleetwood. *On the Diseases of Women including those of Pregnancy and Childbed.* A New American Edition revised by the Author. With notes and additions by M. Francis Condie, M. D. Philadelphia, 1857. Web. *Google Book Search (full view).*

Clerc, Laurent. *Address, Written by Mr. Clerc, and Read by His Request At a Public Examination of the Pupils in the Connecticut Asylum, Before and Governour and Both Houses of the Legislature, 28th May, 1818.* Hartford: Hudson and Co. Printers, 1818. Web. *Google Book Search (full view).*

Cobbe, Frances Power. "The Medical Profession and Its Morality." *Modern Review* 2 (April 1881).

Collins, Wilkie. *Hide and Seek.* Vol. 11 in *The Works of Wilkie Collins.* New York: AMS Press, 1970.

———. *Poor Miss Finch.* Oxford: Oxford World's Classics, 1995.

Critchett, George. *A Case of Blindness from birth: in which sight was restored in a female by an operation at the age of twenty-two.* Deptford, England: J. Anderson, 1855. Web. *Elsevier Science Direct Complete.*

———. "A Course of Lectures on Diseases of the Eye, Lecture XIII." *Lancet* (October 27, 1855): 381–83. Web. Elsevier Science Direct Complete.

Crook, Diana. *Defying the Demon: Smallpox in Sussex.* Dale House Press, 2006.

Crowther, M. Anne, and Marguerite W. Dupree. *Medical Lives in the Age of Surgical Revolution.* Cambridge University Press, 2007.

Dally, Ann. *Women under the Knife: A History of Surgery.* London: Hutchinson Radius, 1991.

Davidson, Luke. "'Identities Ascertained': British Ophthalmology in the First Half of the Nineteenth Century." *Social History of Medicine* 9 (1996): 313–33.

Davidson, Roger, and Lesley A. Hall, eds. *Sex, Sin and Suffering: Venereal Disease and European Society since 1870.* London: Routledge, 2001.

Davis, Lennard J., ed. *The Disabilities Studies Reader.* New York: Routledge, 1997.

Dawson, E., and S. R. Royal, eds. *An Oxfordshire Market Gardener: The Diary of Joseph Turrill of Garsington, 1841–1925.* Phoenix Mill: Alan Sutton Publishing, 1993.

Defoe, Daniel. *The History of the Life and Adventures of Mr. Duncan Campbell.* Ed. George A. Aitken. New York: AMS Press, 1974.

———. *A Journal of the Plague Year.* London, 1722.

Dickens, Charles. *American Notes.* New York: Modern Library, 1996.

———. *Bleak House.* Ed. Nicola Bradbury. London: Penguin Books, 1996.

———. *Great Expectations.* Ed. Graham Law and Adrian J. Pinnington. Peterborough, ON: Broadview Press, 1998.

Digby, Ann. *Making a Medical Living: Doctors and Patients in the English Market for Medicine, 1790–1911*. New York: Cambridge University Press, 1994.

Dowling, William C. *Oliver Wendell Holmes in Paris: Medicine, Theology, and "The Autocrat of the Breakfast Table."* Durham: University of New Hampshire; Hanover, NH: University Press of New England, 2006.

Doyle, Arthur Conan. *Round the Red Lamp, and Other Medical Writings*. Ed. Robert Darby. Kansas City, MO: Valancourt Books, 2007.

Dracobly, Alex. "Theoretical Change and Therapeutic Innovation in the Treatment of Syphilis in Mid-Nineteenth-Century France." *Journal of the History of Medicine and Allied Sciences* 59, no. 4 (2004): 522–54.

Dubos, Rene, and Jean Dubos. *The White Plague: Tuberculosis, Man, and Society*. New Brunswick, NJ: Rutgers University Press, 1987. Orig. pub. 1952.

Duffin, Jacalyn. *History of Medicine: A Scandalously Short Introduction*. Toronto: University of Toronto Press, 1999.

Durbach, Nadja. *Bodily Matters: The Anti-Vaccination Movement in England, 1853–1907*. Durham, NC: Duke University Press, 2005.

Durey, Michael. *The Return of the Plague: British Society and the Cholera, 1831–1832*. Dublin: Gill & MacMillan Humanities Press, 1979.

Eliot, George. *Middlemarch*. Ed. David Carroll. Oxford: Oxford World's Classics, 1998.

Ellis, Richard H., ed. *The Case Books of Dr. John Snow*. (*Medical History*, Supplement No. 14.) London: Wellcome Institute for the History of Medicine, 1994.

Elsevier Science Direct Complete. Web.

Esmail, Jennifer. "The Power of Deaf Poetry: The Exhibition of Literacy and the Nineteenth-Century Sign Language Debates." *Sign Language Studies* 8, no. 4 (Summer 2008): 348–68.

Essays by the Pupils at the College for the Deaf and Dumb, Rugby, Warwickshire. London: Longman & Co., 1845. Web. *Google Book Search (full view)*.

Evans, Richard C. "Cholera in Nineteenth-Century Europe." In Ranger and Slack, eds., *Epidemics and Ideas*.

Farr, William. *Vital Statistics: A Memorial Volume of Selections from the Reports and Statistics of William Farr, M.D., D.C.L., C.B., F.R.S.* London: Office of the Sanitary Institute, 1885. Web. *Google Book Search (full view)*.

Farrell, Gabriel. *The Story of Blindness*. Cambridge, MA: Harvard University Press, 1956.

Flint, Kate. "Disability and Difference." In Taylor, ed., *The Cambridge Companion to Wilkie Collins*, Cambridge University Press, 2006:153–67.

Foucault, Michel. *The Birth of the Clinic: An Archaeology of Medical Perception*. Trans. A. M. Sheridan Smith. London: Tavistock, 1973. Orig. pub. 1963.

Frawley, Maria, ed. *Life in the Sick-Room: Harriet Martineau*. Peterborough, ON: Broadview Press, 2003.

Gairdner, W. T. *Public Health in Relation to Air and Water*. Edinburgh, 1862.

Gaskell, Elizabeth. *Ruth*. Oxford: Oxford World's Classics, 1985.

Gates, Barbara T. *The Journal of Emily Shore*. Charlottesville: University of Virginia Press, 1991.

———. "When Life Writing Becomes Death Writing: *The Journal of Emily Shore*." *Literature and Medicine* 24, no. 1 (2005): 70–92.

Gilbert, Pamela K. *Mapping the Victorian Social Body*. Albany: State University of New York Press, 2004.

Gitter, Elisabeth G. "The Blind Daughter in Charles Dickens's *Cricket on the Hearth*." *Studies in English Literature* 39, no. 4 (1999): 675–89.

Glynn, Ian and Jenifer Glynn. *The Life and Death of Smallpox*. London: Profile Books, 2004.

Goldman, Lawrence, ed. *The Blind Victorian: Henry Fawcett and British Liberalism*. Cambridge University Press, 1989.

———. "Fawcett, Henry (1833–1884)." *Oxford Dictionary of National Biography Online*. OUP, 2004–9.

Grady, Denise. "After a Devastating Birth Injury, Hope." *New York Times*, February 24, 2009.

Grant, Brian. *The Deaf Advance: A History of the British Deaf Association, 1890–1990*. Edinburgh: Pentland Press, 1990.

Gregory, S., and G. M. Hartley, eds. *Constructing Deafness*. London: Pinter, 1991.

Groce, Nora Ellen. *Everyone Here Spoke Sign Language: Hereditary Deafness on Martha's Vineyard*. Cambridge, MA: Harvard University Press, 1985.

Haley, Bruce. *The Healthy Body and Victorian Culture*. Cambridge, MA: Harvard University Press, 1978.

Hamilton, Susan, ed. *Criminals, Idiots, Women and Minors: Victorian Writing by Women on Women*. Peterborough, ON: Broadview Press, 1995.

Hamilton, Thomas, "Kitto, John (1804–1854)." Rev. H. C. G. Matthew. *Oxford Dictionary of National Biography Online*. OUP, 2004–9.

Hanson, Clare. *A Cultural History of Pregnancy: Pregnancy, Medicine and Culture, 1750–2000*. Basingstoke, England: Palgrave Macmillan, 2004.

Hardy, Anne. *The Epidemic Streets: Infectious Disease and the Rise of Preventive Medicine, 1856–1900*. Oxford: Clarendon Press, 1993.

———. *Health and Medicine in Britain since 1860*. England: Palgrave Macmillan, 2001.

Hawkins, Joseph E. "Sketches of Otohistory. Part 2: Origins of Otology in the British Isles: Wilde and Toynbee." *Audiology & Neuro-Otology* 9 (2004): 129–34.

Hays, J. N. *Epidemics and Pandemics: Their Impacts on Human History*. Santa Barbara, CA: ABC-Clio, 2005.

Hempel, Sandra. *The Strange Case of the Broad Street Pump: John Snow and the Mystery of Cholera*. Berkeley: University of California Press, 2007.

"History of the British Sign Language." Web. *Deafsign*.

Holmes, Martha Stoddard. *Fictions of Affliction: Physical Disability in Victorian Culture*. Ann Arbor: University of Michigan Press, 2004.

Hopkins, Donald R. *The Greatest Killer: Smallpox in History*. Chicago: University of Chicago Press, 2002. Orig. pub. as *Princes and Peasants: Smallpox in History*, 1983.

Howarth, Janet. "Fawcett, Dame Millicent Garrett (1847–1929)." *Oxford Dictionary of National Biography Online*. OUP, 2004–9.

Jacyna, Stephen. "Medicine in Transformation, 1800–1849." In Bynum et al., *Western Medical Tradition, 1800–2000*, 11–101.

Jalland, Pat. *Women, Marriage and Politics, 1860–1914*. Oxford: Clarendon Press, 1986.

Jeffries, John. *Lectures on Diseases of the Eye*. Ed. Daniel M. Albert. Belgium: J. P. Wayenbourgh, 1998.

Jewson, N. "The Disappearance of the Sick-Man from Medical Cosmology, 1770–1870." *Sociology* 10 (1976): 225–44.

Johns, B. G. *Blind People: Their Works and Ways*. London: Murray, 1867.

Jones, Greta. *"Captain of All These Men of Death": The History of Tuberculosis in Nineteenth- and Twentieth-Century Ireland*. The Wellcome Series in the History of Medicine. Amsterdam: Rodopi, 2001.

Jordanova, Ludmilla. *Sexual Visions: Images of Gender in Science and Medicine between the Eighteenth and Twentieth Centuries*. New York: Harvester Wheatsheaf, 1989.

———. "The Social Construction of Medicine." *Social History of Medicine*, 07/03 (1995): 361–81.

Kennedy, Meegan. "The Ghost in the Clinic: Gothic Medicine and Curious Fiction in Samuel Warren's *Diary of a Late Physician*." *Victorian Literature and Culture* 32, no. 2 (2004): 327–51.

———. "Syphilis and the Hysterical Female: The Limits of Realism in Sarah Grand's *The Heavenly Twins*." *Women's Writing* 11 no. 2 (2004): 259–80.

Kingsley, Charles. *Two Years Ago*. London, 1857.

———. *Westward Ho!* London: J. M. Dent, n.d.

Kiple, Kenneth F. "The History of Disease." In Roy Porter, ed., *The Cambridge Illustrated History of Medicine*, 15–61. Cambridge University Press, 1996.

Kitto, John. *The Lost Senses: Deafness & Blindness*. (Pagination separate for *Deafness* and *Blindness*.) Edinburgh: William Oliphant and Co.; London: Hamilton and Co., n.d. Reprint. Whitefish, MT: Kessinger, 2003.

Krentz, Christopher, ed. *A Mighty Change: An Anthology of Deaf American Writing, 1816–1864*. Washington, DC: Gallaudet University Press, 2000.

Lane, Harlan, ed. *The Deaf Experience: Classics in Language and Education*. Trans. Franklin Philip. Cambridge, MA: Harvard University Press, 1984.

Lane, Harlan. "Cochlear Implants: Their Cultural and Historical Meaning." In John Vickrey Van Cleve, ed., *Deaf History Unveiled: Interpretations from the New Scholarship*. Washington, DC: Gallaudet University Press, 2002, 272–91.

Lawrence, C. *Medicine in the Making of Modern Britain, 1700–1920*. London: Routledge, 1994.

Lawrence, William. "Lectures on the Anatomy, Physiology, and Diseases of the Eye, I." *Lancet* (October 22, 1825): 145–51. Web. *Elsevier Science Direct Complete*.

Lee, Raymond, ed. *A Beginner's Introduction to Deaf History*. Feltham, England: British Deaf History Society, 2004.

Levy, William Hanks. *Blindness and the Blind; or, a Treatise on the Science of Typhology*. 1872. Web. *Google Book Search (full view)*.

Lewis, Scott, ed. *The Letters of Elizabeth Barrett Browning to Her Sister Arabella*. Waco, TX: Wedgestone Press, 2002. August 31 [1849], v.1, p. 276, August 17 [1849], v.1, p. 271.

Liggins, Emma. "Writing against the 'Husband-Fiend'; Syphilis and Male Sexual Vice in the New Woman Novel." *Women's Writing* 7, no. 2 (2000): 175–95.

Loudon, Irvine. "Childbirth." In Loudon, ed. *Western Medicine*, 206–20.

———. *Medical Care and the General Practitioner, 1750–1850*. Oxford: Clarendon Press, 1986.

———, ed. *Western Medicine: An Illustrated History*. Oxford University Press, 1997.

Mahood, Linda. *The Magdalenes: Prostitution in the Nineteenth Century*. London: Routledge, 1990.

Marten, Benjamin. *A New Theory of Consumptions: more especially of a Phthisis, or consumption of the Lungs*. 2nd ed. London, 1722. Orig. pub. 1720.

Martin, Frances. *Elizabeth Gilbert and Her Work for the Blind*. 1887. Web. *Google Book Search (full view)*.

Martineau, Harriet. *Life in the Sick-Room*. Ed. Maria H. Frawley. Peterborough, ON: Broadview Literary Press, 2003.

Mayhew, Henry. *London Labour and the London Poor*. 4 vols. New York: Dover, 1968.

McAllister, Marie E. "Stories of the Origin of Syphilis in Eighteenth-Century England: Science, Myth, and Prejudice." *Eighteenth-Century Life* 24 (Winter 2000): 22–24.

McClay, John E., "Scrofula." *Emedicine:WebMD*.

McGregor, Todd A., "Syphilis." *Emedicine:WebMD*.

McKeown, Thomas. *The Modern Rise of Population*. New York: Academic Press, 1976.

McLoughlin, M. G. *A History of the Education of the Deaf in England*. Liverpool: G. M. McLoughlin, 1987.

Merians, Linda E. "The London Lock Hospital and the Lock Asylum for Women." In Merians, ed., *The Secret Malady*, 128–45.

———, ed. *The Secret Malady: Venereal Disease in Eighteenth-Century Britain and France*. Lexington: University of Kentucky Press, 1996.

Miller, Genevieve. *The Adoption of Inoculation for Smallpox in England and France*. Philadelphia: University of Pennsylvania Press, 1957.

Miller, John Hawkins. "'Temple and Sewer': Childbirth, Prudery, and Victoria Regina." In Wohl, ed., *The Victorian Family*, 23–43.

Mitchell, Sally. *Frances Power Cobbe, Victorian Feminist, Journalist, Reformer*. Charlottesville: University of Virginia Press, 2004.

Morris, R. J. *Cholera 1832: The Social Response to an Epidemic*. New York: Holmes & Meier, 1976.

Mort, Frank. *Dangerous Sexualities: Medico-Moral Politics in England since 1830*. London: Routledge & Kegan Paul, 1987.

Moscucci, Ornella. *The Science of Woman: Gynaecology and Gender in England, 1800–1929*. Cambridge University Press, 1990.

National Cancer Institute. "Menopausal Hormone Replacement Therapy Use and Cancer: Questions and Answers." Web. *National Cancer Institute*.

Nightingale, Florence. *Notes on Nursing: What It Is, And What It Is Not*. Facsimile of first edition, printed in London, 1859. Reproduced 1946.

O'Connor, Erin. *Raw Material: Producing Pathology in Victorian Culture.* Durham, NC: Duke University Press, 2000.

Oliphant, John. *The Early Education of the Blind in Britain c.1790–1900: Institutional Experience in England and Scotland.* Queenston, ON: Edwin Mellen Press, 2007.

Oliphant, Margaret. "The Condition of Women." In Hamilton, ed., *Criminals, Idiots, Women, & Minors,* 209–30.

Oxford Dictionary of National Biography, Oxford University Press, 2004–9, online. edu.

Pardes, Ilana. "Remapping Jonah's Voyage: Melville's *Moby-Dick* and Kitto's *Cyclopedia of Biblical Literature.*" *Comparative Literature* 57, no. 2 (Spring 2005): 135–57.

Pead, Patrick J. "Benjamin Jesty: The First Vaccinator Revealed." *Lancet* (December 23, 2006): 2202.

Pelling, Margaret. *Cholera, Fever and English Medicine, 1825–1865.* Oxford University Press, 1978.

Peters, Catherine. Introduction to Wilkie Collins, *Poor Miss Finch,* vii–xxiii. Oxford: Oxford World's Classics, 1995.

Peterson, M. Jeanne. *The Medical Profession in Mid-Victorian London.* Berkeley: University of California Press, 1978.

Poovey, Mary. *Uneven Developments: The Ideological Work of Gender in Mid-Victorian England.* Chicago: University of Chicago Press, 1988.

Porter, Dorothy. "The Mission of Social History of Medicine: An Historical View." *Social History of Medicine,* 07/03 (1995): 345–59.

Porter, Roy. "Consumption: Disease of the Consumer Society?" In John Brewer and Roy Porter, eds., *Consumption and the World of Goods.* New York: Routledge, 1993.

———. *The Greatest Benefit to Mankind: A Medical History of Humanity from Antiquity to the Present.* Hammersmith, England: HarperCollins, 1997.

Power, D'A. "Wright, William (1773–1860)." Rev. Anita McConnell, *Oxford Dictionary of National Biography. Online.* OUP, 2004–9.

Quétel, Claude. *History of Syphilis.* Trans. Judith Braddock and Brian Pike. London: Polity Press in Association with Blackwell, 1990.

Ranger, Terence, and Paul Slack, eds. *Epidemics and Ideas: Essays on the Historical Perception of Pestilence.* Cambridge University Press, 1992.

Rée, Jonathan. *I See a Voice: A Philosophical History of Language, Deafness, and the Senses.* Hammersmith, England: HarperCollins, 1999.

Rhodes, Maxine. "Women in Medicine: Doctors and Nurses, 1850–1920." In Brunton, ed., *Medicine Transformed,* 151–79.

Roberts, Shirley. "Blake, Sophia Louisa Jex- (1840–1912)." *Oxford Dictionary of National Biography. Online.* OUP, 2004–9.

Rosenkrantz, Barbara Gutmann. "Introductory Essay: Dubos and Tuberculosis, Master Teachers to Barbara Gutmann Rosenkrantz." In Dubos and Dubos, *The White Plague Tuberculosis, Man, and Society:* xiii–xxxiv.

Rossetti, Dante Gabriel. "Jenny." In Thomas J. Collins and Vivienne J. Rundle, *Broadview Anthology of Victorian Poetry and Victorian Theory,* 809–14.

Peterborough, ON: Broadview Press, 1999. This poem is also available on numerous webpages.

Rothman, Sheila M. *Living in the Shadow of Death: Tuberculosis and the Social Experience of Illness in American History*. New York: Basic Books, 1994.

Roy, Judith M. "Brown, Isaac Baker (1811–1873)." *Oxford Dictionary of National Biography Online*. OUP, 2004–9.

Rubinstein, David. "Victorian Feminists: Henry and Millicent Garrett Fawcett." In Goldman, ed. *The Blind Victorian*. 71–93.

Sacks, Oliver W. *Seeing Voices: A Journey into the World of the Deaf*. Berkeley: University of California Press, 1989.

Schor, Naomi. "Blindness as Metaphor." *Differences* 11, no. 2 (Summer 1999): 76–105.

Sherman, Irwin W. *The Power of Plagues*. Washington, DC: ASM Press, 2006.

Showalter, Elaine. *Sexual Anarchy: Gender and Culture at the Fin de Siècle*. New York: Penguin Books, 1990.

Shuttleton, David E. *Smallpox and the Literary Imagination, 1660–1820*. Cambridge University Press, 2007.

Siena, Kevin P. "The 'Foul Disease' and Privacy: The Effects of Venereal Disease and Patient Demand on the Medical Marketplace in Early Modern London." *Bulletin of the History of Medicine* 75 (2001): 199–224.

———. *Venereal Disease, Hospitals and the Urban Poor: London's 'Foul Wards,' 1600–1800*. Rochester, NY: Rochester University Press, 2004.

Silverstein, Arthur M., and Christine Ruggere. "Dr. Arthur Conan Doyle and the Case of Congenital Syphilis." *Perspectives in Biology and Medicine* 49, no. 2 (Spring 2006): 209–19.

Smith, Andrew. *Victorian Demons: Medicine, Masculinity, and the Gothic at the Fin-de-Siècle*. Manchester, England: Manchester University Press, 2004.

Smith, F. B. *The Retreat of Tuberculosis, 1850–1950*. London: Croom Helm, 1988.

Snow, John. "John Snow." *UCLA Department of Epidemiology*. Web.

———. "The John Snow Archive and Research Companion." *Matrix: The Center for Online Arts, Humanities, and Social Sciences Online*. Web.

———. *On the Mode of Communication of Cholera*. London, 1849; 2nd ed., 1855.

Sontag, Susan. *Illness as Metaphor*. New York: Vintage Books, 1977, 1978.

Spongberg, Mary. *Feminizing Venereal Disease: The Body of the Prostitute in Nineteenth-Century Medical Discourse*. New York: New York University Press, 1997.

Stephen, Leslie. *Life of Henry Fawcett*. London, 1886. Web. *Google Book Search (full view)*.

Stutfield, Hugh E. M. "Tommyrotics." *Blackwood's Magazine* 157 (1895): 833–45.

Summers, Anne. *Angels and Citizens: British Women as Military Nurses, 1854–1914*. London: Routledge, 1988.

Sutton-Spence, Rachel, and Bencie Woll. *The Linguistics of British Sign Language*. Cambridge University Press, 1999.

Taylor, Charles Bell. "Clinical Lectures on Diseases of the Eye, II." *Lancet* (May 8, 1886): 864–66. Web. *Elsevier Science Complete Direct*.

Taylor, Jenny Bourne, ed. *The Cambridge Companion to Wilkie Collins.* Cambridge University Press, 2006.

"U.S. Public Health Service Syphilis Study at Tuskegee: Tuskegee Time Line." *CDC Centers for Disease Control and Prevention.* Web.

Van Cleve, John Vickrey, ed. *Deaf History Unveiled: Interpretations from the New Scholarship.* Washington, DC: Gallaudet University Press, 1993.

Vinten-Johansen, Peter, Howard Brody, Nigel Paneth, Stephen Rachman, and Michael Rip, with the assistance of David Zuck. *Cholera, Chloroform, and the Science of Medicine: A Life of John Snow.* Oxford: Oxford University Press, 2003.

Walkowitz, Judith R. *Prostitution and Victorian Society: Women, Class, and the State.* Cambridge: Cambridge University Press, 1980.

Warne, Vanessa. "'So That the Sense of Touch May Supply the Want of Sight': Blind Reading and Nineteenth-Century British Print Culture." In Colligan and Linley, eds., *Image, Sound and Touch: Media and Literature in the Nineteenth Century.* Ashgate, forthcoming.

Warren, Samuel. *Passages from the Diary of a Late Physician.* Edinburgh and London, 1868.

Webster, Augusta. "A Castaway." In *Augusta Webster: Portraits and Other Poems,* ed. Christine Sutphin, 192–213. Peterborough, ON: Broadview Press, 2000.

Whitbread, Helena, ed. *I Know My Own Heart: The Diaries of Anne Lister, 1791–1840.* London: Virago Press, 1988.

Whitehead, Henry. "The Broad Street Pump: An Episode in the Cholera Epidemic of 1854." *MacMillan's Magazine* 13, no. 74 (1865): 113–22.

Wohl, Anthony S. *Endangered Lives: Public Health in Victorian Britain.* Cambridge, MA: Harvard University Press, 1983.

———, ed. *The Victorian Family: Structure and Stresses.* London: Croom Helm, 1978.

Wright, William. "Causes and Treatment of Deafness." *Lancet* (June 25, 1831): 412–13. Web. *Elsevier Science Complete Direct.*

———. "Causes and Treatment of Deafness, No. II." *Lancet* (July 9, 1831): 464–66. Web. *Elsevier Science Complete Direct.*

———. "Causes and Treatment of Deafness, No. IV." *Lancet* (July 30, 1831): 566–67. Web. *Elsevier Science Complete Direct.*

Yonge, Charlotte M. *The Heir of Redclyffe.* London: J. M. Dent & Co., n.d.

Young, Arlene. "'Entirely a Woman's Question'? Class, Gender, and the Victorian Nurse." *Journal of Victorian Culture* 13, no. 1 (Spring 2008): 18–41.

INDEX

About the Author

Mary Wilson Carpenter is professor emerita of Queen's University, the Department of English, in Kingston, Ontario, Canada. She is the author of *George Eliot and the Landscape of Time: Narrative Form and Protestant Apocalyptic History* and *Imperial Bibles, Domestic Bodies: Women, Sexuality, and Religion in the Victorian Market*. She has also published a number of book chapters and journal articles on Victorian literature and feminist studies.